Southern by the Grace of God

Southern by the Grace of God

RELIGION, RACE, AND CIVIL RIGHTS IN
HOLLYWOOD'S AMERICAN SOUTH

Megan Hunt

The University of Georgia Press
ATHENS

© 2024 by the University of Georgia Press
Athens, Georgia 30602
www.ugapress.org
All rights reserved
Set in 10.25/13.5 Minion Pro Regular by Mary McKeon

Most University of Georgia Press titles are
available from popular e-book vendors.

Printed digitally

Library of Congress Cataloging-in-Publication Data
Names: Hunt, Megan, 1968– author.
Title: Southern by the grace of God : religion, race, and civil rights in Hollywood's American South / Megan Hunt.
Description: Athens : The University of Georgia Press, 2024. | Series: Politics and culture in the twentieth-century South | Includes bibliographical references and index.
Identifiers: LCCN 2024021604 | ISBN 9780820367637 (hardback) | ISBN 9780820367620 (paperback) | ISBN 9780820367644 (epub) | ISBN 9780820367651 (pdf)
Subjects: LCSH: Southern States—In motion pictures. | Religion in motion pictures. | Racism in motion pictures. | Race relations in motion pictures. | Stereotypes (Social psychology) in motion pictures. | Motion pictures and history.
Classification: LCC PN1995.9.S66 H86 2024 | DDC 791.43/65875—dc23/eng/20240604
LC record available at https://lccn.loc.gov/2024021604

CONTENTS

ILLUSTRATIONS

ACKNOWLEDGMENTS

The book began as my PhD project, which brought me to the North East of England over a decade ago. Supervised by Brian Ward and Randall Stephens, the project developed thanks to a Northumbria University studentship and an engaging and supportive group of Americanists. I am eternally grateful for the support I received at Northumbria, not only from Brian and Randall but from my wider community of "Glenamara Expats." That said, the influences for the project were first fostered at the University of Manchester during my masters studies. Here I enrolled on a number of inspiring courses with Eithne Quinn, David Brown, and Michael Bibler, while a last-minute switch to a film history course with Ian Scott undoubtedly changed the entire direction of my work. It was also at Manchester that I first met Brian Ward and learned that almost all the best pubs are in carparks adjacent to university campuses.

I particularly wish to acknowledge the kindness and wisdom of Sharon Monteith, whose work has always been a considerable inspiration but whose feedback on both my initial PhD applications and final thesis proved invaluable.

Post-PhD, I began teaching almost immediately at the University of Edinburgh and held a number of short-term contracts before securing a permanent role in 2021. All the work to wrestle the thesis into this book occurred at Edinburgh, where I have been fortunate to meet some amazing colleagues and even better friends. Navigating academia, especially on precarious and/ or teaching-focused contracts, can be a lonely and dispiriting place. But while our institutions may not always offer much by way of encouragement or investment, my day-to-day life has been improved by the friendship of countless colleagues, especially but not limited to Tereza Valny, Kirsty Day, Stephen McDowall, Bill Aird, Richard Oosterhoff, Wendy Ugolini, Rick Sowerby, and Zubin Mistry. I am particularly grateful to those who have helped develop a conducive environment for writing and research, though as is customary, we do not talk about Fight Club. A "First Book Club" established by Emma Hunter, while relatively short lived, also proved critical at some crucial stages in reworking the book, for which I thank Emma and my fellow "first authors" for their feedback and support. To the countless students I have taught over the last seven years, thank you for your openness and interest in concepts like

"Southern Exceptionalism" and "Atticus Finch's America." Our classes have given me space and reason to reconsider many ideas and topics and have fed into my research in innumerable ways.

At Edinburgh, I joined an impressive community of Americanists, and working with Fabian Hilfrich, David Silkenat, Nick Batho, and Robert Mason, in particular, has helped shape my outlook, teaching, and research in innumerable ways. I have learned much from each of them and am grateful to begin my own teaching journey among such impressive scholars and people. I also must acknowledge Fabian's support while he was head of history, which was only surpassed by the inimitable Diana Paton—a truly inspiring scholar, colleague, and champion.

Away from Edinburgh, my work has benefited from a number of research seminars and invited papers, including at the Institute for Historical Research, the University of Glasgow, Keele University, and the University of Nottingham.

My career thus far has been shaped by my membership in a number of organizations, most notably the British Association for American Studies (BAAS) and Historians of the Twentieth Century United States (HOTCUS). Both have brought me community, friendships, and inspiration and have always provided vital spaces, resources, and connection for Americanists in Britain and beyond. Through these networks, I have met scholars whose support and friendship I value highly, not least Uta Balbier, Lydia Plath, Emily Brady, Kate Ballantyne, Nick Grant, Nick Witham, and Miguel Hernandez. And then there is E. James West, who has probably read more of my ramblings than anyone else and remains my main competition for snarkiest member of the UK Americanist community.

At UGA Press, I would like to extend immense thanks to my anonymous reviewers and to Nate Holly for his courtesy, speed, and reassurance in picking up my project when I was almost convinced this book would never happen. Thanks also to Joyce Li for the copyedits and for Ben Shaw for indexing. Both were a dream to work with. I am so grateful to have gone through this process on a very similar trajectory to my friend, Kate Ballantyne, whose advice kept me sane at some crucial moments!

I want to extend thanks to my family, who have always supported me and this project. You made me the person I am, and I am grateful to have such loving and inspirational people as my first and original community. And to some of my oldest friends, who remain cheerleaders for me and this project, especially Sinead Dyson, Nick Lanigan, and my fellow learned Bedian, Hannah Lyons.

Finally, to Joe, who refuses to read, but has provided an environment of love and calm that made this book (and everything) possible.

Southern by the Grace of God

The Divine and the Depraved

Religion in Hollywood's South

While working on Martin Scorsese's 1991 remake of *Cape Fear,* screenwriter Wesley Strick reconceptualized villain Max Cady as a fundamentalist Christian, designating the character "a monster of the South." A symbol of excessive intolerance, racism, and ignorance, Cady's religion is "the most kind of primitive and, as a New York Jew, the most terrifying."[1] In making such a statement, Strick ensured there was no ambiguity over Cady's southern Pentecostalism; in essence, it is the point of the film. Nonconformist and extreme, Cady's religion indicates and enhances his "white trash" identity, intersecting with other negative stereotypes frequently employed to indicate the poor white South, such as illiteracy, sexual deviancy, and propensity to violence. While the original *Cape Fear* (J. Lee Thompson, 1962) reflects white anxieties around social and racial change in the late 1950s and early 1960s, Scorsese's film implies that the "New South" is little more than a consumerist myth, where contemporary concerns about shifting demographics and religious conservatism blend with much older racial and class anxieties.

Archival evidence shows that Strick was consciously responding to an emboldened and politically powerful southern fundamentalism that had emerged in the aftermath of the civil rights upheavals of the 1950s and 1960s but that had been rocked by a number of high-profile scandals in the late 1980s. Like many of the disgraced televangelists of his era, the new Max Cady (Robert De Niro) treads a fine line between the divine and the depraved: his ostentatious clothes and automobiles indicative of the undeniable economic clout of many southern pentecostals in the 1980s, his upbringing around snake handlers rendering him immune to pain and empathy.[2]

Whether rooted in reality, projection, or a combination of both, southern religiosity remains crucial to the region's functionality as a cinematic site of exoticized premodernism. "From gaunt preachers pointing skyward in eighteenth-century Virginia to Confederate soldiers kneeling in prayer to the spectacular folly of the Scopes trial to the eccentric rituals of Appalachian snake handlers, religion has served as a shorthand for southern exceptionalism," historian Beth Barton Schweiger writes, and can immediately alert viewers to a southern setting.[3] The surreal opening sequence of the HBO series *True Blood* (2008–14), for example, offers a voyeuristic montage of increasingly aggressive images of violence, sex, and decay, resulting in a climactic nighttime river baptism. "It is a cathartic release," according to lead designer Rama Allen, "that allows both sinners and saints to begin the next day anew and is intimately tied to the core of several belief systems in the south, from Christian mysticism to voodoo."[4] A "love letter to the Gothic South," these credits include catfish, swamps, decaying animals, archival footage of the Ku Klux Klan, civil rights protesters, cemeteries, sexualized dancers, and an expressive congregation of African American pentecostals (the last entirely staged and filmed in Chicago, Illinois).[5] The only reference to the show's actual focus on vampires, a church sign that reads "GOD HATES FANGS," recalls the notorious homophobia of the Westboro Baptist Church of Topeka, Kansas. Combined, the images "expose the soft pink underbelly of rural stereotypes" through a "delicate balance of the sacred and profane."[6] Like the first season of HBO's *True Detective* (2014), also set in Louisiana, *True Blood* presents a South populated by highly sexualized, poor, violent whites. "After dipping ourselves in southern gothic," Allen recalled, "we latched onto [the image of] 'the whore in the house of prayer.' This delicate balance of the sacred and profane co-existing creates powerful imagery. . . . Holy rollers flirt with perversion while godless creatures seek redemption."[7]

Allen's reflections reinforce a commonly, if often crudely, understood sectional binary of North-South, constructed by perceived regional polarities of race, class, gender, education, and violence. Building on various cultural myths of insularity and perversion, religious fanaticism conveys the South's alleged disparity from the rest of the nation in films as varied as *Inherit the Wind* (Stanley Kramer, 1960) and *Sling Blade* (Billy Bob Thornton, 1996). Civil rights dramas such as *Mississippi Burning* (Alan Parker, 1988) and *Ghosts of Mississippi* (Rob Reiner, 1996) have helped shape popular understandings of continuing racial tensions in the region, just as more contemporary narratives such as *A Time to Kill* (Joel Schumacher, 1996) and Scorsese's *Cape Fear* demonstrated that the South's uneducated and often violent white underclass could still be relied on to undermine liberal commitment to another

"New South." Indeed, Hollywood's tendency to stereotype poor white southerners is well documented.[8] Like the media coverage of the civil rights era itself, Hollywood dramas have reinforced regional stereotypes of race, class, and gender to cleanse and redeem the wider nation from the implications of systemic racism. However, as this book shows, mainstream Hollywood often relies on certain representations of southern religion, in particular, to further enhance this pattern of difference and regional exceptionalism, consistently displacing broader American racism through a representation of the poor white southerner who is as religious as he (and it is always a he) is racist. By foregrounding the role of religion in these characterizations, *Southern by the Grace of God: Religion, Race, and Civil Rights in Hollywood's American South* contributes to our understanding of southern exceptionalism, a long-standing U.S. nationalist discourse that has assigned racial problems to the errant South alone, enabling white supremacy to not only endure but reproduce.[9]

Far from celebrating Black stories, the civil rights cinema that emerged in the 1980s and 1990s validated a specific form of whiteness, rooted in education, wealth, and secularity. As Justin Gomer has demonstrated, filmmakers and audiences in the post–civil rights era increasingly sought characters with color-blind principles who rejected the bigotry of the mid-twentieth century.[10] But in the midst of a culture wars rooted in debates over affirmative action, feminism, and a distinctly evangelical hostility to the rights and privacies of marginalized others, American audiences sought secular, reasonable heroes.

Symbolic Secularity and Southern Exceptionalism

Southern by the Grace of God examines the presentation and functions of Protestant Christianity in cinematic depictions of the American South. It argues that religion is an understudied signifier of the South on film, used—with varying degrees of sophistication—to define the region's presumed exceptionalism for regional, national, and international audiences. Rooted in close textual analysis and primary research into the production and reception of more than twenty Hollywood films that engage with the civil rights movement and/ or its legacy, this book provides detailed case studies of films that utilize southern religiosity to negotiate American anxieties around race, class, and gender. Dissecting Hollywood's representation of southern Protestantism, *Southern by the Grace of God* is a significant addition to the relatively few existing analyses of civil rights–themed cinema. But it also offers an important new perspective to accounts of the South on film more generally. It posits that religion is an integral trope of the South in popular culture—and especially crucial to the divisions essential to Hollywood storytelling.

The films analyzed in this book all interact with the civil rights era, either because they were released contemporaneously or because they attempted to interpret its legacy in an implicit or explicit manner. The subject of this book's first chapter, *To Kill a Mockingbird* (Robert Mulligan), was released in 1962 and used various cinematic techniques to simultaneously comment on and avoid the controversies of the African American freedom struggle in a fascinating dance of engagement and evasion. In their imagining of actual events, *Mississippi Burning, The Long Walk Home* (Richard Pearce, 1990), and *Selma* (Ava DuVernay, 2014)—each covered in later chapters—have contributed to Hollywood's own interpretation of history, influencing how audiences around the world comprehend the civil rights movement and its legacies. Centered on stories of white redemption and interracial coalition, *Mississippi Burning* and *Ghosts of Mississippi* refracted contemporary concerns about growing racial tensions in the 1980s and 1990s by foregrounding individual stories of racial reconciliation, rather than exploring enduring structural inequalities. In a related fashion, *A Time to Kill* and Martin Scorsese's remake of *Cape Fear* contributed to a late twentieth-century indictment of the South as a region that had, on the whole, failed to emerge reconstructed from the 1960s.

Hollywood's South therefore readily absorbed the religiosity that threatened a particular construction of U.S. history and identity on the eve of the millennium. Filmmakers and studios were seemingly confident that audiences would identify the United States as a modern and secular nation, despite the statistical probability that a large percentage of audiences held religious beliefs and/or lived in the South. This confidence in the nation's symbolic secularity makes the presentation of southern religious intensity appear all the more distant and exotic, echoing David R. Jansson's framework of internal orientalism, itself rooted in Edward Said's conceptual paradigm of postcolonial critique. Jansson's South, "a repository of a set of negative characteristics (such as poverty, racism, violence, and backwardness)," proved the perfect Hollywood backdrop for the battle for America's soul, heightened by liberal fears of a nation undergoing "southernization" via Republican revolution.[11] After all, as Gomer notes, the racial melodramas of the 1980s and 1990s were "less often concerned with the reformation of white racists" that so often preoccupied the mid-century "social problem pictures."[12] Rather, such films worked to construct a color-blind narrative of the past, where, despite the structures and practices of white supremacy, white heroes always existed.

Individual stories of racial reconciliation rooted in white redemption and interracial coalition, the "civil rights melodrama," as it has been designated by Jennifer Fuller, routinely presents a simplistic binary of good and evil that pits recalcitrant southern white racists against brutalized but deserving Black southerners.[13] In this context, Hollywood reflected the obvious political tremors that movement leaders and individuals strategically deployed throughout the freedom struggle itself, courting and utilizing the media to grasp white attention. But the religious symbolism of such Hollywood storytelling, which so often casts a noble yet reductive and static religious African American community against zealous "white trash" operating on the margins of society, offers a further intricacy to Hollywood's southerners. So often to blame for the incendiary racial violence that marks such movies, white trash villains are often associated with Christian fundamentalism, in both rhetoric and actions, enabling filmmakers to offer a clear cause for the South's legacy of racial intolerance and violence. Meanwhile, from *Hallelujah* (King Vidor, 1929) to *The Color Purple* (Steven Spielberg, 1985), Hollywood has reinforced "the code of the 'eternal' or 'static' black," through which "religion becomes a sign and symptom of the perpetual backwardness and outside status of African Americans."[14] Therefore, while much of this book is focused on the apparent divisions within whiteness, it concurrently draws attention to Hollywood's continued representation of religiosity rather than political mobilization as a defining feature of Black southern life. This book also demonstrates how a supposed lack of Black agency often works to imply that racial change happened naturally or through the work of secular, liberal whites.

Entering the small pool of literature on civil rights cinema, *Southern by the Grace of God* therefore explores relationships between the South as reality and the South as representation. It illustrates how cinematic depictions of white southern Protestantism connect to other cultural stereotypes regarding violence, educational attainment, and racism, and how these intersecting images are used to delineate divisions within whiteness. Like other melodramas, the civil rights melodrama returns characters and viewers to "a locus of innocence," restoring faith in the ever-perfecting United States. Meanwhile, "diseased whiteness"—which Allison Graham identifies in Hollywood's white male "cracker"—is "vanquished at the movie's end by the only character capable of driving a stake through the heart of a Delta racist: his alter ego, the man of law, the redeemed" but crucially secular "southern white man."[15]

Such narratives absolve and redeem whiteness as a whole by highlighting racism as a class-based, interpersonal problem detached from larger structures and systems. Notwithstanding these and other genre conventions, there have been very few surveys of civil rights cinema, with volumes focusing largely on the Civil War tradition in southern cinema, seen most recently in Robert Jackson's *Fade In, Crossroads: A History of the Southern Cinema.*[16] This neglect is despite the enduring popularity of films that address civil rights themes, including the Oscar-winning *Green Book* (Peter Farrelly, 2018), and the frequency with which film and media is used to illustrate the civil rights movement to students and the public. The small body of existing scholarship, led by Allison Graham's pioneering work, alongside that of Sharon Monteith, has provided a framework for examining feature films that use the backdrop of the civil rights movement or its legacy to portray interpersonal stories of white redemption.

"Southern Rubes and Obscurantists"

It is not without consequence that much of the religious right's evolution and many of its key figures in the immediate post–civil rights era were centered in the South. Indeed, such a reality must be considered when addressing Hollywood's specific projection of and investment in southern exceptionalism during the latter decades of the twentieth century. Although many of the white southerners who defected from the Democratic to the Republican Party in the 1960s and 1970s held Christian views, theirs was a mostly reactionary movement based on political responses to federal civil rights legislation, feminism, legalized abortion, and the growing gay rights movement. Historians have also argued that southern political realignment manifested as the result of a wider growth of suburban conservatism across the southern and western United States, in particular. However, as E. J. Dionne argues, political realignment from the mid-1960s onward made it easy for liberal politicians and journalists to blame two conflated southern white preoccupations—political conservatism and evangelical Christianity—for almost every subsequent Democratic election defeat.[17] The apparent intersection of these preoccupations is therefore central to how the South is presented and perceived in the wider United States and abroad, compelling a more nuanced understanding of white Evangelicalism's role in continued efforts to project and understand the South and, by extension, the nation.

However, it is not just contemporary studies that have avoided a meaningful discussion of religion when attempting to make sense of the South. Ralph Wood has shown that even the Nashville Agrarians of the 1920s and 1930s, authors of the seminal regional collection *I'll Take My Stand*, "ignored what [journalist H. L.] Mencken rightly saw as the heart of Southern culture—its fundamentalist Christianity." Indeed, although they are hardly nuanced, Mencken's "brittle secularist" critiques remain some of the few works to attempt to communicate the tenacious cultural significance of southern fundamentalism and have endured through stereotype, cultural derision, and projections of irrationality.[18] "From the vantage point of Mencken's desk in Baltimore," W. Fitzhugh Brundage notes, "most of the South was rife with snake-handling religious zealotry, lynch mob barbarism, and unspeakable cultural ignorance."[19] In 1924, Mencken coined the term "Bible Belt" to describe a considerable swath of the nation, stretching from the former Confederacy to the Midwest. By 1925, his role in the media spectacle that surrounded Tennessee's Scopes trial, in which the American Civil Liberties Union (ACLU) challenged a new state law preventing the teaching of evolution in public schools, ensured that "it became fashionable" to dismiss fundamentalists as distinctly "Southern rubes and obscurantists."[20] By the Great Depression, Colleen McDannell writes, "the South had become the symbol for what was wrong with religion throughout the country."[21]

Inherit the Wind, the Broadway play and later Stanley Kramer movie based on the Scopes trial, reflected Mencken's "savage South": populated by "hordes of barbarous peasants." With the region's white aristocracy culturally and economically devastated by the Civil War, Mencken argued that "native stock of excellent blood" had been forced to move elsewhere, rendering Dixie the domain of poor whites.[22] Their vulgarity, Mencken argued, was the product of ignorance and religious excess. But even though historians rarely take Mencken's sentimental, elitist, and racist assumptions seriously, his words forced "professional southerners to speak up from the Potomac to the Rio Grande."[23] As such, Mencken has been credited with awakening the southern literary renaissance of the 1920s and 1930s, with his influence on W. J. Cash particularly well documented. As Cash's editor at the *American Mercury,* Mencken helped Cash hone many of his ideas about poor white southern men, in particular, ideas that would form the basis of Cash's seminal book *The Mind of South* (1941). Rooted in Menckenian assumptions, Cash's vision of southern history implied that "the South has no mind, only feeling."[24]

Writing on the fiftieth anniversary of *The Mind of the South*, Edward Ayers argued that "Cash had plenty to say about religion, all of it bad." However, "most modern historians of the New South grant no more autonomy for religion than Cash granted." C. Vann Woodward's *Origins of the New South* (1951) also maintained "a sort of embarrassed silence on the subject," while *The Burden of Southern History* (1960) addresses religion only in the final essay, where Woodward enters a theological dialogue with Reinhold Niebuhr.[25] Ayers deems Woodward's silence on religion an "inadequate" oversight, but Woodward acknowledged that it was a subject he knew little about.[26] In 1940, Woodward recognized that "if I am going to make the hillbilly and the cracker understandable, I must not neglect his religion." However, in the same letter, Woodward lamented that he was "stumped," as "the hillbilly's religion, like his politics, has left few memorials and documents." Southern white religion was indeed "something interesting," which Woodward, at least in 1940, did not want to neglect.[27] However, on reading *The Burden of Southern History* it is hard to counter Charles Reagan Wilson's argument that Woodward "made no effort to gain insight on southern identity from the region's distinctive religious tradition."[28]

Woodward's overarching preoccupation was with the "hillbilly": a long-standing stereotype of rural whiteness whose supposedly apolitical nature has ensured its continued reproduction despite the societal and political pressures that have rendered other ethnic stereotypes unacceptable. Like scholars of Hollywood's white South, Woodward emphasized class-based distinctions, a predecessor of the "diseased whiteness" at the heart of Allison Graham's civil rights villain. As such, scholars of all stripes have failed to engage with religion when grappling with the villainous white South, something that *Southern by the Grace of God* seeks to correct.[29]

Religion and Southern Studies

Since the early twenty-first century, the globalized, postcolonial focus of the new southern studies has largely worked to undermine the pervasive, oppositional regionalism that marked previous waves of southern scholarship in favor of exploring national, hemispheric, and even global connections. But although the new southern studies has added considerable complexity and stimulated some important new directions in southern scholarship, it has neglected religion almost completely, perhaps because evangelical Protestantism's permeating language, symbols, and rituals remain common and potent signifiers of southern distinctiveness.[30] Whether real or performed, southern religious culture forms a pattern of semiotics, which quickly communicate a perceived South to a national and international audience. Despite scholarly dismissals of performed and consumed exceptionalism, the evident uniqueness of the southern religious landscape can undermine attempts to cement the region within wider national, and international, patterns. Southern distinctiveness may be a complex and brittle concept, disavowed by multiple scholarly efforts, but it continues to have enormous purchase on the popular imagination and, thus, has real-world implications.

According to the Pew Religious Landscape Study (2014), 50 percent of evangelical church members and 60 percent of Americans in historically Black Protestant congregations reside in the South, more than double the figures for the Midwest, the second most religious region.[31] Exploring religious identity at the county level, the Public Religion Research Institute (PRRI) found that evangelical Protestants made up 14 percent of the U.S. population in 2020. But in ten counties across the South, the percentage of white evangelical adherents reached over 60 percent. Counties with the largest percentages of mainline white Christians spread across the Midwest, but their percentage of the population ranged between 34 and 37 percent. The intensity of white evangelical Protestantism's hold in southern counties is therefore almost double that of the strongest mainline denominations in the Midwest. Exploring Black Protestant adherence, PRRI reported that despite making up just 7 percent of the U.S. population, Black Protestants accounted for between 55 and 68 percent of the population in ten counties across Mississippi, Alabama, and South Carolina.[32]

Consistent polls rank Mississippi as the most religious state in the union, with Alabama and Mormon-dominated Utah usually close behind. Based on Gallup polling that began in 2008, southern states make up eight to nine of the ten most-religious states each year, with Utah and, more recently, South Dakota the only nonsouthern states making the top ten.[33] Therefore, despite the suggestion of general religious decline in the United States, the South's statistics remain considerably above the national average. Evangelical church adherents accounted for 25.3 percent of the national adult population in 2014. In the South, this figure rose to 34 percent of the population. But in Oklahoma, Kentucky, Alabama, and Arkansas, evangelicals made up more than 45 percent of the total adult population. This figure rose above 50 percent in Tennessee.[34] Although Southern Baptist numbers are falling, down 2.6 million since a peak of 16.3 million in 2006, the Southern Baptist Convention remains the largest denomination in the nation with 13.7 million members as of 2021.[35]

Only conducted every seven years, the Pew Religious Landscape Study is particularly important because of its nondenominational questions that assess the overall intensity of religious feeling in a state rather than simply denominational membership. While 63 percent of Americans were "absolutely certain" of the existence of God in 2014, this figure was between 10 and 20 percent higher in ten southern states (Alabama, Arkansas, Louisiana, Kentucky, Georgia, Tennessee, Mississippi, West Virginia, North Carolina, and South Carolina), peaking at 82 percent in Alabama and Mississippi. The importance of religion in one's life was again up to 24 percent higher in the South, with 77 percent of Alabamians saying that religion was "very important" in their lives, compared to just 53 percent of Americans.[36] Such nondenominational questions have helped to ensure that religiosity in the South was more broadly accounted for since previous surveys, such as the Glenmary Congregations and Membership Surveys, have depended on denominational records of their own membership. As southern historian Ted Ownby argues, this has often resulted in high numbers of "uncounted" members of "countless evangelical Protestant churches that are part of no denomination," particularly in rural Appalachia.[37]

Despite the difficulties of drawing regional boundaries, data like the Pew Study produce a prototypical Deep South model of substantial Black and white evangelical Protestant denominations that peaks in Mississippi and Alabama but permeates across a wider South encompassing the Carolinas, Arkansas, Tennessee, Kentucky, Georgia, and the Florida panhandle. Florida's peninsula boasts considerable religious diversity due to its popularity with migrants from northern states and Cuba in the twentieth century, long after other regional patterns were set. As a result, Florida is also home to some of the South's largest Jewish and Catholic populations.[38] Both "Southern and not Southern," in Samuel Hill's words, Florida's regional status remains an "abiding question."[39] Equally complex is Louisiana, where a more historically diverse population continues to manifest through closely matched numbers of evangelical Protestants, historically Black congregations, and Catholics.[40]

Directly challenging the work of prominent southern religious historians like Hill, Beth Barton Schweiger contests the notion that religious southerners have historically been more "southern" than they have been religious, an understanding that encourages historians to assume that all white southern behavior is tied to some inimitable religious/cultural experience that has "crippled benevolence" in the South. A southern "preoccupation with personal salvation" often explains "why women demanded the vote in Seneca Falls and not Savannah," and above all, it "meant that slavery stood unchallenged by southern Christians who valued faith over works of benevolence." Schweiger undermines these assumptions of consensus and continuity, demonstrating the adaptations that nineteenth-century churches underwent in response to the changing needs and preoccupations of their congregations. Ultimately, she argues that the white resistance to the mid-twentieth-century civil rights movement has retrospectively shaped understanding of Protestant individualism in the Old South, as Hill and others wrestled to explain the moral complacency of the 1950s and 1960s. Looking to the past to explain the present, these historians failed to explore the religious culture of the antebellum South in its own right, conflating white southern behaviors and identities across the antebellum period, through the Civil War, segregation, and beyond.[41] Brutal lynchings, the visual imagery of the Ku Klux Klan and televised white resistance to the civil rights movement in the 1950s and 1960s helped to form what Charles Reagan Wilson has identified as a "broader ideological view of the South as irredeemably evil."[42] Indeed, half a century later, such images proved central to the aforementioned opening credits of *True Blood,* the first season of which played out as George W. Bush, the latest "avatar" of white evangelical mobilization, left office.[43]

But even though the civil rights era has undoubtedly shaped interpretations of the South and its various waves of resistance to federal intervention and racial change, vengeful white southerners determined to overthrow Reconstruction did not settle on the name "Redeemers" by accident. Rather, as Carole Emberton has documented, they attempted to "legitimize their armed assault on freedpeople and Republican officials as a kind of punishment for the corruption unleashed by emancipation and Union victory."[44] By the 1950s and 1960s, their descendants ensured that mainstream southern politics became increasingly synonymous with white supremacy once again. In direct defiance of federal desegregation decisions, southern states began to incorporate the Confederate battle flag into their state flags, as Georgia did in 1956, or simply place the battle flag above official state buildings, as in South Carolina.

Although many denominational leaders sought to avoid confrontation by quietly complying with desegregation rulings, Paul Harvey argues that lower clergymen and "laypeople in the South articulated, defended, and enforced the theology of segregation" in all aspects of everyday life.[45] Indeed, many white southerners "asserted the whiteness of Christ's blood as part of their defense of the justness of segregation." Their faith in God's justice made compromise less likely and drove an even deeper wedge between the region and the nation. Pamphlets such as "God the Original Segregationist" by Reverand Carey Daniel of the West Dallas First Baptist Church were widely reprinted and "rehashed the familiar racial genealogy that linked African Americans to the Canaanites."[46] Segregation was "deeper than custom," Harvey writes. "The social ordering of the races had been sanctified, and a properly religious cloak thrown over Jim Crow's skeleton."[47]

The continued rise of white Christian nationalism has prompted a revived scholarly interest in the intersections of faith and white supremacy in the twenty-first century; however, earlier scholars of the civil rights era rarely granted segregationist religious thought much care and attention.[48] Even though committed to the "prophetic" nature of the civil rights movement, many civil rights scholars have tended to consider religious segregationists "dupes at best."[49] Indeed, David Chappell claims that segregationists failed "to inspire solidarity and self-sacrificial devotion to their cause" and dismisses their rhetoric as the pragmatic ramblings of an embittered, racist few.[50] Jane Dailey notes that even proslavery arguments have been treated with more sensitivity than those of civil rights–era segregationists.[51] Kevin Schultz and Paul Harvey therefore ask if the "racialized and/or marginalized" status of Black activists in this period makes "it 'safer' [for white historians] to incorporate religion more centrally into intellectual trajectories"? Like the religious right after them, many civil rights activists used theological approaches to comprehend and communicate their marginalization and, indeed, their triumphs. Schultz and Harvey therefore posit that it is perhaps "safer to introduce religion as a central actor in people's lives" when these people self-identify as being outside mainstream American society.[52]

Such attitudes have certainly marked American film, where religion has long proven essential to cinematic representation of Black America.[53] Associating Black people with an exotic, "natural" expressivity, early films like *Hallelujah* and *The Green Pastures* (Marc Connelly, 1936) "situate African Americans outside of history and in the realm of myth."[54] Religion was an important indicator of difference in the 1920s and 1930s, indulging white fantasies about a decadent and primitive Christianity that traveled north during the Great Migration. Static, quaint, and unthreatening, this image of Black spirituality denied the overtly political rhetoric and activism of many African American religious leaders and congregations and shaped white attitudes toward the later work of groups that disassociated themselves from the church, such as the Student Nonviolent Coordinating Committee (SNCC) and organizations associated with the Black Power movement.

An integral resource from which Black southerners apparently draw strength and dignity, Hollywood's depictions of African American Christianity often imply a monolithic religious culture but afford it a positivity frequently denied to white evangelical practice. Rather than meaningfully engage with southern religious cultures, filmmakers have both reflected and helped to cement popular presentations of the region's whites as bitter racists, who pragmatically utilize religious rhetoric to further their own advancement. Reflecting a wider national tendency to distance oneself from the orchestrators and perpetuators of racial violence and subordination, many white filmmakers in Hollywood present segregation and racism as purely southern phenomena, relying on the region's religiosity to further cement this apparent exceptionalism.

It was only with the release of Ava DuVernay's *Selma* (2014) that Hollywood acknowledged white Christian involvement in direct action against Jim Crow. Indeed, the film portrays a broad landscape of religious thought, as clergy from across the United States answer Martin Luther King Jr.'s call to march across Alabama in pursuit of voting rights. Raising an unprecedented discussion about the role of religion in the civil rights movement, *Selma*, which I discuss in chapter 5 of this book, demonstrates cinema's power to shape popular narratives, encouraging white evangelicals to note their denominational forebearers' absence in the voting rights campaign and the civil rights movement, more generally. As such, in presenting—but not centralizing—white involvement in the Selma to Montgomery marches, *Selma* manages to disrupt the dominant narrative that white Christians opposed the civil rights movement, without simply rewriting history to alleviate white guilt. It moves deftly from the pulpit to the strategy meeting, presenting King as both a spiritual and political leader, and provides a welcome alternative to the dominant presentation of African Americans in the civil rights melodrama. Unlike the Black southerners of *Mississippi Burning*, whose "faces reveal them as martyrs, sanctified by centuries of suffering," *Selma*'s activists challenge Hollywood's depoliticization of the southern Black church.[55]

Civil Rights Cinema

Although *Mississippi Burning*'s fictionalization of the search for missing civil rights workers during 1964's Freedom Summer marked Hollywood's first major engagement with the civil rights movement, civil rights analogies were not new. The "social problem pictures" that emerged in the 1940s, like the exploitation movies of the 1960s and 1970s, defied "genrification" as civil rights cinema but demonstrate a longer-standing Hollywood preoccupation with the oppositional South.[56] Documentaries and the made-for-TV movie are also crucial to a broader understanding of civil rights histories on film. Indeed, the latter gradually emerged as "a privileged site for the negotiation of problematic social issues" in the 1970s, beginning with NBC's *My Sweet Charlie* (Lamont Johnson, 1970), which charts a platonic relationship between Marlene, a white, pregnant, Texan teenager and an African American civil rights lawyer from New York (the eponymous Charlie).[57] Originally pitched as a theatrical release with Mia Farrow and Sidney Poitier in the lead roles, *My Sweet Charlie* was reimagined for television, a medium that producer-screenwriter team Richard Levinson and William Link believed could "deal with an intimate personal story better than a large-scale event." [58]

The first made-for-TV movie to be recognized by the Television Academy of Arts and Sciences, *My Sweet Charlie* did not shy from the dangers of white racism: the local sheriff kills Charlie when he seeks help after Marlene goes into labor. "I just thought he was robbing [the] store," the sheriff explains. The film attracted forty-one million viewers on its premiere and scored three Emmys, though *Jet* magazine noted the injustice that the male lead, Al Freeman Jr., left the ceremony empty-handed.[59] Four years later, in 1974, fifty million Americans watched *The Autobiography of Miss Jane Pittman* (John Korty, CBS), a fictional story of a Black woman born into slavery who lives long enough to witness the development of the civil rights movement in the 1950s and early 1960s. It received nine Emmy Awards despite initial funding concerns. Eventual sponsor Xerox would interrupt the narrative only once during the entire two-hour broadcast, which legendary film critic Pauline Kael—in a rare television review that merely enhanced the TV movie's credentials— designated "quite possibly the finest movie ever made for television."[60]

As the result of these successes, the southern TV movie evolved into what Allison Graham and Sharon Monteith call "a generic form that not only [told] stories of social movements and southern communities, but also generate[d] public recognition of their members."[61] Dramatically different from the images of hypermasculine, violent resistance that characterized the 1970s Blaxploitation genre, TV films like *The Autobiography of Miss Jane Pittman* and theatrical release *Sounder* (Martin Ritt, 1972) were rooted in a rural, southern Black past that counterbalanced sensationalized visions of the contemporary urban North. While critical debates raged as to which form of cinematic representation was more "authentically black," Lonne Elder, the African American author of *Sounder*'s screenplay, concluded that perhaps African American audiences wanted to see themselves represented in a variety of ways on-screen after "sixty years" of being "starved for any kind of image at all."[62]

A decade after the success of *My Sweet Charlie*, Levinson and Link would reunite with director Lamont Johnson for *Crisis at Central High* (1981), which focused on the 1957 Little Rock, Arkansas, desegregation crisis but omitted lead organizer Daisy Bates. Focused instead on the memoirs of white teacher Elizabeth P. Huckaby, *Crisis at Central High* presents the personal transformation of a white conservative into an advocate for desegregation, preempting many of the white-centric, interpersonal narratives that would come to characterize Hollywood's representations of the civil rights movement later in the 1980s and 1990s. As white redemption narratives, movies like *Mississippi Burning, Ghosts of Mississippi,* and *A Time to Kill* offered little room for political or theological complexity. Rather, each offered a distinctly negative portrayal of white southern religion, offering clear culprits for the South's, and therefore the nation's, continued legacy of racial intolerance and violence. Particularly derided for its focus on white FBI agents rather than African American activists and communities, *Mississippi Burning*'s white-centric narrative has been the subject of many scholarly critiques.[63] Yet, even though these analyses are justified, they largely fail to examine how director Alan Parker constructs divisions of whiteness along regional, class, and religious lines. Like so many of his successors in the civil rights genre, Parker undoubtedly sidelined Black experiences, but he also flattened the diversity of white responses to the African American freedom struggle, conflating southern white religiosity with reactionary, racist politics. In so doing, Parker established a blueprint for the late twentieth-century racial melodrama, which blended the "social problem pictures" of mid-century with increasingly visceral depictions of overt racism and white-on-Black violence.

Structure

While most readers can identify southern stereotypes and U.S. cultural dependency on the "white savior narrative," *Southern by the Grace of God* is the first book to examine the role of religion in the characterization of southerners and the South itself in civil rights and post–civil rights narratives. Accordingly, it builds on existing explorations of the segregationist, the "southern cracker," and the hillbilly and offers a sustained inquiry into the place of southern religion in Hollywood cinema. Organized into six chapters, *Southern by the Grace of God* explores Hollywood feature films, designed to draw maximum audiences in traditional movie theaters and later through the rental, streaming, and sales markets. Each produced within the conventions of "mainstream Hollywood," the films explored in detail in this book range from the 1960s until the early twenty-first century. The focus of chapter 1, *To Kill a Mockingbird*, provides an interpretive lens through which to examine continuity in cinematic engagement with the civil rights movement and, in particular, Hollywood's uncertain engagement with religion. The chapter therefore challenges the assumption that the key tropes of the civil rights drama evolved solely in the latter decades of the twentieth century. Rather, obvious parallels between the characterization of Atticus Finch (Gregory Peck) and the protagonists of 1990s dramas *Ghosts of Mississippi* and *A Time to Kill* (discussed in chapter 3) reflect the continuing significance and marketability of the secular civil rights hero narrative in the latter decades of the twentieth century, amid a culture war rooted in divergent interpretations of the 1960s that eventually pitted a liberal Southern Baptist president from Arkansas against an emboldened conservative political and religious coalition with a distinctly southern drawl.

The culture wars encouraged many Americans to reconsider the legacy of the civil rights movement, an era that mainstream Hollywood film—fascinated by the seemingly timeless divisions of southern whiteness—was concurrently reshaping. But although these later films have come under significant scholarly and journalistic criticism for their failure to develop Black characters and for scapegoating poor white southerners, they simply reinterpret cinematic tropes of intraracial conflict established in William Faulkner's *Intruder in the Dust*, adapted for the cinema in 1949.[64] Such tropes would prove central to Robert Mulligan's beloved adaptation of *To Kill a Mockingbird*, which largely ignores Harper Lee's host of middle-class Christian hypocrites and bigots and instead isolates the villainous Bob Ewell as a low-class racist and religious anomaly. As such, the celluloid Maycomb, Alabama, like many of its cinematic descendants, is predominantly inhabited by liberal, middle-class whites but threatened by an irredeemable line of racist white trash.

In critiquing the continued reverence bestowed on *To Kill a Mockingbird* as both literary and cinematic phenomena, the first chapter of *Southern by the Grace of God* broadens the critical conversation about the key tropes of civil rights cinema and the place of southern religious cultures in film history. Chapter 2 then briefly explores the legacy of southern Black Protestantism in twentieth-century popular culture, from the ridiculed, hypocritical preacher of minstrelsy to the prophetic clergymen of the civil rights movement. Recognizing the lack of Black agency evident in the civil rights melodrama, this chapter explores religion's central role in the cinematic construction of an impotent, often submissive community. It concludes with *Mississippi Burning*'s representation of a silent Black congregation, paying particular attention to the film's influential use of solemn gospel music to soundtrack white depravity and a seemingly timeless African American faith in eventual deliverance.

Chapter 3 centers the late 1980s and 1990s as a period of considerable racial, cultural, and political tension, which many commentators attributed to the nation's "southernization," perhaps best symbolized by the 1994 Republican revolution, which cemented a considerable overlap between congressional Republicans and the Southern Baptist Convention. As white redemption narratives, civil rights films produced in this period contain little to any reference to liberal white Christianity, as religious preoccupations would presumably complicate the heroes' claims to secular righteousness. As such, the films discussed in chapter 3, most notably *Ghosts of Mississippi* and *A Time to Kill*, offered little room for political or theological complexity. Layering extreme racial views with vengeful religious preoccupations, each of these films presented a distinctly negative portrayal of white southern religion, giving clear culprits for the South's, and therefore the nation's, continued legacy of racial intolerance and violence.

In chapter 4, *Southern by the Grace of God* foregrounds previously unseen archival evidence that Scorsese and his team of filmmakers employed known stereotypes to reconceptualize villain Max Cady as a pentecostal Christian and "monster of the South" in their 1991 remake of *Cape Fear*. The chapter therefore spotlights perhaps the crudest manipulation of southern religion onscreen, reflecting the "social deprivation" theories of the 1980s, the distinctly southern accent of the newly dominant religious right, and the numerous scandals that rocked televangelism in the late 1980s. In exploring the specifics of Cady's reincarnation, chapter 4 expands this book's focus on the culture wars of the late twentieth century as a backlash to the gains of the civil rights movement and argues that the film's presentation of Pentecostalism updates the racial and class tensions of the 1962 film of the same name without featuring a single Black character.

Chapter 5 shifts to the more recent civil rights dramas, *Selma* and *The Butler* (Lee Daniels, 2013), examining their representations of the civil rights movement, religion, and the significance of Black filmmaking in the promptly defined "age of Obama." In its coverage of *Selma* in particular, the chapter documents a considerable divergence from the white-centric civil rights melodrama, reflected in storytelling, cast, crew, and the noticeable discomfort provoked by director Ava DuVernay's imagining of President Lyndon Johnson. It therefore raises questions about the evolution of the civil rights genre and its rightful reimagining at the hands of Black directors, where African Americans are no longer secondary characters and where religiosity becomes an agent of solidarity, power, and political strength.

By a way of conclusion, the final chapter then returns to the mid-1990s and charts the reception of two 1996 films associated with Arkansan actor-turned-writer-turned-director Billy Bob Thornton: *Sling Blade* and *A Family Thing* (directed by Richard Pearce). In exploring these films, the conclusion offers summative thoughts on the exoticized mythology of white southern "authenticity" in the age of the civil rights melodrama and Thornton's efforts to redeem a region that he argued was continually reduced to its racist history. Using interviews to simultaneously lament and claim ownership over Hollywood's South, Thornton argued that films "like *Ghosts of Mississippi* or *Mississippi Burning* are just ridiculous."[65] Proving that the civil rights drama had become a recognizable Hollywood preoccupation by the mid-1990s, Thornton was concerned that narratives spotlighting "all these horrible things that happened over civil rights" shaped popular opinion about the contemporary South and overshadowed films about reconciliation, including his own. Both *A Family Thing* and *Sling Blade* therefore offered a rebuttal to the ubiquity of the civil rights melodrama in the mid-1990s, even while they echoed the racial melodrama's themes of white male sacrifice and redemption.

Furthermore, Thornton's portrayal of a violent and all-encompassing Christianity was crucial to *Sling Blade*'s perceived southern authenticity, reinforcing the extent to which religion is crucial to presentations of the South as a region apart from the rest of the nation. This concluding chapter therefore reinforces the significance of *Southern by the Grace of God*'s detailed analyses of religion's intersections with other key coordinates of the South in mainstream cinema and the methodology it provides to better examine the enduring and evolving consequences of the 1950s and 1960s and the resulting culture wars.

CHAPTER 1

"They Take the Bible Literally You Know"

To Kill a Mockingbird and the Origins of Hollywood's Secular Civil Rights Hero

In December 1996, Janet Maslin wrote in the *New York Times* of *Ghosts of Mississippi*'s "'To Kill a Mockingbird' moment," when white southern attorney Bobby DeLaughter (Alec Baldwin) tucks his daughter Claire (Alexa Vega) into bed and explains to her (and the audience) why it is no longer appropriate for them to sing "Dixie."[1] Just as Atticus Finch once attempted to alleviate daughter Scout's bedtime fears of the ghostly Boo Radley, DeLaughter tells Claire, "I'm not so sure all ghosts like 'Dixie.'" Less than a month later, Ty Burr contended in *Entertainment Weekly* that another new southern legal drama, *A Time to Kill*, owed "half of its plot, three quarters of its title, and all of its good intentions" to *To Kill a Mockingbird*.[2] Indeed, the publishers of John Grisham's original novel had been keen to highlight such connections, encouraging teachers to "enhance students' experiences as they read *A Time to Kill* by drawing comparisons to Harper Lee's classic," which they argued "addresses the same cultural issues."[3] Despite noting twenty-six-year-old Matthew McConaughey's admirable performance as Mississippi lawyer Jake Brigance, Ty Burr concluded his comparison of *A Time to Kill* and *To Kill a Mockingbird* by arguing that, ultimately, "the difference between the two movies comes down to the moral weight of their respective hunks [and] Jake Brigance, sir, is no Atticus Finch."[4]

It perhaps goes without saying, therefore, that Peck's Academy Award–winning white hero cast a significant shadow over the representation of Brigance and DeLaughter onscreen. As attorneys, all three represent what sociologist Jennifer Pierce calls "arbiters of the law, justice, and morality." Each suffers considerable personal turmoil, usually at the hands of bitter white supremacists, but all endure as "'civilizing' figures," who use the law to bring about southern redemption.[5] "In this country, the courts are the great levelers," Atticus advocates in *To Kill a Mockingbird,* just as Jake Brigance will insist that "in the New South, justice will be colorblind." Even in 1996, Donald Bogle writes, "the white attorney has to inform the white jury of its own racism."[6]

The seemingly timeless cynicism toward white southern juries can be traced back even further than *To Kill a Mockingbird,* most notably to *Intruder in the Dust,* the 1949 adaptation of William Faulkner's novel of the same name, which, like *Mockingbird* and *A Time to Kill* in particular, follows a central narrative of a Black man accused of a capital offense against a white southerner. But Faulkner's presentation of the white lawyer was much less noble than Harper Lee's and John Grisham's. In Faulkner's tale, it is explicitly stated, rather than merely implied, that middle-class white men are too concerned with "notions" to challenge white supremacy and the status quo. The town lawyer, John Stevens (David Brian), is cold and condescending toward his potential client, Lucas Beauchamp (Juano Hernandez): "Has it occurred it to you that if you just said 'mister' to white people, and meant it, you might not be sitting here now?" The threat of a public lynching does not even warrant being late for dinner according to Stevens's brother-in-law, Mr. Mallinson: "It's happened before and it's bound to happen again." Those looking to challenge injustice must find their allies in women and children.

Lucas Beauchamp, who understandably chooses not to trust the didactic Stevens with the truth, seeks instead the help of Chick Mallinson (Claude Jarman), the white lawyer's teenage nephew, who is then assisted by his childhood African American friend and an elderly white woman. Thus, where *To Kill a Mockingbird* "celebrates lawyerly paternalism," encouraging white Americans to "serve others in a way that confirms our superiority in a system we have made in our own image," *Intruder in the Dust* "challenges the rule of lawyers if not law itself."[7] *Intruder in the Dust* was, according to Ralph Ellison, "the only film that could be shown in Harlem without arousing unintended laughter."[8] Yet, as this book will attest, Hollywood cinema firmly adopted the *Mockingbird* rather than the *Intruder* model.

A Time to Kill and *Ghosts of Mississippi,* which are both further discussed in chapter 3, enjoyed neither the critical acclaim nor cultural longevity of *To Kill a Mockingbird.* But their reliance on the earlier film demonstrates that the reconstructed southerner/white savior narrative far preceded the 1990s, when it became a recognizable trope. Rather, it had been constructed alongside and in relation to the civil rights movement itself. Equating privileged white masculinity with heroism, *To Kill a Mockingbird* set a cinematic precedent that endured through the construction of later southern white lawyers, each ennobled by their participation in cases involving comparatively underdeveloped African American characters.

Smarter than his neighbors, Hollywood's white civil rights hero lawyer propels the apparently national agenda of consensus liberalism and secular equality rather than the sectional obsessions of zealous Christianity and racial division. Robert Mulligan's 1962 adaptation of *To Kill a Mockingbird*, arguably the first white-hero civil rights melodrama, therefore sacrifices the religious diversity and moral complexity of Harper Lee's novel in a manner that would prove exemplary to later generations of filmmakers. *To Kill a Mockingbird's* cinematic morality, inextricably bound to Gregory Peck's paternal, liberal humanism, is rooted in a learned rationality that transcends small-town racial bigotry and exists beyond the influence of religiosity.

But arguing that Atticus's "serious moral values" are rooted in secular humanism rather than Christian theology, as some scholars have, only makes sense if readers accept Atticus as both entirely nonreligious and infallible, or at least the book's sole moral compass.[9] As this chapter will show, Atticus is simply one of many characters in Lee's novel to offer a worldview, and he is far from the omnipotent voice of secular egalitarianism that the later film implies. Lee's Atticus is a prominent character, the idealized father of Scout's retrospective narration. But Scout's precocious ability to absorb, critique, and refashion numerous philosophies and belief systems is crucial to the novel's structure and appeal. Atticus is therefore one of many voices Scout recounts. However, in Mulligan's cinematic adaptation, Maycomb appears uncomplicated by the influence of religious faith—specifically the Methodism that is so important to the Finch lineage that it is mentioned on the novel's second page. Aside from Jem's request that Atticus play football "for the Methodists," there is nothing in the film to suggest denominational adherence and the family do not attend church as they do in the novel. Such narrative omissions make Mulligan's *To Kill a Mockingbird* a significant example of how southern religion has been represented, misrepresented, and sometimes elided in popular culture.

More recent debates over *To Kill a Mockingbird's* morality, stimulated by the 2015 publication of Lee's only other novel, *Go Set a Watchman*, and the deeply personal grief many readers exhibited at Lee's death in early 2016, only confirmed *To Kill a Mockingbird's* lasting and immutable power in both literary and cinematic form.[10] This chapter will therefore explore how each manifestation of Lee's narrative continues to influence popular dialogue around race, religion, and poverty in the American South despite numerous scholarly attempts to complicate its legacy.[11] It ultimately concludes that the cinematic Atticus Finch—notably a more prominent character in the movie than in Harper Lee's novel—enabled the development of an enduring Hollywood trope in the southern liberal lawyer, offering an apparently timeless, color-blind, and commonsense approach to racial progress rooted in gradualist paternalism at the height of the civil rights movement. By foregrounding Atticus, the film omits a range of other characters, scenes, and themes that Lee's novel explored, especially those relating to women and religion, culminating in a whiter, more secular, and more masculine interpretation of Maycomb that would prove influential across decades of cinema.

Religion: "Maycomb's Principal Recreation"

According to Rebecca Best, Harper Lee's fictional town of Maycomb, Alabama, is comprised of Foucauldian "disciplinary mechanisms" designed to uphold strictly defined race, gender, or class norms. Scout ("almost six") and her older brother Jem ("nearly ten") "develop their personalities and find their places in society by copying the behavior of people in similar social positions."[12] Constantly under family and community surveillance, the children are discouraged from drifting too far from the status quo. Their questioning and eventual acceptance of middle-class, liberal, white southern Christian values form the subsequent basis of the novel's lasting moral code. Therefore, while Maycomb abounds with gossip and contradictory characters, its inhabitants—like those of Faulkner's novels—are of what Cleanth Brooks called "a Christian environment": from Jem's lament that the only movies that come to town are "Jesus ones" to Miss Stephanie's exclamation about the crowds gathering for Tom Robinson's trial: "You'd think William Jennings Bryan was speakin.'"[13]

Lee was a lifelong member of her local United Methodist Church in Monroeville, Alabama, where stained glass windows were donated in honor of her parents.[14] But her first—and for fifty-five years her only—published novel is by no means kind to organized religion. Rather, it abounds with the hypocrisies and elitism of supposedly Christian people, from the dubious paternalism of the women's missionary circle to the societal exile of the Radleys, a family of "foot-washing Baptist[s]." It does, however, offer an inclusive view of the numerous strands and intensities of southern Christianity found within Maycomb's white social spectrum. The misinterpretations and hierarchies that govern relationships between white Baptists and Methodists, for example, are every bit as complex to Scout as those between the races but offer a constant reference point within a child's changing world, as perhaps they did for Lee herself. When Jem and Scout suffer racist taunts as a result of their father's legal defense of African Americans, Atticus specifically informs them that he "couldn't go to church and worship God if [he] didn't try to help" Tom Robinson. As such, Atticus appeals to his children's burgeoning sense of Christian principle to justify his implicit undermining of white supremacy, something that governs their lives but that they are too young to fully understand.[15]

Characterized by Scout as "Maycomb's principal recreation," church attendance appears compulsory in the novel.[16] However, allowing religion to take over one's life can be as harmful as alcoholism, according to the Finches' Baptist neighbor Miss Maudie Atkinson, who teaches Scout to be suspicious of excessive religion, especially that of the rural or secluded. "There are just some kind of men who—who're so busy worrying about the next world they've never learned to live in this one," Miss Maudie says of their other neighbor, Mr. Radley, whom she denounces as a "foot-washing Baptist." Here, Maudie and Scout assume a distinctly middle-class feminine bond that transcends their generational and denominational differences, illuminating the broad Protestant spectrum in Maycomb, while simultaneously reinforcing ideas about what is "appropriate."

As a Methodist, Scout assumes that Baptist insistence on closed communion separates her from all Baptists, foot-washing or otherwise, but Miss Maudie decides that "it was easier to define primitive baptistry than closed communion." As such, she instructs Scout, "Foot-washers believe anything that's pleasure's a sin. Did you know some of 'em came out of the woods one Saturday and passed by this place and told me me and my flowers were going to hell?" Scout begins to instantly question the intent of any religion that might banish Miss Maudie to "various Protestant hells" simply for enjoying her flowers. "Thing is, foot-washers think women are sin by definition," Miss Maudie continues. "They take the Bible literally you know." Absorbing her adult neighbor's concern that the Bible can be dangerous, "worse than a whiskey bottle" for some men, Scout concludes that for Mr. Radley, disturbed religious understandings have manifested in a violent and reclusive son, Boo. [17]

Through her discussions with Miss Maudie, Scout therefore discovers that there are differing opinions on the correct purpose and place of organized religion in southern society. In her own life, the Bible is much more than a moral guide; it is an educational gateway—a book she must grapple with if she is to make sense of any other. Her precocious literacy, so often attributed to Atticus's teaching, is actually the result of copying Bible passages with Calpurnia, the family's African American maid. Although she had read law files over Atticus's shoulder for as long as she could remember, Scout asserts that "Atticus ain't got time to teach me anything," and so it is Calpurnia she blames when her literacy causes her and her first schoolteacher to start "off on the wrong foot."[18] Although theology is not the crucial element in this aspect of the novel but rather Scout's tempestuous entrance into the public school system, the Bible's physical presence is testament to the pervasive nature of Maycomb's distinctly southern Protestantism. Indeed, the physical item, as the primary example of the written word in southern culture, takes on a meaning and purpose far beyond its theological function.

Like racism, then, Scout's religious characterizations, discussions, and experiences are crucial to Lee's evocation of the small-town rural South. Indeed, Atticus argues that the injustice evident in Tom Robinson's conviction for raping a white woman is "just as much Maycomb County as missionary teas." However, like in *Intruder in the Dust*, the threat of a lynch mob is thought to be reduced on Sundays, when poor whites "go to church all day." It is fitting, therefore, that Scout and Jem's only glimpse of Black Maycomb comes through religion, when they attend First Purchase African Methodist Episcopal Church with Calpurnia. "The men stepped back and took off their hats; the women crossed their arms at their waists, weekday gestures of respectful attention," Scout remembers. "They parted and made a small pathway to the church door for us."[19] Whereas Robert Butler argues that these scenes demonstrate that the African American congregation, unlike its white counterparts, "warmly welcomes outsiders," Scout's use of the word "weekday" to describe the African Americans' "respectful attention" makes it clear that Maycomb's Black population is accustomed to behaving in a certain manner around white people, including children.[20] Indeed, their weekday employment almost certainly depended on them adhering rigidly to these conventions. Although Jem and Scout are invited guests, other whites "trespass with apparent impunity," using First Purchase as a gambling den on weekdays, "bring[ing] illegal activities under the protection of an unwritten rule that allows them to take whatever they please from the Blacks."[21]

Only Lula, a Black woman dismissed by her own community as "a troublemaker from way back," with "fancy ideas an' haughty ways," points out the hypocrisy of white children attending "n****r church," a situation that would never be accepted in reverse. When Calpurnia asserts that Jem and Scout are her "comp'ny," Lula's response is acerbic: "Yeah, an' I reckon you's company at the Finch house during the week."[22] Deliberately confrontational, Lula is apparently not even a practicing Christian; she has turned up purely to express her distaste. She is therefore implicitly separated from the upright, respectable, church-based African Americans working with dignity to improve race relations in both Maycomb and Lee's contemporary 1950s.[23]

Rather than portray ideological divisions within the Black community about how best to dismantle white supremacy—divisions that were becoming considerably more pronounced by the time most audiences saw the film in

1963—Mulligan's film omits the scenes at First Purchase altogether, ensuring that the film never enters Maycomb's African American "quarters." This is just one of many scenes in which Lee attempts to navigate Maycomb's complex, intersecting religious and political fault lines, and its omission from the film enables the movie to deny the existence of the Black assertiveness that Lula represents, as well as Scout's recognition of Calpurnia's "modest double life," which calls to mind W. E. B. DuBois's concept of "double consciousness."[24] It is also here that Scout observes that "the Impurity of Women doctrine that seemed to preoccupy all clergymen" stretched beyond racial boundaries.[25] As such, Scout's developing awareness of what it means to be a southern woman is closely linked to her experience with both Black and white organized religion.

An inquisitive tomboy, Scout is used to a rough-and-tumble existence with her brother Jem and summertime companion Dill Harris. However, as the novel and the children develop, Scout is increasingly left out of the boys' games and expected to adhere to gender standards that both startle and stifle her. In noticing the sexism that marks the rhetoric at both Black and white churches, Scout begins to appreciate that divisions between the sexes run much deeper than her brother's adolescent awkwardness. As such, Lee's coverage of Maycomb's religious landscape provides interesting context for a young girl's developing awareness of intersections between gender, race, and religion, all of which is conspicuously absent from the film, compromising what Dean Shackelford defines as "the novel's feminist center."[26] Indeed, Lee's intricate and often feminized religious landscape was omitted so that the film might build toward Tom Robinson's trial (and the case for Atticus's secular sainthood) in a more streamlined manner, ignoring much of Scout's growing relationship with Miss Maudie and omitting Aunt Alexandra altogether.

In making such narrative decisions, director Robert Mulligan, who had largely worked in television before embarking on a career-defining series of collaborations with *Mockingbird*'s producer Alan Pakula, distorted what literary scholar Bradley Shaw calls "Lee's Southern religious complexities" in favor of what he "reasonably could assume was the primary Gothic horror of the South: persistent and irrational hatred inflamed by a degenerating poverty."[27] Analyzing *To Kill a Mockingbird* in relation to the films that followed it, the aforementioned *Ghosts of Mississippi* and *A Time to Kill*, thus highlights that the earlier novel and film has been shielded from the criticism that marked the release of subsequent civil rights dramas that follow a broadly similar narrative. The comparison also exemplifies why *To Kill a Mockingbird* remains, in the words of Ryu Spaeth, "absolutely essential to the white understanding of America's racist past," while being completely irrelevant to the Black experience, a point reiterated by influential African American writer Ta-Nehisi Coates, who revealed on the release of Lee's second novel *Go Set a Watchman* in 2015 that he had never read *To Kill a Mockingbird* and did not intend to.[28]

To Kill a Mockingbird in Context: Scottsboro, *Brown v. Board of Education*, and Emmett Till

While seminal Black intellectuals like James Baldwin and Ralph Ellison never saw fit to write about *To Kill a Mockingbird* in the 1960s or beyond, critics and fans alike have consistently drawn parallels between *To Kill a Mockingbird*'s depiction of race relations in the Deep South during the Depression and the civil rights movement that punctuated the period in which Lee wrote and published her novel, culminating in its cinematic adaptation, first released in December 1962. Writing of a spell in jail during the Freedom Rides in 1961, James Farmer, the director of the Congress of Racial Equality (CORE) recalled being given a copy of *To Kill a Mockingbird* by National Association for the Advancement of Colored People (NAACP) chairman Roy Wilkins.[29] Although Farmer did not express an opinion on the novel, his memory nevertheless reflects what Eric J. Sundquist calls "the book's popular appeal at the height of the civil rights protest."[30] Likewise, Andrew Young, a key member of Martin Luther King Jr.'s Southern Christian Leadership Conference (SCLC), who went on to serve as U.S. ambassador to the United Nations in the late 1970s, has credited the novel with giving Americans "a sense of emerging humanism and decency."[31] However, despite these apparent connections to the anti-racist activism of the early 1960s, *To Kill a Mockingbird*'s filmmakers, like Lee herself, seemed reticent to openly support the civil rights movement. "The big danger in making a movie of *To Kill a Mockingbird*," Mulligan recorded in the production notes, "is in thinking of this as a chance to jump on the segregation-integration soapbox. The book does not make speeches. It is not melodramatic with race riots and race hatred."[32]

Indeed, despite its seemingly obvious themes of equality and anti-racism, *To Kill a Mockingbird*—published in July 1960—made only guarded references to contemporary events; the story is very much sequestered in the historical 1930s. Because of this, numerous fans and critics have argued that Tom Robinson's story must have been based, at least in part, on the lengthy and well-publicized Scottsboro cases in which nine African American boys (aged between twelve and nineteen) were wrongfully convicted of raping two white women on a train passing through Alabama in 1931. Jill May has observed that "Scout Finch faces the realities of southern society within the same age span that Harper Lee faced Scottsboro" and that both the novel and Scottsboro questioned the meaning of "rape"—a term Scout admits she does not understand—when implied as "a rhetorical justification for lynching . . . sectional resistance to the nationalization of constitutional rights [and] a judicial procedure employed to codify a predetermined guilt." Indeed, when defense attorney Samuel Leibowitz objected to a prosecutor's continued "ranting about 'n****rs' and rape" during the second Scottsboro trial, the offending prosecutor appealed earnestly to the judge, "Your Honor knows I always make the same speech in every n*****r rape case."[33] In the aftermath of Tom Robinson's conviction, even ten-year-old Jem is forced to conclude, "I know it's not right, but I can't figure out what's wrong—maybe rape shouldn't be a capital offense. . . . Lots of folks have been hung—hanged—on circumstantial evidence."[34]

Efforts to overturn the convictions of the Scottsboro boys led to two Supreme Court cases, *Powell v. Alabama* (November 1932) and *Norris v. Alabama* (April 1935), both rooted in considerations of the Fourteenth Amendment. Both cases should have borne considerable influence on the Tom Robinson case, which takes place in the summer of 1935. The former is likely the reason why Tom has legal assistance at all, having reversed the convictions of those who lacked effective assistance of counsel during capital cases. Indeed, Atticus Finch is no Samuel Leibowitz and is distinctly unromantic about how he came to take on Tom's case, advising his brother, "I'd hoped to get through life without a case of this kind, but [Judge] John Taylor pointed at me and said 'You're It.'"[35] The latter of the Scottsboro cases offered Tom a solid basis for appeal, ruling that the systematic exclusion of African American jurors at the selection process was unconstitutional, noting that even though there was no direct ban on nonwhite jurors in Alabama, voter registration exclusions ensured that all-white juries, such as Maycomb's, were inevitable and denied Black defendants the equal protection of the law.

Although it seems unlikely that any novel told from the perspective of a child would engage with the specifics of recent Supreme Court jurisprudence, noted parallels between Tom Robinson's case and Scottsboro seem limited to the well-documented significance of the "southern rape myth," which Scout very well understands: "Tom was a dead man the minute Mayella Ewell opened her mouth and screamed."[36] But none of Lee's characters—not even Atticus in his concluding argument—make any reference to Scottsboro, including the Supreme Court rulings that fundamentally altered Tom Robinson's rights in the courtroom. Indeed, historian Joseph Crespino has shown that Lee's father, A. C. Lee, long thought to be the inspiration for Atticus, did not even acknowledge the powerful decision to overturn the original Scottsboro convictions in his position as the editor of the *Monroe Journal*. Rather, the elder Lee's prime concern regarding the case was the unwelcome publicity it brought on the state of Alabama, which he blamed on the meddling of outside forces. Therefore, as Crespino concludes, if the pioneering lawyers of the Scottsboro case did have any influence on Harper Lee's work, "it was not because her father took much note of [them] in print."[37] It therefore appears, to echo Isaac Saney, that *To Kill a Mockingbird* does not only fail to reflect on its apparent parallels with Scottsboro but rather exists in a world where the infamous case "never happened," creating "the indelible impression that the entire Black community existed in a complete state of paralysis."[38]

For all their constitutional significance, *Norris v. Alabama* and *Powell v. Alabama* left Jim Crow largely intact. So too did the New Deal despite, as Atticus notes, "pressure from the distaff side of the Executive branch," itself a fairly archaic reference to First Lady Eleanor Roosevelt, whose articulations of Black equality were far more convincing than her husband's. Indeed, as Mrs. Merriweather notes in Lee's novel, the sentiment among white southerners was that "Mrs. Roosevelt's lost her mind—just plain lost her mind coming down to Birmingham and tryin' to sit with them." Referring to Eleanor Roosevelt's challenge to the segregated seating plan imposed by Bull Connor's Birmingham police at the Southern Conference for Human Welfare in 1938, Mrs. Merriweather's concern reflects one of the novel's chronological lapses.[39] After all, by this point in the novel, it is only 1935, creating what Patrick Chura calls "an amalgam or cross-historical montage, the novel's 'historical present' diluted by the influence of events and ideology concurrent with its period of production."[40] Writing in the mid-1950s, it is clear that Lee was driven by a more recent Supreme Court case than those that emerged from the Scottsboro scandal, one that sent the white South into a spiraling hysteria.

If Scottsboro was "a call to arms" for the white South, *Brown v. Board of Education* (1954) produced the all-out war of massive resistance. The 1955 murder of Emmett Till then resurrected "Judge Lynch," exposed not only through the literal act of killing but also the failure of Mississippi courts to convict Till's murderers.[41] Recalling the trial of her son's murderers, Mamie Till-Bradley wrote that the defense focused not on the murder of her son but on "showing who was in charge." Even though she was an hour away from the courthouse, Till-Bradley heard celebratory gunshots on the day of the verdict. The acquitted were on the front page of every newspaper; the whole of white Mississippi, it seemed, celebrated the outcome of the trial.[42]

In their confession to *Look* magazine, Till's murderers implicitly admitted that they were motivated by the threat of interracial sex, arguing that the fourteen-year-old Till had boasted of white girlfriends up North.[43] In the aftermath of *Brown*, they connected Till's childish confidence with sexual threat—a physical manifestation of the specter of racial mixing that segregationist preachers and politicians argued loomed within any federal attempt to enforce de-segregation. As Heather Pool has written, "Till's mutilated body signalled the South's intention to reject racial integration and equality offered by the Supreme Court in *Brown v. Board*, a refusal accomplished through a spectacular act of violence against the very image of a new generation's promise: a smart, confident African-American youth."[44]

Although it remained easy for white northerners to blame the South (rather than the nation) for this most recent display of racist violence, Till's lynching cut through the usual national silence that met Black death in the South, something that many historians and activists have attributed to Till's mother's decision to display his mutilated body in their hometown of Chicago, photographs of which were published in *Jet* magazine.[45] However, in a wider assessment of what made the Till case so unique, Pool argues that its breakthrough nature, especially among white northerners, cannot be separated from its proximity to the *Brown* decision, which ensured that African American inferiority before the law was no longer a given. Indeed, the Supreme Court's unanimous ruling, overturning the concept of "separate but equal," demonstrated levels of federal intervention into the status of African American citizenship not seen since Reconstruction. Therefore, all who engaged with the Till murder did so under extremely new legal and cultural conditions. Although scholars have addressed the significance of the *Brown* decision to the United States' wider objectives in the Cold War, it remains clear that it unleashed particular anxiety in the white South because it implied a contestation—and eventually a worrying validation—of Black citizenship and equality, where previously there had been no question. For African Americans, the Till case starkly exposed the limitations of the Supreme Court's "symbolic" ruling in *Brown*, establishing what Pool calls "a twilight zone between two legal realities" that would both inspire and compel future activism.[46]

While Atticus may not refer to Scottsboro in his courtroom defense of Tom Robinson, parts of his speech omitted from the film nevertheless exhibit a skeptical understanding of the fundamental principles of the *Brown* decision and a predominant white southern discomfort with outside agitation, which Atticus argues is a perversion cloaked in the sentiments of American exceptionalism: "Thomas Jefferson once said that all men are created equal, a phrase that the Yankees and distaff side of the Executive Branch in Washington are fond of hurling at us. There is a tendency in this year of grace, 1935, for certain people to use this phrase out of context, to satisfy all conditions." In making such an argument, Atticus manages to both anticipate and undermine the 1954 *Brown* decision, particularly the overarching principle of the Supreme Court's unanimous opinion, that "segregation of white and colored children in public schools has a detrimental effect upon the colored children": that "the policy of separating the races is usually interpreted as denoting the inferiority of the negro group [affecting] the motivation of a child to learn."[47] For Atticus, "all men are *not* created equal in the sense some people would have us believe— some people are smarter than others, some people have more opportunity because they're born with it" (emphasis mine). However, "the people who run public education promote the stupid and the idle along with the industrious— because all men are created equal, educators will gravely tell you, the children left behind suffer serious feelings of inferiority."[48]

At other points too, Lee's novel implies serious inadequacies with public schooling and the sentiments behind it; indeed, the pathetic state of Maycomb's elementary school may invite further scrutiny of what was really at stake in the *Brown* decision. If the ruling sought to afford all American children with an equal education, Harper Lee's novel questioned what the value of that education actually was. If African Americans were admitted to Maycomb's white schools, something that the Atticus of *Go Set a Watchman* argues would ensure a further degradation of public education "to accommodate Negro children," Scout's creativity would (in *Mockingbird*'s logic) be even further stifled, while the Ewells would still play truant.[49] Such is the inequality of values and opportunity that Atticus gestured to in his summation speech. In an age where high-profile desegregation cases ended in violence, from Little Rock, Arkansas, to the University of Alabama, Lee—ever the gradualist—implies, "what is the point?" She was not alone. A combination of vehement segregationists and ambivalent moderates ensured that just over 1 percent of Black southern children attended desegregated schools by the time most cinemagoers saw *To Kill a Mockingbird* in 1963.[50]

Go Set a Watchman

Atticus's concluding speech, delivered before Maycomb's courtroom in *To Kill a Mockingbird*, is much longer in Lee's novel than it is in Mulligan's film. Although some key points remain—the fallacy at the heart of the South's rape myth, the wretched poverty endemic to the Ewells' diseased whiteness—others, including Atticus's veiled indictments of *Brown*, are obscured. In Lee's novel, Atticus manages to undermine the principal mythology of white southern womanhood, its use to justify segregation, as well as the philosophies of equality bestowed by *Brown*. For Atticus, the courts are America's "great levelers"—from "the Supreme Court of the United States or the humblest J.P. court in the land." Although this may appear somewhat contradictory to readers, given Atticus's clearly derogatory allusions to *Brown*, the controversial publication of Lee's only other novel, *Go Set a Watchman*, in 2015 confirmed what Lee had always implied in *To Kill a Mockingbird* but that Mulligan's film could never admit: that Atticus (and all of white Maycomb) would oppose the *Brown* decision.

Go Set a Watchman therefore fostered a new dialogue between critics and fans about the lasting significance of Lee's *To Kill a Mockingbird* and the subsequent film adaptation. Because fans and critics had grown to accept Harper Lee's withdrawal from public life in the years after her first novel's release, the apparent "reappearance" of the *Watchman* manuscript in the last year of her life appeared cynical and financially motivated.[51] However, such controversies significantly intensified when it was revealed that the Atticus of *Go Set a Watchman*—set approximately twenty years after *To Kill a Mockingbird*—was a Citizens' Council member committed to the separation of the races. In fact, the new Atticus even resented the modest civil rights gains of the Scottsboro era, dismissed as part of his wider attack on "NAACP-paid lawyers standing around like buzzards . . . demand[ing] Negros on the juries."[52]

Although some reviewers pointed out that a flawed and even contradictory Atticus was probably reflective of white southern thought in the 1950s, most seemed to see Atticus's "transformation" as some kind of personal betrayal. Heartbroken fans and critics alike responded with a flurry of op-eds, blog posts, and articles, while some vowed not to read the book at all. One Michigan bookstore even contended that its customers were owed "refunds and apologies" over the manner in which the book was promoted. According to Brilliant Books of Traverse City, *Go Set a Watchman* was a mere academic curiosity: an insight into the editing process rather than a legitimate prequel or sequel to *To Kill a Mockingbird*, or even a novel in its own right. "To see our noble industry parade and celebrate this as 'Harper Lee's New Novel' . . . is pure exploitation of both literary fans and a beloved American classic (which we hope has not been irrevocably tainted)," the store's management stated on its website. Yet, rather than focus on the editorial hand undoubtedly missing from *Watchman*'s prose, the booksellers suggested that the novel would sit uneasy with readers because of the distasteful attitudes espoused by many of its characters. *Go Set a Watchman* "is a first draft that was originally, and rightfully rejected," the piece reads. "The book, and some of the characters therein, are very much a product of this era in the South."[53]

It is certainly true that *Go Set a Watchman* is a complex, often frustrating look at the hardening racial attitudes of many white southerners following the 1954 *Brown* decision, acknowledging the lingering racism of what the adult Scout, now using her real name Jean Louise, calls "men of substance and character . . . of all varieties and reputations."[54] Brilliant Books and many others therefore castigated *Watchman* for its realism, a criticism that is testament to the hallowed place that Mulligan's adaptation of *To Kill a Mockingbird* occupies in the popular (white) memory of the civil rights movement. After all, racist attitudes abound in Lee's *To Kill a Mockingbird* but did not cost the novel many fans. It is only in Mulligan's film—which omits the middle-class bigotry of Mrs. Dubose and the women's missionary circle—that racism is confined entirely to its most overtly poor, violent, and masculine manifestation, Bob Ewell. Described, as if by W. J. Cash, in the 1998 documentary *Fearful Symmetry* as a "southern cracker . . . the twisted, decayed remnant of the lively braggarts of Scotch-Irish descent . . . who despised machines and money and ambition and who dueled at the hint of an insult," Bob Ewell became the cinematic blueprint for the southern racist, carefully detached from the middle-class whites who shared many of his viewpoints but delivered them in more genteel settings.[55] The willful denial among some critics and readers that Atticus could even harbor racist views, something that has been advocated by numerous scholars in the decades since *To Kill a Mockingbird*'s publication, suggests that for some readers, Atticus is an actual person, whose words and actions have been callously misrepresented in *Watchman*.[56]

The fact that the president of the American Bar Association has risen to Atticus's defense in the past is testament to the character's exceptional cultural and ideological significance in the minds of countless, predominantly white Americans.[57] After publishing Crespino's critique of Atticus's enduring legacy in 2000, the editors of *Southern Cultures* were forced to reflect that it had "been some time since an essay has provoked as much debate around here." Noting that "readers found [Crespino's reappraisal] to be a narrow and inaccurate portrayal of Harper Lee's most famous creation," the editors then printed three responses to Crespino's article. The first, written by North Carolina attorney Marcus Jimison, argued that "Atticus displayed the principle of nonviolent resistence [sic], years before Martin Luther King Jr., when he refused to respond violently after the racist Maycomb spat in his face."[58] Jimison's conflation of Atticus's fictional words and deeds with the realities of civil rights history confirms the unique place *To Kill a Mockingbird* (as both film and novel) holds in the white American imagination and implies that Finch and King are of equal historical value. It also ignores the fact that Lee's novel, while set in the 1930s, was written in the mid-1950s, immediately after the Montgomery bus boycott presumably influenced her understanding of what constituted noble nonviolence. After all, it was after a Christmas 1956 donation from her benefactor, Michael Brown, that Lee began writing full time.

Like the debate generated by Crespino's article, then, the controversy surrounding the publication of *Go Set a Watchman* has proven "fascinating, if a bit depressing." Those boycotting the book "don't know what they're missing," Stephen L. Carter has contended, arguing that even though many views espoused in the novel may seem shocking or unsavory to *Watchman*'s contemporary readers, they are very much entwined with the historical evidence of progressive white opinion in the Alabama lowlands of the 1950s.[59] Indeed, many of *Watchman*'s critics would have done well to read Lee's disappointed letter to a friend in 1961, after a "pastiche" piece she had written was rejected by *Esquire* magazine on the basis that the editor did not believe that segregationists could oppose the Ku Klux Klan. "This is an axiomatic impossibility, according to *Esquire*!" Lee seethed. "I wanted to say that according to those lights, nine-tenths of the South is an axiomatic impossibility."[60] Although the exact content of Lee's rejected piece remains a mystery, it seems apparent that she was still attempting to navigate the seemingly endless manifestations of southern white racism a year after *To Kill a Mockingbird* hit the bookshelves. Whereas editorial guidance appears to have persuaded Lee to present readers with obvious heroes and villains of the more child-centric *To Kill a Mockingbird*, her earlier effort, *Go Set a Watchman*, frequently represents the incongruity of many a white southerner's behavior in the mid-1950s. Jean Louise, though physically sickened after witnessing her father and boyfriend attend a White Citizens' Council meeting, admits that the *Brown* decision left her "furious" and that after reading about it in the newspaper, "she stopped at the first bar she came to and drank down a straight bourbon."[61] She shares her father's opinion that African Americans are "backward . . . that the vast majority of them here in the South are unable to share fully in the responsibilities of citizenship."[62] "If Atticus is a bundle of contradictions," Allen Mendenhall writes, "so is Jean Louise."[63]

As she attempts to account for the rising racial tensions in her hometown and across the South, Jean Louise is forced to confront her own inconsistent and evolving racial attitudes. She starts to doubt the faith she has put in others, especially Atticus, and therefore begins to question the security she once felt in such an apparently blighted and bigoted town. Crucial to Lee's vision of small-town southern life, religion forms a considerable part of this texture, as it did in *To Kill a Mockingbird*. Visiting home, Jean Louise is again expected to comply with the social requirements of her family's distinctively southern Methodism. Passages in which Atticus's brother, Jack Finch, lambasts the local minister's musical direction show that southern whites could be just as protective of their distinct religious identity as they were of racial segregation. Horrified that his minister has attended a course "in what was wrong with

Southern church music," led by an instructor from New Jersey, Jack contends that "apparently our brethren in the Northland are not content merely with the Supreme Court's activities. They are now trying to change our hymns on us."[64]

Although primarily focused on dissecting Maycomb's racial issues, Jean Louise is nevertheless reminded that religion and white supremacy are the two seemingly integral yet intertwined elements of Maycomb's identity. "There's nothing like a blood-curdling hymn to make you feel at home," she thinks on her first Sunday back in Maycomb, suggesting that religion plays little role in her New York life. Picturing her childhood, she remembers Maycomb's frequent revivals: "Revival time was a time of war: war on sin, Coca-Cola, picture shows, hunting on Sundays; war on the increasing tendency for women to paint themselves and smoke in public, war on drinking whiskey . . . at least fifty children per summer went to the altar and swore they would not drink, smoke, or curse until they were twenty-one." Transfixed by oratory performances and descriptions of hell ("a lake of fire exactly the size of Maycomb, Alabama"), Scout, Jem, and Dill would enact their own revivals, "repeating [their] own version of everything they had heard for the past three nights," before plunging each other into "the black water of the fishpool" in the name of baptism.[65]

Back in Maycomb as an adult, Jean Louise attends Bible class, where she "slept with her eyes open through the lesson, as was her custom." More observant and overtly critical of the hypocrisy of Maycomb's Christians than her childhood incarnation in *To Kill a Mockingbird*, Jean Louise asks, "Why doesn't their flesh creep? How can they devoutly believe everything they hear in church and then say the things they do and listen to the things they hear without throwing up? I thought I was a Christian but I'm not. I'm something else and I don't know what."[66] But she comes to tolerate the religiosity of her home just as she comes to terms with its racism. Sleeping with her eyes open therefore becomes a fitting metaphor for Jean Louise's eventual acceptance of Maycomb, as she chooses to put her own objections to one side for the sake of maintaining familial and indeed regional/racial connections.

An alarming ending to a book determined to document what Michiko Kakutani calls "the worst in Maycomb in terms of racial and class prejudice," Jean Louise's acceptance of her father's bigotry—and that of the white South in general—illuminates one of the novel's more problematic insinuations: that "the civil rights movement roiled things up, making people who 'used to trust each other' now 'watch each other like hawks.'"[67] Variants of these debates marked *Watchman*'s July 2015 publication, as ideological battles raged over the place of Confederate iconography in the twenty-first-century South, following the massacre of nine African American worshippers at a Charleston church exactly a month earlier, the white perpetrator of which had frequently posed with the Confederate battle flag. "The toppling of Atticus as a moral icon feels attractively modern and nuanced," Katy Waldman noted for *Slate*. Indeed, it seemed "true to this ambivalent racial moment, in which white police officers can gun down black teenagers, but we're beginning to perceive the poison stitched into the Confederate flag."[68]

But for all its contemporary significance, *Watchman*'s ending is very much of the 1950s, as Jean Louise—and therefore the reader—succumb to the idea that there is something worth preserving about Maycomb's way of life after all and that southern whites across the political spectrum need to address these issues together, as a family, rather than splinter under the duress of national bodies such as the Supreme Court or the NAACP. "In the wake of intrafamilial tragedy," then, Lee echoes what Waldman defines as "Lost Cause talking points," ultimately restoring Atticus's morality: "a compromised but beloved part of Scout's past . . . a small Confederate redemption."[69]

Just as Lee's *To Kill a Mockingbird* implied there were no simple answers—"perhaps no answers at all"—*Go Set a Watchman* denies African Americans a voice in its discussions of their goals and tactics in an atmosphere enflamed by the *Brown* decision. Indeed, to Jack Finch, African Americans are simply "incidental" to intra-white conflict: "what was incidental to the War Between the States is incidental to the issue in the war we're in now."[70] *Watchman*'s plot is therefore driven not by the realities of racism and massive resistance in the postwar South but by their encroachment on Jean Louise's idealized home. Through Jean Louise, Robert H. Brinkmeyer writes, Harper Lee directed her anger not at white supremacy itself but Atticus's support of it and the implication that he has joined the "trash." The same could be said for the many fans of the "original" Atticus, who refused to accept the "betrayal" contained within *Watchman*'s pages; Maycomb's "ruling elite has now cast off its mask of Southern paternalism and is openly embracing the virulent racism that they had previously displaced upon poor whites."[71] In many ways, the Atticus and Scout Finch of *To Kill a Mockingbird* "may be less characters in a novel than the embodiment of the nation's profound, continuing, and frequently self-deluding need for racial salvation."[72] To make an icon, one must know her audience.

African Americans in *To Kill a Mockingbird*

Despite its apparent sympathy for Calpurnia ("the 'good Mammy'") and Tom ("the disempowered 'naif'"), *To Kill a Mockingbird*'s presentation of Black and white relations is distinctly hierarchical.[73] While Tom's trial forms the story's main plotline, Scout, our narrator, is much more preoccupied by the ghostly Boo Radley.[74] As such, it is "Tom's predicament (rather than Tom as a character)" that stimulates the narrative, his trial, and death significant only for the lessons they teach middle-class white children who are treated like royalty by the noble Black community.[75] Similarly, while Atticus assures his sister that Calpurnia "knows what she means to this family," the Finches' beloved housekeeper must ride in the back seat of his car when the two travel together.[76] The film removes this awkward evidence of Jim Crow within the Finches' prized domesticity by omitting Calpurnia from the relevant scenes.[77]

Despite these omissions, Mulligan's adaptation owes much to the novel when it urges Black patience and trust that the white liberalism and decency that Atticus represents will triumph. Recommending his son read speeches by Henry W. Grady, the late nineteenth-century advocate of an industrial "New South" where only white men could vote, Lee's Atticus never implies that African Americans will drive their own emancipation. He is a member of the state legislature but brushes off Jem's demands that he "go up to Montgomery and change the law." Although it is easy to dismiss Jem's naive requests, the point remains that Atticus is committed to gradual change in the South and makes no demands of his region. He defends Tom Robinson because he is required to by court appointment and because he believes him to be innocent, not because he intends to pursue overarching racial change. While Lee makes it clear that some white townsfolk resented Atticus because "he aims to defend" Tom rather than simply letting the case run its usual course, his role as a defense lawyer seems akin to his political career, rooted in racial, gender, and class privilege and a sense of civic rather than civil duty.[78] Equating tolerance and statesmanship with class status and education, as the novel often does, neighbor Miss Maudie reminds Aunt Alexandra that Maycomb, or at least "the handful of people in this town with background," trust Atticus "to do right," which she renders "the highest tribute we can pay a man."[79]

Indeed, Atticus is often called on to strike down that which threatens his community, standing in for the lawmen who fail to act. "They're perfectly willing to let [Atticus] do what they're too afraid to do themselves," Alexandra laments in the novel.[80]

After all, it is County Sheriff Heck Tate who implores Atticus to shoot the rabid dog that many scholars have argued represents unfettered white supremacy: "For God's sake Mr. Finch . . . I can't shoot that well and you know it!"[81] In the novel, Miss Maudie declares that Atticus's marksmanship is "a gift of God," which, along with Calpurnia's whisper of "Sweet Jesus, help him," adds a metaphysical dimension to Jem and Scout's growing appreciation of

Sheriff Heck Tate (Frank Tate) watches on as Atticus Finch (Gregory Peck) raises a shotgun to shoot a mad dog (off-screen) in *To Kill a Mockingbird* (Robert Mulligan, 1962).

the father they had previously dismissed as "feeble" and "nearly fifty." As Miss Maudie says after the trial, "We're so rarely called upon to be Christians, but when we are, we've got men like Atticus to go for us." Unfortunately, as Jem realizes, "can't any Christian judges an' lawyers make up for heathen juries." [82]

Crespino argues that "[Sheriff] Tate in this scene may well refer to the elected officials of the South, such as Arkansas governor Orval Faubus in Little Rock, who through fear, incompetence, or narrow-mindedness were unable to face down the mad dog of southern racism."[83] But for all its vitality during the New Deal era, the southern racial liberalism that Atticus represents was inherently gradualist, and by the turn of the 1960s, Tony Badger argues, it was in a state of paralysis. Whereas southern segregationists launched a huge campaign of propaganda and massive resistance in the wake of *Brown v. Board of Education*, racial moderates and liberals failed to communicate a visible, gradualist alternative. The change that readers and viewers know will eventually come to Maycomb will therefore have little to do with the work of southern moderates like Atticus Finch. In fact, as Badger demonstrates, it will happen in spite of them and will be far from gradual. "After 1960," Badger writes, "no southern white could dictate the timetable of racial change. Segregation collapsed under the combined assault of the Black civil rights movement from within the region and the federal government and judiciary from outside."[84] Unlike Atticus, countless Black Americans were very much prepared to go up to Montgomery and change the law, literally marching to the state capitol from Selma in the 1965 battle for voting rights.

Harper Lee does not completely ignore working-class African Americans; the dissatisfaction that many of Maycomb's "cooks and field hands" felt following Tom Robinson's trial proved evident to many an unsympathetic white employer.[85] And of course, it is Calpurnia, the lone Black presence in the Finches' all-white neighborhood, who recognizes the danger of the rabid dog, commands Atticus home to resolve the issue and warns everyone else to stay off the streets. Through Calpurnia, Crespino writes, Lee acknowledges the persuasiveness of Black concerns about Jim Crow, "[but] their role is limited to that of warning the liberal white hero of the danger to come." [86] However, although Calpurnia issues the bulk of her warnings by telephone, she is forced to put herself in physical danger to alert the Radleys, who do not have a phone, indicative of their status as reclusive religious and cultural outsiders. "They won't come out anyway," Jem advises as Calpurnia makes her way to the Radley house, implying a hardheaded resistance to change among classes of white southerners alongside but unlike the Finches. But in issuing her warning, Calpurnia violates southern racial custom, taking the front steps rather than entering via the rear of the property. But as Jem surmises, such regulations "don't make any difference now."[87] Conflict, and change, has reached Maycomb.

With Lula omitted from the film, Atticus becomes the only Maycomb resident prepared to explicitly acknowledge the town's "usual disease" and therefore assumes, if not invents, the role of the white civil rights hero who identifies and attempts to rectify the problems that African Americans themselves cannot even put into words. But although the novel endows Atticus with religious symbolism, screenwriter Horton Foote found a much more concise manner in which to ensure that Atticus's sense of justice was unavoidably apparent: by dedicating twice as much time to Tom Robinson's trial as the novel does.[88] As such, Foote's adaptation reflected predecessors in the courtroom genre, such as 12 *Angry Men* (Sidney Lumet, 1957), as the cinematic Atticus seemingly "bases his decision on belief in a moral law that transcends man-made laws and must be followed by all human beings."[89] Through this reconstruction of the novel's narrative, the adult, masculine world of the courtroom and the contemporary 1960s tensions it reflected replaces Scout's naive and unassuming interpretations about the Depression-era world around her. Atticus becomes central to the story but also to the wider narrative of a white South divided by class and religious fanaticism.

Maycomb's Women and Religion

Uncomplicated by many of the book's pressures, the cinematic Atticus appears all the more exceptional. His siblings, Jack and Alexandra, are both absent from the film, which presents Atticus and his children as an isolated but contented family unit. In the novel, Alexandra significantly disrupts this liberal sanctuary, constantly reminding readers of the family's often-fractious internal and external relationships. Especially significant to Scout's development, Alexandra actually moves in with her brother and his children to assist the motherless Scout's transition into womanhood. The perennial southern busybody, Alexandra is obsessed with matters of lineage and class status. Committed to the racial, class, and gender boundaries that divide Maycomb's residents, she provides a helpful commentary on the town's social structures, which she personally polices wherever possible. Because Atticus is less committed to these societal rules, Alexandra's presence is crucial in reminding readers of the reality of southern middle-class life. To deny Alexandra's presence, as the film does, is to deny the frictions and divisions within the Finch family (and by extension the middle-class white southern liberalism they represent) and to suggest that the only opposition or criticism Atticus and the children faced was from less educated, lower-class outsiders.

Alexandra is also significant because her interests and occupations are just one of the many ways that Lee's novel reinforces the significance of organized, mainline Protestantism in the small-town South. A member of the women's missionary circle, she invites many of the neighborhood women into the Finch household to discuss "the squalid lives of the Mrunas," an African tribe seemingly incapable of living up to the women's moral standards. "It was customary for every circle hostess to invite her neighbors in for refreshments," Scout narrates, "be they Baptists or Presbyterians."[90]

Scout describes Mrs. Merriweather, one of Alexandra's guests, as "the most devout lady in Maycomb." Her "large brown eyes always filled with tears when she considered the oppressed," Scout recalls, as Mrs. Merriweather describes "the poverty . . . the darkness . . . the immorality" blighting the Mrunas.[91] The women's sense of Christian responsibility to these far-flung tribes, though laden with colonialist overtones, offers an ironic comparison to their attitudes toward the people of African descent living in poverty across the tracks from their own neighborhood. In reference to Maycomb's racial divide, Mrs. Farrow, "the second most devout lady in Maycomb," laments that "we can educate 'em till we're blue in the face, we can try till we drop to make Christians out of 'em but there's no lady safe in her bed these nights." Mrs. Merriweather then offers a thinly veiled criticism of Atticus's defense of Tom Robinson, noting that such "good but misguided" actions had done little more than "stir 'em up." Such denunciation is too much for Miss Maudie, who bitterly reminds Mrs. Merriweather that she is enjoying Finch hospitality while making such remarks.[92]

The hypocrisy of the missionary circle is in keeping with white southern attitudes of the time, with historian Mark Newman noting that until the civil rights era, "most Baptists saw no conflict between their desire to evangelize non-white peoples and their support for racial segregation in the South."[93] Missionaries themselves, however, often articulated very different attitudes in the pages of their denominational publications. In the late 1940s and early 1950s, for example, the Methodist *World Outlook* "displayed black and white youth together in interracial institutions, conferences, and retreats." The publication even ran articles by high-profile Black leaders, including representatives of the United Nations and the NAACP. In its report to the Southern Baptist Convention in June 1954, just two weeks after the *Brown* decision, the Christian Life Commission advocated that American "treatment of minority peoples in our citizenship weakens the witness of our missionaries in other lands even more than in our own. . . . Our missionaries have left China and are finding it more and more difficult to work in Africa, Asia, and other areas of the world."[94] "A few more Montgomerys and Birminghams and we might as well call home our SBC [Southern Baptist Convention] missionaries ministering to the black people of the world," the editor of North Carolina's *Biblical Recorder* lamented in June 1961.[95] Nevertheless, as Carolyn Dupont recognizes, progressive evangelicals often only advocated "better treatment of black Americans" rather than systemic change.[96]

It is amid the bigotry and hypocrisy of the women's missionary society that Atticus emerges with the news that Tom has been shot dead, reminding readers, as Maureen Markey writes, "that such bigotry and prejudice have violent and deadly consequences in the real world." Thus, it is through her participation with the apparently Christian missionary society that Scout learns most about hypocrisy and prejudice, undercutting what Markey recognizes as "Atticus' valiant efforts to convince Scout and Jem that the people of Maycomb are not as bad as the jury that convicted Tom."[97] Scout's experience of the missionary circle therefore contrasts with her memories of attending First Purchase with Calpurnia, where Reverend Sykes converts his Christian principles to direct, local action, refusing to let the congregation leave until ten dollars had been raised for Tom's family.

"Placating Dixie Audiences"

Omitting the missionary circle, presumably in the interests of a simplified plot, the film's producers declined to implicate the Finches' middle-class Christian neighbors in the degradation of Maycomb's African Americans. Key scenes with elderly neighbor Mrs. Dubose were filmed but then omitted for a similar reason, with producer Alan Pakula recalling that "the film builds up so gradually to the courtroom" that any distractions from this meant that "the narrative of the picture began to crumble."[98] Pakula's admission confirms that Atticus and the trial were recentralized as the point of the narrative at the expense of scenes that added further nuance to Maycomb's racial, religious, or cultural landscape, which includes Atticus himself. In the novel, Mrs. Dubose hides a Confederate pistol beneath her "numerous shawls and wraps" and argues that Atticus "is no better than the n****rs and trash he works for."[99] Jem responds by beheading her camellias—themselves perhaps a reference to the Knights of the White Camellia, a white supremacist terrorist organization that emerged in the aftermath of the Civil War—only to be punished by Atticus and forced to read Sir Walter Scott's medieval romance *Ivanhoe* to the cantankerous old bigot.[100]

Atticus's graciousness toward Mrs. Dubose confuses his children, and so after her death he informs them of the morphine addiction she had been battling, telling them that "she died beholden to nothing and nobody."[101] But Jem appears to learn a different lesson than the one Atticus intended: that hatred, like the camellia root, runs much deeper than he first expected. Even though the Knights of the White Camellia were obsolete by the 1930s of the novel's setting and Mrs. Dubose dead by the novel's end, her white camellias persist and grow back just before she dies. "You thought you could kill my Snow-on-the-Mountain, did you?" she taunts Jem. "Well, Jessie says the top's growing back out. Next time you'll know how to do it right, won't you? You'll pull it up by the roots, won't you?" Atticus later returns from the old woman's deathbed with a gift for Jem: a boxed "white, waxy, perfect camellia."[102]

Although seemingly unaware of Pakula's explicit rationale for cutting the scenes with Mrs. Dubose, Thomas Shaffer's speculation about the symbolic reason for her absence from the film remains convincing: "the American civil-rights agenda when Horton Foote wrote the screenplay could not find a way to come to terms with Mrs. Dubose—with the fact that Atticus Finch could endure an old woman's ruthlessness and racist attack on him and his client and at the same time hold her out to his children as the bravest person he ever knew."[103] Indeed, the adaptation's stark reconfiguring of the novel's narrative could simply not allow the toxic racism of a genteel southern lady living alongside the Finches. Such close proximity would damage the easy production of a class-based understanding of racism: a construction that provided a convenient buffer for a nation struggling to come to terms with the reality that the civil rights movement was holding up to scrutiny. Although Mrs. Dubose still appears briefly in the film, calling Scout an "ugly girl" for her lack of appropriate manners, she makes no further comments or appearances after being appeased by Atticus. Thus, her racism is omitted and intolerance banished entirely to the Ewells—Tom's accusers—and the other poor whites who make up the jury that convicts him.

Atticus admits that the middle classes of Maycomb always excused themselves from jury duty, turning over legal and ethical decisions to the "white trash" that they nevertheless disdain.[104] "You never see anyone from Maycomb on a jury," Jem observes. "They all come from out in the woods."[105] Such realities relieve the middle classes of any guilt or shame regarding Tom's murder, especially in the film, where the specific events leading to Tom's death are both literally and symbolically altered from the novel's description. Although Tom is still shot (off-screen) by law enforcement officers, it is one stray bullet while the well-meaning officers were "taking him to Abbottsville for safe-keeping" rather than seventeen shots during a regular exercise period. In the novel, the cause of Tom's death is so heinous that even the racist proprietor of the *Maycomb Tribune* describes it as a "senseless slaughter."[106] In the film, Atticus tells Miss Maudie and the children that "Tom broke loose and ran. The deputy called out to him to stop. Tom didn't. He shot at him to wound him and missed his aim: killed him. The deputy says 'Tom just ran like a crazy man.'"

It goes without saying that there is a considerable difference between accidentally killing a man with a warning shot and shooting a man seventeen times. It is also significant that Atticus's description of Tom's killer, simply "the guards" in the novel, becomes "the deputy" in the film. Although the deputy is not named, the fact that he is known to the Finches simply by his rank and title implies that he is a more senior and therefore trustworthy narrator than the novel's group of anonymous guards. Atticus clearly trusts the deputy's memory of the events even though, as Andrew Sarris noted on the film's release, "the disinterested spectator is aesthetically justified in questioning the truth of something not shown on the screen," especially "the word of the local constabulary on a matter concerning the rape of white womanhood."[107] But in recalling the story to Maudie and the children, Atticus implies little cynicism. This was an individual tragedy: an accident of Tom's own making, rather than the murder of a scared victim of an inherently racist justice system by its indifferent and faceless guards. This narrative shift is especially significant when one considers the contemporary context of the civil rights movement in early

1963, when most cinemagoers saw the film, as Black men, women, and children were arrested and held in southern jails knowing that any abuse inflicted on them would go unpunished.[108]

Screenwriter Horton Foote's decision to alter this aspect of Lee's story signified more than simply a departure "from the sacred text of the novel," Sarris continued in his biting *Village Voice* review. Rather, it was "to placate Dixie audiences," alleviating much of the novel's implicit white guilt. Where in the novel Atticus acknowledges that he "couldn't in truth say we had more than a good chance" of an appeal and resigns that "Tom was tired of white men's chances and preferred to take his own," in the film he is damning of Tom's attempts at autonomy, reflecting, as Sarris continued, "some inverted logic understood only by Liberal Southerners."[109] Almost aggressively, Peck's Atticus laments, "The last thing *I told him* was not to lose heart; that we'd ask for an appeal. We had such a *good* chance. We had *more* than a good chance."

Atticus's frustrations echoed across American cinemas in early 1963, including in Birmingham, Alabama, where some of the era's most significant civil rights protests were concurrently taking place. There, Martin Luther King Jr. also found himself in an Alabama jail. Like Tom Robinson, King was "sick of white men's chances." Writing from his cell, King composed one of the most well-known pleas for liberty in the English language and harangued a class of white moderates "more devoted to 'order' than to justice." For "'Wait' has almost always meant 'Never,'" King concluded. "It rings in the ear of every Negro with a piercing familiarity."[110]

"The Disgrace of Maycomb": Divided Whiteness in *To Kill a Mockingbird*

Tom's trial is only significant to *To Kill a Mockingbird*'s narrative (both literary and cinematic) because it enables audiences to determine the hierarchies of whiteness. It is explicitly clear in the novel that the middle classes are easily exempted from jury duty, absolving them of the prejudice evident in Tom's trial. But characters like Mrs. Dubose and the women's missionary circle demonstrate a wider culture of racism and Christian hypocrisy that Lee's Ewells are but a part of. Without those other characters, the Ewells emerge as an openly religious anomaly, the natural harbingers of racial terrorism, unparalleled and irredeemable. Indeed, their entire sordid existence is played out in the courtroom for all to see. Here, Bob Ewell (James Anderson), the film's only "really totally dark person," according to producer Alan Pakula, claims to be "a God-fearing man," the victim of "tricksy lawyers like Atticus Finch."[111] He pragmatically adopts a language of race and Christianity that appears desperately out of touch with the secular, middle-class Maycomb the film has otherwise

Atticus Finch stares at Bob Ewell (James Anderson), after the latter spits in Atticus's face in *To Kill a Mockingbird* (Robert Mulligan, 1962).

exposed us to. However, while these appeals to the jury's basest anxieties render Ewell all the more pathetic in the film's logic, they are ultimately what score his victory in the case. As such, the narrative reflects a wider liberal rejection of southern white recalcitrance despite failing to offer a viable alternative. Atticus and his acolytes can do only so much. They offer hope of change, but those on the periphery can always reemerge to scupper long-needed progress. Such is the divided whiteness of the South that would drive many a subsequent Hollywood film, from *A Time to Kill* to Scorsese's *Cape Fear*.

After all, the Ewells are not a momentary blip but a clear indictment of rural, southern poverty: "the disgrace of Maycomb for three generations." Employing a child's naive and honest narration, Lee was able to offer judgment on the Ewells without facing criticism. As a child, Scout cannot be blamed for her opinions; in fact, her "natural" distrust of the Ewells proves to be entirely justified. Through Scout's growing suspicion of lower-class families, Lee is able to offer her own cynical interpretation of the divisions of whiteness and the differences between a good family and "trash."[112] Certainly, no one seems to care that by the end of the novel/film, the underprivileged and abused Ewell children are now orphans. Mayella may have lied about Tom Robinson, Diann Baecker writes, but "her testimony is motivated less by shame than by fear—not of Robinson, but of her father. Atticus calls her a victim of 'cruel poverty and ignorance,' but what she is most clearly is a victim of incest and physical abuse." However, as Baecker continues, "the incestuous relationship of a white trash man with his white trash daughter is a part of the novel often glossed over by scholars who probably find it unremarkable anyway." Indeed, most readers and viewers seem to concur with Atticus that Mayella does not deserve protection.[113]

If Atticus and Bob Ewell are Maycomb's opposites, their status as widowed fathers rounds out the comparison. Ewell's violent abuse of his daughter certainly sets him apart from Atticus but establishes a precedent for the violent misogyny that almost all white supremacist villains will enact in later southern dramas, from *Mississippi Burning*, where Deputy Sheriff Clinton Pell (Brad Dourif) violently beats his unnamed wife (Frances McDormand), to *A Time to Kill*, where Klansmen kidnap and abuse northern law student Ellen Roark (Sandra Bullock). In all of these films, violence against women—often specifically sexual violence—contributes to a wider characterization of mindless depravity that is deeply gendered. Theodore and Grace-Anne Hovet point out that all "points of conflict in [*To Kill a Mockingbird*] are marked by the absence of a female presence, particularly the maternal. Mrs. Finch, Mrs. Ewell, and Mrs. Radley have all died before the key events in the stories. Thus, there are no mothers who . . . have implicated themselves in Mayella's abuse by her father, or exonerated Atticus's failure to act more decisively in the state legislature to combat segregation and lynching."[114] Maycomb's lynch mob, like that of *Intruder in the Dust* and the Klan chapters of *Mississippi Burning* and *A Time to Kill*, is entirely male. Likewise, though Atticus may trivialize the fact that women cannot serve on juries in 1930s Alabama ("I doubt if we'd ever get a complete case tried—the ladies'd be interrupting to ask questions"), women are nevertheless absolved of the blame the narrative directs at those who convicted Tom Robinson.[115] Even though the novel's presentation of Mrs. Dubose and the women's missionary circle makes it clear that the vast majority of white, middle-class Maycomb women harbor distinctly racist views, the film's omission of these characters encourages viewers to see southern racism as a distinctly male phenomenon, a cinematic trope that has been replicated by numerous civil rights melodramas.

With the future of whiteness locked in a battle of masculine opposites, the irredeemable Robert E. Lee Ewell—"who saw no resemblance to his namesake"—must die at the hands of an upstanding white man. But rather than Atticus, this task falls to the "sickly white" hands of Boo Radley, whom Graham describes as "the fading specter of southern gentility."[116] Protecting the Finch children on Halloween, a pagan occasion on which evil spirits roam, Boo converts Ewell's heresy into what Butler calls "a kind of All Saints' Day, the day after Halloween devoted to honoring unrecognized saints who do not have celebratory days of their own."[117] But because the film "completely avoids the theological explanation for Boo's character," the isolated son of "foot-washing Baptists," Boo emerges simply as a ghostly white hero, cementing the film's commitment to the neighborhood as one of unusual but ultimately redeemable white, liberal, secular, middle-class allies.[118] Here, Boo enters Scout's world as an equal—"Boo was our neighbor." In the novel, Scout takes the time to explain that she never saw Boo again and that although he had given them so much, including their lives, she and Jem had given him nothing in return and so they could not really be neighbors.[119] "Ultimately an inexplicable Gothic mystery," according to Shaw, Boo simply returns home.[120]

Events of the early 1960s ensured that *To Kill a Mockingbird*'s filmmakers were less interested in Lee's subtle invocations of the southern gothic and more concerned with the demonization of lower-class, evangelically tinged racism and the subsequent redemption of the white middle classes. Although the Finches had never been able to hold back Maycomb's racist hysteria alone, by 1962–63 they needed secular alliances to keep the tensions from their neighborhood. The film thus creates the impression that in battling the racist, religious Bob Ewell, Boo Radley (played by Robert Duvall) has built a lasting relationship with Scout and the Finches. Together, as neighbors, they will shoot down any further mad dogs that threaten their community.

Once a "displaced phantasm of racial fear," Boo Radley thus emerges as what Sundquist calls "the domesticated 'gray ghost' of harmonious integration."[121] After all, as Atticus tells Scout in the novel, "most people are [nice], when you finally see them."[122] For Sundquist, Atticus's "integrity is circumscribed by his admonition that moral action must respect the prejudices of 'our friends' and ultimately abide by local ethics." As such, "the novel's undeniable power is circumscribed by its own narrative strategies."[123] Upholding Atticus's teaching, producer Alan Pakula described the story's failed lynch mob as having "an essential decency." Those gathered to murder Tom Robinson may be "a different class" from Atticus and other bastions of Maycomb's legal system, including Sheriff Heck Tate and Judge Taylor, but "they all come from the same communities."[124] Pakula's comments, like Lee's novels, suggest that these people understand and guide each other better than cynical, federal legislation ever could. Walter Cunningham, leader of the mob, is "basically a good man," Atticus tells his children. "He just has his blind spots along with the rest of us."[125] Unfortunately, as Monroe Freedman points out, "Cunningham's blind spot (along with the rest of us?) is a homicidal hatred of black people."[126]

Indeed, Atticus has so much faith in the Cunninghams that he refused to strike one from the juror's list, thereby letting a man who just the night before had been determined to terrorize and presumably murder Tom Robinson (and indeed Atticus himself) onto the jury that then held Tom's fate in its hands. Jem is incensed: "How could you take such a risk, Atticus, how could you?"[127] But Atticus regularly makes decisions in the novel and film that be-lie any argument that he is committed to the law in an abstract sense, instigating conflict resolutions based on his own interpretations of what is best for Maycomb. Thankfully, for Atticus anyway, he is always supported to do so by the only person who could actually hold him to account, Sheriff Heck Tate. Although both Finch and Tate are well intentioned and framed as appropriate cultural and legal gatekeepers (as opposed to the poor whites represented by the Ewells and the Cunninghams), their actions nevertheless echo the white South's frequent demands for time and autonomy in dismantling racial segregation despite the fact—as Tom Robinson's trial shows—that there was little reason for African Americans and sympathetic whites to put any faith in the capacity of southern legal systems to deliver racial justice.

But if the white South's recalcitrance in the face of federal desegregation decisions is remembered by historians as a repulsive manipulation, Atticus's seemingly intractable status as Maycomb's (or America's) hero is rooted in the same racial, gender, and class privilege. In the 1998 documentary *Fearful Symmetry: The Making of* To Kill a Mockingbird, prominent African American attorney Cleophus Thomas Jr. argued that the story's events transformed Atticus from "a defense lawyer to the benign figure of the state: the legislator, the state official that decides when the power of the state ought to be used." But rather than seeing this as problematic, Thomas warns that "we, as individuals, have to make sure we don't characterize these people in a pejorative way and say they're soft on crime."[128] Literary scholar Claudia Durst Johnson concurs, arguing that in giving up "what means most to him"—the law—to protect Boo Radley, Atticus performs "one of his most unselfish and heroic acts."[129]

Atticus Finch: "That Part Is Greg's for Life"

Adapting Lee's fiction to better position Atticus Finch as a hero, Mulligan's film irreparably determined the popular understanding of the character and established cinematic precedent. By 1962, Gregory Peck was already famous for his virtuous, upstanding roles in films such as *The Yearling* (Clarence Brown, 1946) and *Gentleman's Agreement* (Elia Kazan, 1947), bringing considerable and deliberate star power to *Mockingbird*. Indeed, Peck was the only casting decision that contradicted Mulligan's demand for unrecognizable faces and lesser-known Broadway actors.[130] Peck was also fresh from playing another upstanding southern lawyer terrorized by the white trash underbelly of the South in the original *Cape Fear*. He formed Brentwood Productions with Mulligan and Pakula, becoming heavily involved in *To Kill a Mockingbird*'s development, including its casting and creative development.[131] Having watched a rough cut in June 1962, Peck sent a lengthy report to his agent and executives at Universal Pictures. Concerned that the film was too committed to the children's stories, Peck argued that "Atticus has no chance to emerge as courageous and strong."[132] In a follow-up letter, he stressed that "the picture will begin to look better as Atticus' storyline emerges, and the children's scenes are cut down to proportion."[133]

Diverging considerably from the novel, Peck's sense of "proportion" helped inflate Atticus far beyond his literary significance. The actor's association with the fictional southern lawyer would last his entire career—a connection Peck actively supported, commenting in March 1963, "I never had a part that came close to the real me until [Atticus]."[134] His agent argued that he would "lose the entire South" by taking the role, but Lee's happiness with Peck's performance surely legitimized the actor's ascendency. Lee asserted that "the man and the part met. As far as I'm concerned, that part is Greg's for life."[135]

Ever the patriot, Peck was confident during filming that *To Kill a Mockingbird* "will have a good effect in Europe, Asia and Africa, where people too often think the Negro is without rights and friendless in the South. They will see that there were southerners who fought for justice even in the '30s." He cited the importance of white moderates, including the *Atlanta Constitution*'s Ralph McGill and Harper Lee herself in the South's "amazing" racial progress. "They are the ones who make sense, not the ones who want everything changed at once or the ones who want no changes."[136] Indeed, Harper Lee assured the *Birmingham Post-Herald* in 1962 that *To Kill a Mockingbird* was "not a racial novel. It displays an aspect of civilization, not necessarily Southern civilization."[137] Never ostracized in her hometown of Monroeville, Lee told *Life* in 1961, "I'm not Thomas Wolfe; I can go home."[138]

For his part, *To Kill a Mockingbird*'s director, Robert Mulligan, dismissed claims on the film's release that it was "a chance to jump on the segregation-integration soapbox."[139] In keeping with a general tendency to "contain" the civil rights implications of movies in the early 1960s, Mulligan's comments reflected the initial universal marketing of the "southern melodrama" or "social problem picture." But although the novel may not have been "melodramatic with race riots and race hatred," concurrent white resistance to the efforts of the civil rights movement, particularly in Birmingham, Alabama, ensured that the environment within which the film was consumed certainly was. At the Cannes Film Festival, Peck was quizzed on his racial views, the questions prompted by the disturbing images circulating from Birmingham, where Bull Connor's police met marching high school and college students with attack dogs and fire hoses. "I have never felt intolerance," the Californian-born actor confirmed. "I judge Negroes on personality, intelligence and quality, as I would anyone else. I'm thankful that I was born in an area where this type of prejudice doesn't exist."[140]

Whereas Peck had previously celebrated *To Kill a Mockingbird* as a film that was kind to the white South, describing it as the one picture about the region "that isn't sick," he now resorted to deflecting racial tensions to the South alone, entangling himself in a web of national mythmaking and southern exceptionalism.[141] Screenwriter Allen Rivkin, head of the American delegation to Cannes, praised Peck's performance before the journalists, arguing, "This was the first time that an American performer has been questioned by the European press on the U.S. race question. It is still a great problem, but we are solving it and we are not afraid to talk about it and or bring a picture on the race question to an international film festival such as Cannes."[142] The film was dutifully awarded the Prix Gary Cooper, which on just two occasions (1961 and 1963) rewarded the film with the most social and human significance at the festival. First awarded to *A Raisin in the Sun* in 1961, the Prix Gary Cooper proved a useful tool "whenever the American selections weren't up to scratch," Richard Roud recalled.[143] Despite criticism of both films at the festival, the Prix Gary Cooper nevertheless implied international recognition for their engagement with racial themes at the height of the civil rights movement and the Cold War.

Conclusion: "Minds of Their Caliber"

In comparison to the more overt social commentary of films such as *Nothing but a Man* (Michael Roemer, 1964) and *The Cardinal* (Otto Preminger, 1963), discussed in the next chapter, *To Kill a Mockingbird* appears distinctly detached from the reality of America's most publicized period of racial turmoil. Establishing a cinematic trope that has endured for more than half a century, Mulligan's adaptation of *To Kill a Mockingbird* helped define the southern civil rights melodrama as a simplified battle, exposing class anxieties within white communities rather than meaningfully tackling racial issues. The dichotomy of a liberal, secular middle class alongside an irredeemable dynasty of white trash—whose appeals to Christianity appear as misguided as their claims to racial privilege—would prove vastly influential, becoming a prominent trope of the South on-screen.

But even though it is hard to defend Harper Lee's omission of Black voices, her presentation of white thought was more developed than Mulligan's adaptation suggests. Lee's novels acknowledge hypocrisy, contradiction, and difference among Maycomb's middle class and, indeed, within the Finch family itself. But in denying numerous strata of the town's society, from Aunt Alexandra and the missionary circle to the congregation of First Purchase, and in failing to develop storylines involving Mrs. Dubose and the Radleys, Mulligan and his team not only ignored much of Maycomb's diverse texture but also moved the narrative toward a decisive battle of good versus evil personified by Atticus and Bob Ewell. Religious and political diversity were cast aside to provide an instantly recognizable, uneducated, redneck menace that absorbs the town's hypocrisy. After all, as Atticus concludes, with a dismissive gesture toward the Ewells during his closing argument, "the assumption—the evil assumption—that *all* Negroes lie, *all* Negroes are basically immoral beings, *all* Negro men are not to be trusted around our women" can only ever be associated "with minds of their caliber."[144] The rest of white Maycomb, the South, and even the United States is therefore redeemed from the implications of Tom's trial and subsequent death in a manner that proved irresistible to future generations of white filmmakers and unrecognizable to Black audiences.

CHAPTER 2

"How Come the Only Cheek Gets Turned in This Country Is the Negro Cheek?"

African American Christianity and
Civil Rights in Cinema, 1920–1990

When President Barack Obama delivered a searing eulogy for slain South Carolina state senator Reverend Clementa Pinckney in June 2015, he referred to the Black church as "our beating heart." Serving as "rest stops for the weary along the Underground Railroad; bunkers for the foot soldiers of the Civil Rights Movement," Obama's image of the Black church inspired radical action and embedded itself in the national historical consciousness.[1] Linking the racially motivated murder of Pinckney and eight of his parishioners to a long history of violent terrorism directed at African American churches, Obama's speech was likened to a performance, "deploying the inflections and oratorical rhythms of a pastor."[2] When the president embarked on a rendition of the hymn "Amazing Grace," the clergy around him appeared pleasantly surprised and were soon on their feet to join Obama in song. Yet at the end of what *Bloomberg Politics* called a "vindicatory and legacy-insuring" week in which the Supreme Court endorsed his policies on gay marriage and health-care expansion, Obama nevertheless found himself at "the altar of a black church to mourn people lost to the kind of racial hatred that his presidency was supposed to relegate to a dark chapter of American history."[3]

Political scientist Reverend R. Drew Smith argues that "the association between black churches, civil rights activism, and the mid-twentieth century South has become mutually reinforcing. When mentioning black churches and civil rights activism, one thinks of the mid-twentieth century South; when mentioning civil rights activism and the mid-twentieth century South, one thinks of black churches." The "heroic activism mobilized from the mid-1950s through the mid-1960s against the segregationist juggernaut of the American

South" provided a "historical stage," Smith writes, on which "black churches were spotlighted for their substantial role." As such, the civil rights movement changed "perceptions in the minds of many about the potential political significance of black churches."[4]

Yet for many historians, the political role of the Black church remains ambiguous. In their studies of Mississippi and Louisiana, respectively, John Dittmer and Adam Fairclough have shown that many Black churches failed to support the freedom struggle in any meaningful fashion.[5] Taylor Branch notes that Martin Luther King Jr. only threw "himself into the escalating civil disobedience of the movement" in late 1961, after his attempt to "gain control of the National Baptist Convention [NBC]" ended in disunity and eventual excommunication. King had hoped to cement the NBC as "the institutional basis of the civil rights movement," reflecting his "stature as a prince of the Negro church." However, although around one-fifth of NBC clergy would resign with King when the convention failed to adopt a serious civil rights platform in 1961, "others, including old family friends and eminent preachers such as Adam Clayton Powell Jr. could not bear to tear away."[6] Since the mid-1950s, Wallace Best writes, King's main adversary in the NBC—autocratic president Joseph Harrison Jackson of Chicago—represented himself as "a legitimate participant in discussions about racial equality, following a political approach that resonated with a wide spectrum of Americans and a social vision that reflected the longing for national unity and commonality" at the height of the Cold War. The conflict between King and Jackson, often simplified to a battle of radicalism and conservatism, was instead rooted in "Jackson's espousal of post–World War II political values and the desire to extend the reach of black Baptists worldwide."[7] Meanwhile, mid-century sociologists argued that African Americans, like other Americans, were becoming more secular. By the late 1960s, in particular, sociologists argued that increasing numbers of Black Americans had lost faith in the power of religious institutions, doubting their "function for social change."[8]

Despite such accounts, contemporary historians are still working to complicate popular ideas of a united, progressive Black church. In 2008, Barbara Dianne Savage argued that popular perceptions of the civil rights movement have "eclipsed the history and memory of intraracial conflicts about the place of religion in political struggle."[9] Similarly, Eddie Glaude has written of "a reductive historical narrative about African American religion," where internal theological and political differences are ignored and ideas about the African American "'public' (or 'publics')" become extremely limited. Although Glaude does not mention film specifically, his critique of outdated perceptions about a monolithic, politically progressive Black church offers a useful framework for considering cinematic projections. While ideas of a collective "black church" have limited value, because "all African American churches were not and are not politically engaged in some recognizably progressive or prophetic sense," very few feature films focus on socially or politically engaged Black churches.[10] In fact, many more downplay or even degrade church-organized Black political activity in favor of a more static, unthreatening spirituality that appears to be at odds with the dominant narrative that scholars note and to which Obama appealed in Charleston. Although still an instrument of solidarity, Hollywood's Black church often becomes little more than a sanctuary, where African Americans sing and pray for eventual deliverance, but make little attempt to instigate earthly change.

Relatedly, when politics is acknowledged within a Black church, it can be in a reductive, dismissive manner. *A Time to Kill*, for example, is deeply cynical about Black Christian involvement with the NAACP, which is presented as a manipulative, self-serving group of elite African Americans determined to raise their own profile. In 2014, *Selma*'s acknowledgment of the vital role of churches in organizing mass mobilization for voting rights in 1965, despite the internal political and methodological tensions that threatened the civil rights movement's public-facing cohesiveness, proved revelatory in its divergence from existing tropes. Whereas a small body of more interrogative made-for-television films had probed various issues of civil rights history and representation, the long-standing depoliticization of African Americans in Hollywood movies generally suggested to audiences that racial change occurred naturally in the United States or through the work of liberal, usually secular, whites.[11] As a result, mainstream Hollywood repeatedly denies the sacrifices of countless African Americans in a movement that, although supported by some whites, was developed, fostered, led, and sustained by Black people. This narrative not only negates the numerous theological and political contributions of Black churches to the mid-twentieth-century struggle but also the efforts and achievements of groups that increasingly or always distanced themselves from the church-led movement, including the Student Nonviolent Coordinating Committee (SNCC), the Congress of Racial Equality (CORE), and the Black Panther Party.[12] In this chapter, a select examination of independent Black-centered cinema, from Oscar Micheaux in the 1920s to Ossie Davis in the 1960s provides a range of Black responses to the purpose and place of the church in racial protest and uplift, adding further nuance to cinematic depictions but rarely commanding the same audiences as Hollywood studio films.

Reliant on the construction of diametrically opposed groups, post–civil rights Hollywood repeats a dichotomy of dignified African American

Protestantism versus zealously racist white evangelicalism in order to simplify one of the most significant ideological battles of the twentieth century: whether and how to dismantle racial segregation in the United States. While basic historiographical questions about the African American freedom struggle remain hotly debated by scholars, popular culture ensures that it is "pressured toward moral legibility."[13] The apparent evil of poor southern whites is central to the construction of this narrative, as is the goodness of liberal, secular whites. However, both must be cast against an overarching southern "Blackness" that lacks denominational, class, or political distinctions but that gives meaning to these conflicts within whiteness. This chapter therefore briefly explores the long history of African American religiosity on-screen, noting how, since the earliest days of American cinema, Hollywood has associated African Americans with an exotic, natural religious expressivity and formed a composite lens through which to explore the nature and place of Black people in the United States. From the childlike reverence of *The Green Pastures* to the affective irreverence of Ossie Davis's independently financed *Gone Are the Days!*, filmmakers exploring the civil rights era via the late twentieth-century civil rights melodrama had decades of representations to consider when developing their Black churches. The chapter therefore concludes with a discussion of Black religiosity as represented in *Mississippi Burning*, Hollywood's first major civil rights picture, with a particular emphasis on the film's use of religious music to soundtrack white supremacist violence.

Making Meanings out of Blackness: Representing the Black Church in Early Cinema

Civil rights lawyer Loren Miller conceded in 1934 that "the movies but reflect the traditional American outlook" but nevertheless charged filmmakers with "doing more than their fair share to whip up prejudice." He argued that "millions of white Americans of all ages confirm their beliefs about Negroes at the neighborhood theaters" and chastised Hollywood pictures that demonized African cultural and religious practices, as well as "news reels that poke fun at Negro revivals or baptisings [sic]."[14] For many whites, the distinct, enthusiastic worship styles that traveled north with southern African Americans during the Great Migration were excessive and undignified. Initially overcrowding the mainline Black churches of their new cities, many migrants formed their own, smaller, more informal places of worship in storefronts and houses.[15] Here, as Teresa L. Reed notes, congregants could "sing, shout, clap, emote, and praise in the manner to which they were most accustomed." By 1928, "66 percent of Chicago's Black Baptist churches and 86 percent of its

Holiness/Pentecostal churches met in storefronts and houses, most of which were on the more economically depressed part of the city's South Side."[16]

Although Wallace Best's study of early twentieth-century Black Chicago undermines the notion that the storefront church was solely a lower-class phenomenon, these makeshift churches often proved embarrassing for mainstream, middle-class Black denominations and sociologists. Influential African American writers such as E. Franklin Frazier and Richard Wright adhered to what Best calls "Darwinian metaphors" to distinguish between the apparent "backwardness of black southerners and the civility of urban blacks."[17] Migrants were encouraged to join established mainline churches, but with such a crowded religious market in northern cities, displaced southerners were free to find the church that best suited them.[18] Reflecting their southern roots, many new churches prioritized personal salvation over social reform, leading prominent interwar critics such as Howard University dean Kelly Miller to lament expressive religion as a distraction from the more pressing issues of racial justice and uplift. Other critics, including journalists from the *Crisis* and the *Chicago Defender*, argued that such religions often constituted active collusion with white supremacists.[19]

However, historian Daniel R. Bare has highlighted the distinct ways that interwar African American fundamentalists articulated a vision of racial equality overwhelmingly absent in white fundamentalist circles, arguing that scholarly emphasis on white fundamentalists engaged in adversarial politics—mostly in defense of white supremacy and against the teaching of evolution in schools—has neglected the existence of self-designating Black fundamentalists altogether. Whereas whites often sought separate fundamentalist institutions, publications, and socialization, Bare argues African American fundamentalists drew connections between earthly racial inequalities and their faith, seeking wider community outlets through which to advance their ideas—from the secular Black press to mainline congregations. From these visible positions, Black fundamentalist preachers explicitly rejected the apparent need for the social gospel, noting that previous commitment to biblical literalism had lifted the race from slavery to emancipation.[20]

Perhaps most important, storefront churches drew members and money from the established congregations. Middle-class critics warned of uneducated preachers leading fundamentalist flocks, arguing, as sociologist Ira Reid did in 1926, that while the "sincere and well-established churches in Harlem . . . steadily prod at social problems with instruments both spiritual and physical and methods religious and humanitarian, the others are saying, 'Let us prey.' And they do."[21] Meanwhile, the pioneering independent Black filmmaker Oscar Micheaux tended to represent religious figures as hypocritical and predatory, most notably in his surviving films *Within Our Gates* (1920) and *Body and Soul* (1925). In the latter, Old Ned encourages other African Americans to accept second-class citizenship, while allowing whites to openly ridicule him for amusement. Whereas some scholars have noted Micheaux's distaste for religion as a likely comment on his detested father-in-law, others have argued that Micheaux's middle-class outlook, which favored education as racial uplift, sought to spotlight the cultured, upright "New Negro."[22]

Outside the storefront walls, Reed writes, both Black and white Americans "seemed to agree that black religion—particularly, Southern-born black religion—was comical." Although recorded sermons by southern clergy such as J. M. Gates proved huge business from the mid-1920s and early 1930s, many secular blues musicians manipulated religious compositions to reflect growing dissatisfaction with organized religion, which they deemed unable and unlikely to enhance the material and political needs of its congregations.[23] Through recording and reproduction, Black Christianity had become what religious historian Lerone Martin calls "a mass-produced commodity."[24] By the 1930s, many artists were deliberately targeting the crossover market, selling entertaining, lighthearted records rather than overt social commentary. However, a consistent feature remained: the distortion of Black religious worship and clergy. Ignorant, hypocritical preachers and deacons were often central figures, caricatured much as they were in minstrelsy, where white audiences had long indulged their fantasies of a decadent African American religious culture.

In his study of antebellum blackface, William John Mahar notes that "religion was a powerful indicator of difference" and that performers often emphasized "the charismatic role of the African American preacher." More than simply "delineating" African Americans, Mahar writes, Black dialect was used to enhance "prevailing racist theories that linked difference with some form of deficiency," reassuring those whites unsettled by the articulate rhetorical performances of prominent African American orators like Frederick Douglass.[25] Thus, as a recognizably Black or interracial worship style, the exuberance of pentecostal or Holiness traditions became tied to ideas of rural Blackness, reflecting a regional and class bias that easily intersected with minstrelsy's use and production of racial stereotypes. For many white audiences, minstrel shows did not simply entertain; they confirmed what Reed calls "the huge cultural gap between themselves and blacks."[26]

With the rise of Hollywood, many of these tropes made the transition to the big screen. But white filmmakers were attracted to more than just "the significance of religion in black culture," Judith Weisenfeld argues, noting the particular potential for Black religious music and aesthetics in the eyes of early filmmakers. For white audiences, representations of African American religion helped "make meanings out of blackness," just as they had in minstrelsy. King Vidor's *Hallelujah* (1929), for example, reflected the prominent white director's interest in the "sincerity and fervor of [Black] religious expression [and] the honesty and simplicity of their sexual drives." Citing his Texas roots, Vidor promoted himself as an authority on "the negro" on the film's release, while promotional materials from Metro-Goldwyn-Mayer claimed Vidor had "caught the rhythm of [Black] existence and has reproduced, for the first time, a section of humanity so little understood by those who do not know this colorful race."[27] While the film reaped rave reviews in the white press, its simultaneous New York premieres in Harlem and Times Square revealed much about its intended audiences and the practical assumptions of Jim Crow.[28]

As Weisenfeld has demonstrated, many Black critics and journalists hoped that the emergence of sound film would usher in a more diverse range of roles for African American performers, not least because of the opportunities around religious music, already a key contribution to American audio culture. However, the apparent realism of the religiosity on display in Vidor's *Hallelujah* "served as the most potent justification of its racism," with *Variety* noting that the film represented "a camera reproduction of the typical southland with its wide open cotton spaces, where the good natured singing negro continues to eke out a bare existence. . . . It brings realistically to the screen how he lives in nondescript surroundings with continual evidence of illiteracy that even remains unpolished when becoming hysterically religious." Although the film presented authentic African American music in the form of spirituals, blues, and folk, thus "lend[ing] an air of dignity to some of the characters," the consistent connection drawn between religion and sexuality, alongside Vidor's frequent assessment of his actors as "untrained, naturally emotional and religious," is difficult to overlook. While *Hallelujah* may have brought a range of music to the screen, it is clear that Black religion as imagined by white filmmakers proved a static and grounding force that pacified and justified broader cultural difference. An examination of Black responses to *Hallelujah* presents pride in the performances and acknowledgments of truth in its expressions of worship, alongside anxieties surrounding the high stakes such visibility engendered. Indeed, one reviewer noted that Vidor "should be willing to understand if the Negro is a bit sensitive about going on the block."[29]

Representing a commodification of—rather than dialogue with—Black religious cultures, *Hallelujah*'s influence could be seen long after its day, as Hollywood entranced generations of white audiences with simple premises of voyeurism. "Thousands of Negroes in the Deep South visualize God in terms of people and things they know in their everyday life," states the prelude to *The Green Pastures* (1936), based on Marc Connelly's hit Broadway play; "*The Green Pastures* is an attempt to portray that humble, reverent conception." A representation of "what southern blacks believe," rather than a theological engagement with the Bible, the central premise of *The Green Pastures* thus makes it clear that its intended audience is white and unlikely to expect a representation of God as a Black man.[30] To simply label the film racist, Weisenfeld argues, denies the important cultural dialogue it contributed to: how it helped shape and reinforce white ideas about African American religion and the decisions white America subsequently made about the roles of Black people in national life. White audiences clearly responded well to the idea of childlike African Americans, incapable of bearing a grudge. However, such qualities—"so attractive to those who appreciated *The Green Pastures*"—exasperated many Black critics.[31] When a high-profile Broadway revival of *The Green Pastures* played for less than a month in 1951, *Ebony* magazine celebrated the show's folding as "one of the most heartening signs of the growing maturity of race relations in America. . . . The number of paleface Americans who will pay to see their darker brothers swishing switch blades and yassuh'ing has reached a point of diminishing returns."[32] The Black church had proven a powerful force against "irreligion and communism," the Right Reverend Decatur Ward Nichols of the African Methodist Episcopal Church argued in an open letter to other religious leaders. Distortions such as *The Green Pastures* must therefore "be condemned to the scrap heap."[33]

Gone Are the Days!: Purlie Victorious and the Black Preacher in the Civil Rights Era

Ten years after the short-lived Broadway revival of *The Green Pastures*, Ossie Davis—one of its biggest stars—would present his own satirical account of race and religion in the American South, *Purlie Victorious*. Opening in September 1961, Davis's play ran for 261 performances before being adapted to film in 1963 as *Gone Are the Days!*, directed by Nicholas Webster.[34] Determined to "preach freedom in the cotton patch," fast-talking Purlie (played by Davis himself) intends to wrestle a stolen inheritance and a disused barn from his former Confederate master Capt'n Cotchipee (Sorrell Booke) so that he can build a church and lead his people.

By the summer of 1963, the undeniable significance of the civil rights movement was beamed across the world through coverage of Project C in Birmingham and the June desegregation of the University of Alabama. The highs of the August 28 March on Washington and the devastating lows of the September 15 bombing of Birmingham's Sixteenth Street Baptist Church cemented the year's poignance. Initially released just eight days after the bombing, on September 23, 1963, Davis's independent film moves deftly between the numerous strands of the evolving freedom struggle in a unique manner that is ripe for reevaluation alongside the later civil rights melodramas that offered nothing of Purlie's radical critique of segregation and embryonic calls for Black Power. The dramatic financial failure of *Gone Are the Days!*, like that of *A Raisin in the Sun* two years earlier, also contributed to the subsequent scarcity of Black-centered films that characterized the rest of the 1960s. Indeed, Davis and his white collaborators—director Webster and first-time producers Milton and Thomas Hammer—planned future ventures that never reached production following the financial failure of their debut.[35] An unlikely yet significant figure in the history of civil rights cinema nevertheless, Purlie Victorious is worthy of some exploration here.

Where *A Raisin in the Sun* probed generational debates around theistic belief and secular humanism among inner-city families of the Great Migration, Davis returned to minstrel stereotypes to imagine a Black plantation preacher prematurely equipped with the nascent language of Black Power. The satirical nature of Davis's writing quickly establishes his characters as critiques rather than advancements of white supremacy, while the actor-turned-playwright admitted to using comedy to draw attention to the ridiculousness of segregation, an exercise one reviewer compared to "blow[ing] up [stereotypes] like Macy parade balloons, [making] them fatter and more preposterous than an old-fashioned cartoonist could ever have conceived."[36] Yet this farcical self-awareness did not protect Davis from considerable critical disdain, and liberal whites in particular were said to be uncomfortable with the implications of a play that they heard "made fun of Negroes."[37] One reviewer of the original play argued that Davis's work was "based on the assumption that there is a humorous side to the racial problem," while Jesse H. Walker of the *New York Amsterdam News* deemed it "a howl a minute," likely to draw a laugh from even Alabama governor George Wallace.[38] Despite many positive reviews like the latter, the farcical satire of *Purlie Victorious/Gone Are the Days!* proved too close to older, more disparaging styles for some critics, jeopardizing efforts of the civil rights movement to reconstruct popular ideas about the southern Black preacher and his congregation.

However, far from an attack on Black religious leadership, *Purlie Victorious/ Gone Are the Days!* manages to explore what Carol Bunch Davis calls "linkages between integration, black Christianity, and self-affirmation," all of which become "equally important functions in resisting racial oppression."[39] In this respect, Davis's work was more culturally significant than many of his critics gave him credit for, moving between various ideological strains of the evolving Black freedom struggle with ease and humor. The contemporary context of high-profile leadership and grassroots organization adds humor to Purlie's pompous sense of importance that only he can lead his people out of ignorance and into freedom. "Who else they got?!," Purlie asks with almost a wink to the camera for audiences aware of Davis's commitment to the existing movement. Beyond such obvious allusions, the film brims with what Christopher Sieving calls "watchwords from the civil rights movement ['You tryin' to get non-violent with me, boy?'] and cutting references to serious events and topics."[40] For some, however, the proximity to real events, especially the Birmingham church bombing that left four young girls dead, rendered Davis's attempts at humor callous. Indeed, the timing was unfortunate. Davis himself later noted that "maybe, at this point in our history, Negroes do not feel like laughing."[41]

Contemporary events and emotions aside, there was a more practical reason for the relative failure of *Gone Are the Days!*, as the desegregation of southern movie theaters gained momentum. The NAACP had called a high-profile press conference in June 1963 arguing for the fairer treatment of African Americans in cinema and television, building on decades of protest, while the Kennedy administration included cinema owners among the influential groups invited to the White House in anticipation of the president's proposed civil rights legislation.[42] By the time *Gone Are the Days!* was released in September, increasing numbers of southern cinemas were desegregating under Justice Department pressure. However, as Sieving writes, Davis's film "stood little chance of playing the ever-expanding number of integrated houses below the Mason-Dixon line."[43] Although Davis was confident that his well-reviewed film could be "the electric example of [financial] success" needed to change the industry's attitude toward Black stories—with grittier, more "authentic" films like *Black like Me* (Carl Lerner, 1964) and *Nothing but a Man* (Michael Roemer, 1964) waiting in the wings—the topicality of his film was considered to be of little appeal to white arthouse audiences and would likely have fared better in Black-only theaters.[44] Following a disastrous first run in Manhattan, distributors began to consider *Gone Are the Days!* "too controversial" for release. "It's dead," coproducer and distributor Milton Hammer lamented after five weeks of what the *New York Times* called "meager public support."[45] Despite some passionately supportive reviews and publicity in the Black press and a handful of showings in big cities such as Houston, Chicago, and Baltimore, exhibitors largely rejected the film, ending the hope of national distribution.[46] The "topicality" that had seemed so promising had become a liability.

Others questioned the necessity of a film that offered little diversion from a Broadway show seen by an estimated forty thousand people. The *New York Times* described the movie as "filmed facsimile" that had "taken little advantage of the versatility and motion of the movies."[47] More specifically, Sieving notes that *Gone Are the Days!* lacked the authenticity that the NAACP demanded from Black-centered cinema.[48] Overtly stylized and artificial, Davis's vision relied on comedy and the overblown stereotypes of the plantation past rather than providing an intimate examination of contemporary African American life. Its knowing satire and sparse theatrical sets, rather than location-specific filming, differs considerably from the realism of *Nothing but a Man*, for example, the story of a restless Black railroad worker frustrated with the limitations of life in segregated Alabama. And yet, *Gone Are the Days!* manages to acknowledge the fast pace of racial change through a cinematic genre that had no precedent for African American artists and audiences. Much of Purlie's self-affirming rhetoric would become increasingly associated with the Black Power movement later in the 1960s (as well as the connected Black arts movement of the mid-1960s–1970s) but within the play/film's retrospective southern narrative (and indeed within the civil rights context in which it opened), it was perceived as the evidence of an anger unbefitting of a preacher.

In a considerable break from the dominant ideology of nonviolence that inspired the clergymen central to the established movement, Purlie describes how "the wrath of a righteous God" led him to become a preacher and ultimately whip his former master. "How come the only cheek gets turned in this country is the Negro cheek?" he asks. Although Purlie's description of "murder" was a subversive parable, a fantasy of the violence he would like to inflict on Capt'n Cotchipee, his sermon has a profound effect on his friends and family, leading them to finally rebel against white authority. When the old Confederate Cotchipee drops dead from shock, the congregation celebrate the death of their former master with adapted spirituals and minstrel songs including "Massa's in the Cold, Cold Ground."

Purlie's first and final sermon (the film both begins and ends with Capt'n Cotchipee's funeral) concludes with what critic Edward Mapp later deemed the first "explicit statement of the 'black is beautiful' credo" in American film.[49] "Today, my friends, I find in being black a thing of beauty, a joy, a strength, a secret cup of gladness. . . . Be loyal to yourselves, your skin, your lips, your hair, your southern speech, your laughing kindness," Purlie advises before passionately bestowing the protections of American citizenship on his congregation in a sure nod to the patriotic appeals of the civil rights movement: "May the Constitution of the United States go with you; the Declaration of Independence stand by you; the Bill of Rights protect you and the State Commission against Discrimination keep the eye of the law on you, now and forever, amen!" The congregation then descends into a rendition of the spiritual "Oh Freedom," a song popular with civil rights activists, that contains the improvised lyrics: "No more Capt'n Cotchipee, No more crawling on our knees, Tell the NAACP we are free!" Sieving notes that such congratulatory references to the civil rights movement and Black pride assumed "viewers' solidarity . . . and their familiarity with black culture and folklore." While this proved crucial to the attempts to market the film to African American audiences, it proved problematic to Davis's hope of a crossover, interracial audience.[50]

At the beginning of the film, Purlie questions if his congregation's joyful response to the death of Capt'n Cotchipee is "Big Bethel on her best behavior?" aware of the presence of whites both within the narrative and, by extension, among the audience. In recognition of "the first integrated funeral in the sovereign segregated state of Georgia," Purlie encourages his congregation to "put on their Sunday-best-go-to-meeting-self," reflecting the respectability central to the church-led southern freedom movement working under a white gaze. Although Davis's delivery is satirical, the box office failure of *Gone Are the Days!* suggests that the film itself could have benefited (in commercial terms, at least) from a stronger commitment to the "Sunday-best-go-to-meeting-self." Despite Davis's best efforts to cement a farcical examination of the falsities of white supremacy as a meaningful and financially viable method of cinematic analysis, it was the alternative intersection of cinematic realism and political gradualism that would endure as the dominant cinematic representation of southern African Americans facing racial repression and/or violence.

The Cardinal

As we learned in the previous chapter, there is no evidence that *To Kill a Mockingbird*'s producers made any comment on the contemporary racial situation in Alabama and across the South, apart from when put on the spot by French journalists at the Cannes Film Festival. Like many other southern-set racial dramas of the era, the film was marketed as a "social problem picture." While such descriptions could never fully determine audience reactions, they could nevertheless "lead the terms of audience engagement and reception," Sharon Monteith argues. "They certainly indicated that influential film reviewers rarely correlated southern cinema with racial politics."[51]

Like Robert Mulligan, director Otto Preminger looked to a best-selling novel set in the 1930s to comment on the early 1960s, independently adapting Henry Morton Robinson's *The Cardinal* (originally published in 1950) for the screen in 1963. Yet, unlike Mulligan, who frequently omitted *To Kill a Mockingbird*'s religious elements in pursuit of a more streamlined articulation of white liberal politics, Preminger forced his viewers to acknowledge the religious and racial complexities of the Deep South, admitting that he was inspired by the 1962 desegregation rows at Catholic schools in New Orleans. He also developed an additional character, an African American Catholic priest named Father Gillis (played by Ossie Davis), who travels to the Vatican in 1934 seeking support to desegregate Catholic schools in his Georgia parish. Despite the story and the connections to real issues in New Orleans, Preminger expected the film to play in the Crescent City and many others across the South without edits. "If they don't want to accept it like it is in Georgia [for example], then we won't play there. I have a contract with all my pictures saying that not one scene can be cut without my permission."[52]

Preminger had previously offered Martin Luther King Jr. a minor role as a southern senator in his 1962 film *Advise and Consent*, arguing that "his appearance will make a positive statement for this country here and abroad. It should indicate that it is possible for a Negro to be elected to the United States Senate at any time, now or in the future."[53] The press erupted with news of the casting after the SCLC administrative committee agreed (in King's absence) that King would accept the role on the basis of a $5,000 contribution to the organization. However, on the same day that the *New York Times* presented the story on its cover, King issued a statement to the press confirming that although "well-meaning associates of mine felt that a positive contribution might be made by my appearance in a film as a Negro Senator . . . I feel that the brief role could not be of any significant value in advancing civil rights, and therefore have not accepted the proposal."[54]

In *The Cardinal*, Father Gillis's church is burned by white supremacists, and even though his request for papal support is denied, the film's protagonist, Stephen Fermoyle (Tom Tryon), then a bishop, covertly follows Gillis to Georgia. Although it is but one sequence of events in a three-hour film spanning over twenty years of Fermoyle's life, the plotline was what *Ebony* magazine called "a gripping episode . . . [that] dramatizes the crucial racial problem which faces the church in America today." An important event for African Americans in cinema, *Ebony*'s five-page spread included numerous images of the film's racial violence and portraits of Ossie Davis and his family in Rome during filming. The film also received coverage in *Jet*, which printed Preminger's comments about the need for African Americans to be "aggressive" in their pursuit of cinematic success.[55]

In Preminger's narrative, Fermoyle encourages Gillis to testify against the arsonists, contradicting the advice of the local bishop who frequently refers to Gillis as "boy" and Fermoyle as a "Yankee agitator." Denied a room at a local hotel as a result of his "meddling," Fermoyle is kidnapped along with Gillis and attacked by "Dixie"-singing local Klansmen, who whip him in front of a burning cross when he refuses to spit on his crucifix.[56] While Preminger admitted that the scenes were designed to show Fermoyle "was far ahead of his time and took an uncompromising stand on behalf of racial equality" in 1934, exactly twenty years before any major desegregation rulings, the characterization reflects the considerable opposition such a pioneer was likely to face, rather than simply elevating its protagonist to unrealistic heights.[57] It is important to note that Gillis too is ahead of his time, attempting to desegregate southern parochial schools two decades before his demands would carry any legal, never mind social, weight. As victims of white supremacist violence, Fermoyle and Gillis are unlikely to dismiss the Ku Klux Klan—as Atticus Finch does during the 1930s—as a defunct "political organization" unable to "find anyone to scare."[58] Enduring ecclesiastical passivity and white terrorism together, Fermoyle and Gillis foster a lasting acceptance that is built on a mutual understanding of equality before God.

Ossie Davis described Preminger as understanding his role in *The Cardinal* "as a black man would, without any condescension or patronization." Unlike whites "embarrassed by racism," Davis continued, Preminger "was direct and clear and compassionate." Despite such praise, Preminger's film received mixed reviews in the mainstream press, with many critics commenting that its depth did not match its length. Even though the visually spectacular film addressed a range of important topics, its primary actor, Tom Tryon, was overshadowed by definitive supporting performances from John Huston in particular. Indeed, Davis recalled that by the time he joined the cast in Rome, Tryon was visibly exhausted as the result of Preminger's constant frustration and ridicule. According to the *New York Times*, Tryon's Fermoyle "is no more than a callow cliché, a stick around which several fictions of a melodramatic nature are draped." The film's engagement with segregation was therefore cited as simply one of many moments in "a bumpy gamut of crudely contrived episodes."[59]

Nothing but a Man

White reviewers seemed particularly determined to strip *Nothing but a Man* (1964) of its racial and cultural significance despite, or perhaps because, its producer and director spent months living among African American activists and communities in the Deep South, "armed with a letter of introduction from the NAACP." Producer Robert Young had previously directed a documentary for NBC's prestigious *White Paper* series called *Sit-In*, focusing on the civil rights activism of Nashville students in 1960.[60] While researching their new feature film, Young and director Michael Roemer stayed with numerous civil rights workers from the SCLC and CORE—including James Bevel and Diane Nash, veterans of the Nashville movement—and were frequently tailed by local sheriffs. The one request their activist hosts imparted was that the film's protagonist not leave the South, as so many "energized men" had.[61]

Although *Nothing but a Man* does not directly mention the civil rights movement, it is clear that when Duff Anderson (Ivan Dixon) berates his coworkers for "acting the n****r" and his conservative preacher father-in-law for "stooping so long . . . you don't even know how to stand straight" that he is expressing his desire for African American empowerment and self-determination. Duff's quarrel, as Donald Bogle summarizes, "was not only with his white oppressors but with those blacks who permit oppression."[62] Such a message, integral to Duff's identity as a politically astute African American protagonist, presumably inspired Malcolm X's apparent admiration of the film. Yet it drew limited attention in the film's marketing campaign, which attempted to attract audiences through the movie's more universal themes of heteronormative romance and family. Writing for *America*, Moira Walsh praised the film for being "scrupulously non-propagandistic and . . . not even primarily about race."[63] Thomas Goldthwaite likewise reassured his readers that Roemer's film "is not a violent racial documentary and the sympathy felt is for a poor uneducated man rather than specifically for the plight of the Southern Negro." It was unlikely, he concluded, "that this celebrated

Duff (Ivan Dixon) and his father-in-law, the conservative preacher (Stanley Greene), in *Nothing but a Man* (Michael Roemer, 1964).

picture . . . will inspire denunciations of the South."[64] The movie's soundtrack, mostly Motown numbers, provided a contemporary sound to an otherwise fairly timeless picture and further enhanced the film's crossover potential with liberal white audiences.

White critics proved "lavish in their accolades," Hoyt. W. Fuller noted in the *Negro Digest*, but this did not convert into box office success.[65] White praise—rooted in the film's apparent reality and universality—proved offensive to those who, like Albert Johnson, recognized the film's "exceptionally tame" indictment of white southern racism.[66] As if to prove this point, *Life* magazine appeared to celebrate the idea that *Nothing but a Man* "is one [film] whites can see without bleeding to death if they're liberals, or breaking the kitchenware if they're not."[67] Such emphasis on what the film could offer white audiences "merely adds up to the fact that *Nothing But A Man*, while low-keyed and plausible, lets the White South off the hook," Fuller continued. "Its white villains are of the variety calculated to be irrelevant—hoodlums and straw bosses." Often little more than disruptive caricatures, Roemer's white characters all have distinctly southern accents, while the film's African Americans do not. "The [true] source of viciousness which pinions the Negro hero against the wall is never probed, never even suggested," Fuller wrote. As such, the true realities of Duff's attitudes and behaviors are never explored. "Every Negro knows that the price of being *that kind* of man in the South is prison or death, or both," Fuller concluded.[68]

In its depiction of religion, *Nothing but a Man* implies accommodationism and conformity. Its clergy are the "go-between of the black community and the white power structure," and they serve to isolate the protagonists, thus bringing them together.[69] Josie Dawson (Abbey Lincoln) is the preacher's daughter and later becomes Duff's wife. The couple's shared dissatisfaction with the status quo attracts them to each other—"I never had much use for hellhowlers," Duff tells Josie on their first meeting. Meanwhile, the church, which although headed by Josie's father seems mainly composed of women, restricts them both. Even though Reverend Dawson's accommodationist stance was well presented in the Black South, Khalil Gibran Muhammad points out that it nevertheless confines the range of Black political philosophies the film could explore and limits Black women—especially older Black women—to a lack of agency. Indeed, *Nothing but a Man* contains "no counternarrative of a black church or black preachers challenging segregation or brokering with the white power structure," which Muhammad argues "had already proven to be an effective way of challenging white supremacy in the South," particularly when harnessed through community boycotts developed and sustained by women.[70]

The film's depiction of religion is distinctly Marxist, Muhammad continues, associating expressive faith with worldly acceptance and placing the impetus for change in labor activism. Such a presentation denies the fact that for every "accommodationist preacher" like Josie's father, "you could have a Wyatt Walker, or a C. T. Vivian, or a Fred Shuttlesworth, or ultimately a Martin Luther King Jr." It therefore denies the radical potential of Black Christianity, its achievements thus far in the movement, and, according to Muhammad, implies something of a misunderstanding on the part of the film's white leftist producers. In their coverage of the movement, including *Sit-In*, Roemer and Young did not see "activists in their own religious identities." Rather, Muhammad posits, they "perhaps saw them more as young people challenging the status quo, representing again a liberal secularist tradition or a Marxist tradition of class warfare." According to Muhammad, it was perfectly plausible in the Black South for individuals to embrace NAACP integrationist politics, left-wing labor unionism, and the church if such organizations offered effective means of addressing the material or spiritual conditions of their lives. Belief in Jesus Christ did not prove incompatible with other affiliations, as secular Marxists might assume. But how could Roemer and Young "capture and harness" the power of religion if they did not believe in it?[71]

The following year, in 1965, critic Albert Johnston lamented that "it seems impossible for writers and film-makers to capture the essence of courage or dedication that drives many Negroes toward self-sacrificial death in the Southern states." Yet Johnson had some sympathy for Hollywood as "to release a fiction film based on the true-life horrors experienced by white and Negro civil rights workers in the backward counties of Mississippi, Georgia, and Alabama . . . would be inflammatory and raise cries of anarchy." Although a series of exploitation films quickly capitalized on the tensions surrounding the Freedom Rides and Freedom Summer, Johnson would have to wait almost twenty-five years for mainstream Hollywood releases that purported to show the dangers facing civil rights workers in the Deep South. Yet, that first wave of films—most notably *Mississippi Burning* and *The Long Walk Home*—were far from the vision of "the Negro and his struggle for freedom and personal integrity in the American South" that Johnson had invited in 1965.[72] *Mississippi Burning*, in particular, through its construction of a victimized, stoic Black community bears little resemblance to the vibrant grassroots activism that characterized the civil rights movement at this time. It also constituted a considerable shift in the intentions of white directors when positioning issues of race. If King Vidor promoted himself as an authority on Black southern life and religious culture in the 1920s and Michael Roemer sought to live among civil rights workers in the 1960s, the white directors of *Mississippi Burning* and *The Long Walk Home* made no such claims to expertise. Rather, they established a new direction for the southern-set racial narrative—one that repositioned civil rights history as the story of white bravery.

The Long Walk Home

As one of the first mainstream Hollywood films to engage with the civil rights movement, Richard Pearce's *The Long Walk Home* (1990) deserves considerable criticism for its emphasis on a middle-class white housewife—a narrative strategy that centers a white feminist awakening rather than anti-racism and incongruously presents white women as integral to the Montgomery bus boycott of 1955–56. However, when compared to its immediate predecessor, *Mississippi Burning, The Long Walk* Home appears sensitive, at least, to the significance of the Black church to the boycott, reflecting a period of the civil rights movement centered on respectability, patriotism, and church-centered leadership. What is less clear in the film, however, is that the boycott was instigated and developed by Black women as the visible on-screen organization, including carpools, is initiated from the (male) pulpit. Nevertheless, the key initial output of the Women's Political Council—the infamous flyers that were distributed to Black schools and workplaces to advertise the boycott in response to Rosa Parks's arrest—feature prominently, as does their message of a racial discrimination and humiliation that impacted Black women in particular. The flyers are immediately effective, sparking discussion among school-

Workers read a leaflet prepared by the Women's Political Council of Montgomery, Alabama, detailing the plans for a boycott of city buses following the arrest of Rosa Parks in December 1955, in *A Long Walk Home* (Richard Pearce, 1990).

children, female domestic workers, and male laborers. Rosa Parks is discussed by name, and the "[Claudette] Colvin case" is also mentioned, implying that both women are known to the film's Black characters. The content of the flyers is read aloud by characters in both domestic and industrial settings, demonstrating how its message disseminated through the community.

When Herbert Cotter (Ving Rhames) returns home from his job at a glass manufacturer armed with a flyer, he joins hands with his family to say grace over the dinner table. However, before leading his family in prayer, Herbert speaks his mind: "I'm tired of hanging my head in the shadow of crackers. I want to ride the front of the bus." After issuing thanks for the food on the table, he concludes his prayer: "Watch over our souls tonight, and help us live Your word tomorrow. In Jesus's name, Amen." In the next scene, by dawn's light, Herbert's prayer seems answered, as the excited Cotter family rush onto the porch to watch the first bus go by. "That bus is as empty as my grave," Herbert's wife, Odessa (Whoopi Goldberg), exclaims.

None of the family rides the buses that day, nor do any other Black residents of Montgomery as the film presents a montage of downtown walkers and empty buses. Odessa, feet bloody from her long commute on foot, barely makes it home in time for the "mass meeting," where crowds stream into the Holt Street Baptist Church. Although Martin Luther King Jr. is not presented visually, his words are heard over loudspeaker—a recording from the first mass meeting of the Montgomery Improvement Association (MIA) on December 5, 1955.[73] In this short snippet of King's original speech, he appeals to ideas of equality before God but also U.S. civic ideals. King tells those gathered that "the only weapon we have in our hands this evening is the weapon of protest. And we are not wrong. If we are wrong, then the Supreme Court of this nation is wrong. If we are wrong, the constitution of the United States is wrong. If we are wrong, then God Almighty is wrong."[74] As such, viewers are encouraged to invest in the patriotic legitimacy of the early civil rights movement, which is juxtaposed against the senseless violence enacted against King later in the film, when it is revealed that his home has been bombed.

When examining King's December 5, 1955 speech, Kirt H. Wilson documents a range of themes within it, ultimately concluding that King's rhetoric, though essential to the boycott's eventual success, "effaced the gender and class implications of the protest," particularly through his representation of Rosa Parks. King positioned Parks as the center of the "bus situation in Montgomery" despite several other high-profile cases in recent years he could have drawn on. While celebrating Parks's integrity, King denied her agency, Wilson argues, and her "person was lost from sight precisely [as] her persona transformed her into a national and international hero." Although it is unlikely that a Hollywood film would ever present King's speech in its entirety, the snippet chosen prioritizes national themes, rather than King's discussion of Parks, and positions the church-led movement as a righteous crusade established and maintained by American principles that audiences are likely to value in their own lives. Focusing on the extract chosen for *The Long Walk Home*, Wilson notes the significance of King's use of the pronoun "we," as well as the frequency with which King repeated many of the phrases and images evoked here across his career. Conflating "the decisions of the Supreme Court, the Constitution of the United States, the theology of several religions, and the teachings of Jesus," King would return to the themes of his first MIA mass meeting "for many years to come."[75] The speech and particularly the extract selected are therefore an unsurprising choice for the film, cementing legitimacy but also appealing to familiarity. At the end of the film, as on-screen text alerts viewers to the outcome of the boycott and the development of the wider civil rights movement, extracts from King's March 1965 speech at the end of the Selma to Montgomery march can be heard, signifying both the successes of the postboycott movement and King's triumphant return to Montgomery, where—it is implied—it all began.

Montgomery was about more than buses, as Odessa testifies. Soon it will be about "the parks and the restaurants . . . colored teachers in white schools," Odessa tells her white employer, Miriam Thompson (Sissy Spacek). "What about when we start voting, Ms. Thompson, 'cos we are. And when we do, we are going to put Negroes in office. What about when the first colored family moves into your neighborhood?" Drawing strength from rallies and church services, Odessa is prepared to walk miles and risk unemployment to secure a better life for her children, one of whom is tellingly named Selma: a sign of the fights and victories is to come. "You come into town and go to one of those mass meetings," Odessa tells a colleague, "you'd feel like you could walk forever." Whereas one critic perversely argued that the Cotter "family's frequent churchgoing" in *The Long Walk Home* "and its belief in nonviolent resistance are overemphasized, *no matter how true they are to the attitudes of the black community of this place and time*" (emphasis mine), the film cements the position of civil rights activity in the lives of its Black characters much more centrally than many later films, including the female-driven narrative that it is most regularly compared to, *The Help* (Tate Taylor, 2011), which offers no exploration of the theological or political preoccupations of its African American characters other than the fact that they do, of course, attend an unspecified church.[76] This lack of development contributes to a narrative that seems to willfully deny the reality of Black life in Jackson, Mississippi, in 1963–64, as a hyperfeminized sphere diverts attention from the very real events exploding across Mississippi and the rest of the South in favor of interpersonal conflict.[77]

In *The Long Walk Home*, a Black preacher explains some of the boycott's logistics at a mass meeting: "If you have a car, but you must be at work during the day, we have fine young men who can drive your cars, allowing you to still contribute to the boycott." Following the preacher's request, the choir sings "We're Marching to Zion," a song that takes on a more literal meaning for the large number of congregants that are now walking to work and school rather than use segregated transport. For the Cotter family, whose young son Theo (Richard Habersham) bears the scars of a beating by racist whites after an incident on the segregated buses, the service and indeed the song seem to cement their sense of righteousness, and gradually they all join in the singing. "Everybody would . . . clap and hold hands in the meeting," Jo Ann Robinson of the Women's Political Council—who first instigated the Montgomery boycott—would later recall: "Oh, you just loved everybody."[78] Indeed, when racists surround Odessa and other Black women at the carpool headquarters, the women respond to the chants of "Walk, n****r, walk" with a rendition of the hymn "I'm Going Through," which situates their struggle within a larger spiritual and moral framework:

> I'm going through, I'm going through,
> I'll pay the price, whatever others do;
> I'll take the way with God's despised few;
> I'm going through, Jesus, I'm going through.[79]

Civil rights memoirs and histories are filled with stories of those who entered the political and physical battlefield of the civil rights movement armed only with their sense of righteousness before God.[80] However, in relation to the described scene from *The Long Walk Home*, Rosa Parks herself doubted that such a hymn would have been enough to silence a racist mob. "People adamant about harassing blacks wouldn't have been affected by someone stepping forward to sing a song," Parks commented on the film's release. "They just weren't Christian enough to fall silent."[81]

Mississippi Burning

Set almost ten years later, in 1964, *Mississippi Burning* evidences the horrors of white violence but denies African American agency in its dignified yet simplistic depiction of a silent, frightened community. *Mississippi Burning*'s Black population seems entirely estranged from both the plight of missing civil rights workers and the brutality that marks their own everyday lives. As George Will

Water fountains marked "WHITE" and "COLORED," depicted in the opening credits of *Mississippi Burning* (Alan Parker, 1988).

argued in 1989, African Americans appear in *Mississippi Burning* merely "as sufferers, a background chorus to a melodrama of white FBI agents battling white conspirators."[82] Music is a fundamental component of this construction. For example, almost every scene of Black suffering in *Mississippi Burning*—from the beating of an African American congregation by Klansmen, to house bombings, and the subjugation of Black protesters by angry whites—is accompanied by a slow-tempo gospel hymn. The film's opening credits play over images of a slowly burning church, sound tracked by Mahalia Jackson's mournful rendition of "Precious Lord, Take My Hand," a version commonly associated with Martin Luther King Jr.'s funeral. A scene of an African American boy using a drinking fountain marked "COLORED" provides clear visual introduction to the segregated South, while the music evokes one of the lowest moments of the civil rights movement—the assassination of its nonviolent talisman. These sights and sounds of the South betray a place of violence and hopelessness, while the developing narrative makes little effort to understand racial realities.

Parker's direction of the beating of a Black congregation deserves particular attention, as it positions the film's most symbolic religious groupings—the stoic but defenseless Black community and the irredeemable violence of the Klan—against each other, illuminating Paul Harvey's contention that the southern civil rights movement reflected "American Christianity . . . at its most tragic and its most triumphant."[83] As an African American congregation sings "When We All Get to Heaven," men in white hoods begin to form a counterassembly outside. The animated chatter of the departing churchgoers then descends into terrified screams on recognition of the waiting mob, as Klan members begin to chase and assault members of the congregation.

A Klansman looms over a young Black boy, who prays as his church is attacked by white supremacists in *Mississippi Burning* (Alan Parker, 1988).

"When We All Get to Heaven" can then be heard yet again, this time sang at a slower tempo by Lannie Spann McBride, who served as director Alan Parker's "Gospel Music Consultant" on the movie.[84] Through McBride's reserved delivery, the song loses the previous triumphalism of its lyrics ("When we all get to heaven, what a day of rejoicing that will be! When we all see Jesus, we'll sing and shout the victory!"). There is no inspirational or confrontational element to the music here; rather than encouraging resistance, the song acts as a salve, promoting dignity in the face of tragedy or potentially indicting religion's failure to deliver worldly justice. As one young Black boy simply kneels in prayer, a Klansman kicks him in the face and threatens him with death.

Mississippi Burning ends with a choral performance of "Walk on by Faith," again led by Lannie Spann McBride. This final scene unfolds in the remains of a burned church, as an interracial choir of faces previously unseen in the film gather to mark the departure of the FBI agents charged with investigating the disappearance and murder of three civil rights workers. The agents watch from a respectful distance before heading back to their car and presumably Washington, D.C. As such, the scene will be their (and the audiences') lasting glimpse of Mississippi. Little more than a "southern cliché," according to historian Roger Fischer, "after two hours of nonstop white depravity and black victimization, the scene rings fundamentally false."[85]

This repeated use of somber religious music, rather than the freedom songs activists and historians have consistently linked with the movement, is not unique to *Mississippi Burning* and deserves attention as a fundamental component of the civil rights melodrama. Such musical accompaniment implies that a righteous but besieged African American community is resigned to their earthly fate, placing their hope in eventual redemption through death in Christ. Although musicologists such as Philip Tagg have debated the musical evidence of "specific skin colour or continental origin" in a given piece of music, they neglect, as Ruth Doughty has noted, "to address that 'black music' is systematically deployed by the film industry to gain swift entrance into the African American condition."[86]

"Black music" is, of course, a contentious term, yet it remains evident that certain musical forms—including blues, jazz, hip-hop, and gospel—often facilitate a "concise and unambiguous" attempt at connoting the geographic location and racial makeup of a film's setting.[87] Black religious music, and specifically gospel, has long been crucial to Hollywood's evocation of the southern Black community despite the fact that scholars have consistently linked gospel music to the distinctive experiences of African Americans transplanted to the urban North during the Great Migration.[88] Nevertheless, because "gospel has frequently been depicted as some kind of pure, unmediated, expression of Black 'folk' mentality," as Brian Ward has argued, it is apparently immune "to the crass and distortive business considerations which have made other forms of black popular music, like black rock and roll, pop and soul, somehow less 'authentic.'"[89] Disavowing rhythm and blues (R & B) and soul as derivative and commercialized, Charles Hobson agued in 1968 that "nothing in soul can match the best in Gospel."[90] The continuing influence of this sentiment in Hollywood film implies that gospel speaks to and for all African Americans, uniting them to a common past that endures through collective racial consciousness and cultural forms.

Of course, sociologists and historians have linked African American social and cultural movements ever since W. E. B. DuBois explored the "souls of black folk" in 1903.[91] "For DuBois," Ron Eyerman and Andrew Jamison write, "slave songs were not merely music, they were an expression of a life rooted in a rural past, and more generally they reflected an experience all African Americans could recognize."[92] In Hollywood film, where Black stories and cultural forms have been routinely co-opted by white directors and producers, spiritual music offers a dignified salve but lacks the sense of resistance and opposition that so many have attributed to it across African American history. In a cinema primarily for and about white Americans, Black music tends to constitute little more than "local color," reflecting a static and monolithic understanding of Black religious cultures, while conveying a sense of regional and racial distinction. Rather than compelling social action, gospel music in particular often pacifies communities facing senseless violence; providing comfort, it replaces the politicized with a stoic and gracious faith.

The use of Black religious music was therefore as crucial to *Mississippi Burning* as it was to *Hallelujah*, providing what Doughty calls "an associative link" to Black America and specifically to the Black South.[93] However, whereas *Hallelujah* attempted to provide a voyeuristic insight into the childlike faith of African American caricatures known to audiences through minstrelsy, *Mississippi Burning* uses sorrowful religious music to evoke a time and place rooted in racist exploitation and violence. Like much of *Mississippi Burning*, the music is more important as an evocation of the hellish South than of Black history and culture, an invocation of southern exceptionalism and internal orientalism.[94] Similarly, because most late twentieth-century civil rights narratives imply that the boundaries of racism and segregation have been largely overcome, relegated to the past through the actions of liberal whites rooted in a national rather than sectional culture, somber religious music transports audiences back to a darker time when race relations were considerably worse.

Less than a year after *Mississippi Burning*'s release, three-quarters of whites polled believed that opportunities for African Americans had improved under Ronald Reagan's administration despite statistical evidence to the contrary. For George Lipsitz, such responses did not necessarily indicate "ignorance of the dire conditions facing black communities, but . . . that many whites believe that blacks suffer deservedly, that they do not take advantage of the opportunities offered them."[95] Rather than harvesting the fruits of progress secured in the 1960s, contemporary African Americans, especially those residing in urban ghettoes, "suffer[ed] from poor housing and employment opportunities because of their own lack of willpower," survey results suggested.[96] For whites harboring these attitudes, *Mississippi Burning* presented stoic, rural African Americans worthy of viewer sympathy and FBI protection. Silently hopeful that America would one day embrace them as full citizens, these characters apparently knew that change was gradual and they waited with dignified patience.

Such faith in American progress constructs the contemporary "agitation on the part of activists and organizations still struggling for equality [as] unwarranted and illegitimate," Kelly Madison writes.[97] It is easy to see why the angry urban African American of the late 1980s and 1990s—so threatening to what Jennifer Fuller calls America's relatively recent "sense of itself as a successfully integrated nation"—was symbolically replaced by his cinematic ancestor: the submissive but deserving poor Black southerner.[98] Just as earlier fictions such as *The Green Pastures* "joined broader discussions about the Great Migration and the kind of religion that was deemed 'good' for the black masses," late twentieth-century civil rights melodramas like *Mississippi Burning* offered reassuringly rural Black communities that seemed to have resisted industrialization and secularization. During the uncertainty of the Depression, Curtis J. Evans continues, "white admirers tended to laud what they saw as the peculiar qualities of African Americans exhibited in *The Green Pastures*." His description could be easily applied to *Mississippi Burning*: a "lack of vindictiveness, resignation under suffering, a joyful carefree spirit, and a simple innate religiosity."[99] Relegated to mere props, African Americans in Alan Parker's film are, to use David Jansson's words, "used or abused by white Southerners depending on the degree to which the latter group has achieved some level of American enlightenment."[100] Whereas scholars have long noted the film's omission of Black mobilization for voting rights, jobs, education, and housing, the film's presentation of African American religion remains a commonly underacknowledged part of its construction.

In over two hours, *Mississippi Burning* offers just one rallying call from the pulpit as an unnamed Black orator (played by Frankie Faison) delivers a eulogy for a slain civil rights worker, closely based on CORE's Mississippi director Dave Dennis's impassioned speech at James Chaney's funeral on August 7, 1964. In this rarely discussed scene, the speaker explicitly expresses his continued anger and frustration at the slow progress of racial change: "I have no more love to give. I have only anger in my heart today . . . and I want you to be angry with me! Now, I am sick and I am tired . . . and I want you to be sick and tired with me! I . . . I . . . I am sick and tired of going to the funerals of black men who have been murdered by white men! I . . . I am sick and tired of the people of this country who continue to allow these things to happen!" Because *Mississippi Burning* fails to "focus on one local black leader," Donald Bogle writes, the eulogy scene "seems almost like an afterthought." Bogle likens this underdeveloped scene to the "poorly conceived black FBI agent who threatens a white character with castration." Indeed, these communications of Black anger bear a stark contrast to the rest of the film, which otherwise limits African American assertiveness to the willingness of two Black children to testify before the FBI. Yet, although the black FBI agent is, as Bogle writes, "a complete falsification of history" (the FBI had no African American agents at this time), the eulogy scene was not.[101] It may even have been familiar to some audiences who had previously seen Dennis's original speech in episode 5 of *Eyes on the Prize*. *Mississippi Burning*'s re-creation, while reflecting Dennis's anger, nevertheless lacks his uncompromising call to action. Although Dennis gave a damning account of the actions of state and federal officials, including the president, he also cursed local African Americans who refused to act in pursuit of their own liberation. The congregation had an obligation, Dennis implied, to not simply mourn Chaney's death but continue his work to ensure he did not die in vain: "I've got a bitter vengeance in my heart tonight. . . . If you do go back home and sit down and take it, God damn your souls! Stand up! Your neighbors down there who were too afraid to come to this memorial, take them to another memorial. . . . Make them register to vote and you register to vote. I doubt if one fourth of this house is registered. Go down there and do it. (Pause) Don't bow down anymore! Hold your heads up!"[102]

In her study of the African American funeral, Suzanne E. Smith compares Dennis's speech with Martin Luther King Jr.'s February 1965 eulogy for Jimmie Lee Jackson, who was killed by an Alabama state trooper during a voting rights march in Marion, Alabama.[103] Both Dennis and King exalted the fallen as martyrs but sought to instigate further political action, noting that the list of those implicated in such murders stretched beyond the eventual gunmen. For William Lawson, both tributes "function less like eulogistic discourse and more like [speeches] attacking complacency."[104] Both seem to suggest that salvation is not simply awarded by God but something that requires personal action, inspired by a righteous anger. However, rather than representing a sudden engagement with the Black community, *Mississippi Burning* presents its adaptation of Dennis's eulogy for Chaney within a longer montage designed to communicate a wider shift in the film's white-centric narrative, as Agent Ward (Willem Dafoe) of the FBI agrees to join the Ku Klux Klan "in the gutter" and "fight dirty," a decision made in response to the Klan's violence toward a white female informant rather than the continued intimidation and persecution of African Americans.

In keeping with the film's wider connections to the western genre, FBI mobilization following the attack on Mrs. Pell (Frances McDormand) enables a Quentin Tarantino–esque revenge fantasy in which the much-maligned, entirely fictional Black FBI agent threatens the town's mayor with castration.[105] Writing in 2005, Alan Parker admitted that the studio, Orion Pictures, wanted the film to be "a detective story that just *happened* to be set against the civil rights struggle" (emphasis Parker's).[106] As a result, *Mississippi Burning* offers no judgment or punishment for the FBI's aggressive behavior; they are now "in the gutter" with the Klan, an irredeemable enemy. Agent Ward therefore stands aside and allows Agent Anderson (Gene Hackman), a Mississippi native, to take control, the implication being that Anderson is the only agent who knows "how to 'talk southern.'"[107]

Presenting the Klan as the natural manifestation of a pathologized town,

FBI Agents Ward (Willem Dafoe) and Anderson (Gene Hackman) disagree on tactics while footage of their enemy, the Ku Klux Klan, is projected in the background in *Mississippi Burning* (Alan Parker, 1988).

Mississippi Burning makes no attempt to account for the radicalization of white locals. Unlike some post–civil rights dramas, such as *A Time to Kill*, we do not see the initial development of a Klavern or any sense of how the Klan recruited its membership in the fictional Jessup County, a stand-in for the real Neshoba County. On the one hand, there is a strong implication that the Klan is a timeless factor of small-town southern life, one that has entrapped generations of resentful, uneducated white men. However, as businessmen and police officers, the Klansmen of *Mississippi Burning* are hardly marginal figures as they are in *A Time to Kill*. Nevertheless, *Mississippi Burning* offers no theological, social, or political alternative to the Klan. Instead of contrasting the Klan against a local religious or political organization, *Mississippi Burning* pits the Klan entirely against the secular, federal power of the FBI, ensuring that the film's heroes and villains are starkly projected, with little room for theological or political complexity; white churches and other institutions seemingly do not exist.

But even though scholars and critics have dissected the film's presentation of its white heroes and its subjugated, silent Back community, *Mississippi Burning*'s construction of its villains rarely figures in the critical literature.[108] *Mississippi Burning* does not, as some critics suggest, simply celebrate whiteness at the expense of Black activism; rather, it creates divisions *within* whiteness along regional, class, and religious boundaries, projecting the idea that secular, consensus liberalism is stronger and more resilient than the values of an anomalous, racist region. Such constructions of both the region and the nation would prove vastly influential in the developing civil rights genre of the 1990s as American audiences were increasingly encouraged to reimagine the civil rights era as a period of color-blind white heroism rather than the historical reality of Black radicalism, bravery, and political assertiveness. Whereas Ralph Ellison may have dismissed the "social problem pictures" of midcentury as "not [being] about Negroes at all" but rather "about what whites think and feel about Negroes," the racial melodramas of the 1990s went one step further. These films were not about how white Americans "thought and felt" about Black Americans at all. Rather, they increasingly reflected how white Americans thought about *themselves* on the eve of the new millennium.[109]

CHAPTER 3

"When Things Made Sense, When We Were the Good Guys"

Reconstructed White Southerners in the Mid-1990s Civil Rights Melodrama

In February 1996, the Clinton administration announced a federal investigation into a sequence of suspected arson attacks at Black churches across the South.[1] Described as "an epidemic of terror" by the assistant attorney general for civil rights, this wave of destruction brought back painful memories of the civil rights era, when African American churches were frequently targeted by white supremacists. "They're not burning down black barbeque joints [or] pool halls," Randolph Scott-McLaughlin of the Center for Constitutional Rights observed, "they're burning down black churches. It's like they're burning a cross in my front yard. They're burning down symbols of resistance and community and hope and refuge."[2]

For a short while in 1996, stories of church burnings dominated the news cycle, culminating in a considerable federal and public response that was remarkably different from the silence of the 1960s. Congress made it significantly easier to prosecute arson attacks on places of worship, increased the punishment for those convicted, and promised a $10 million federal loan program to help affected congregations to rebuild.[3] Even Ralph Reed, executive director of the staunchly conservative Christian Coalition, met with Black pastors in Atlanta, offering "ready hands to fight this senseless violence." Pledging to raise a special fund of up to $1 million for the rebuilding of damaged churches, Reed acknowledged that his predominantly white evangelical following had seldom committed to bridging racial divides in the past but argued that "we come today bearing the burden of that history with broken hearts [and] a repentant spirit." Few African Americans were convinced by Reed's contrition. Joseph Lowery, president of the Southern Christian Leadership Conference (SCLC), boycotted the meeting along with several other Black leaders, arguing that Reed's outreach was little more than a cynical effort to boost the Christian Coalition's conservative agenda among Black Christians. It was this very agenda, Lowery contended, that was responsible for the rise in racial violence in the first place.[4]

Bill Clinton's newly appointed National Church Arson Task Force would later report that at the height of the 1995–96 wave of arson attacks, a fire occurred at an African American church roughly every five days. Over the next four years, the task force investigated 827 arsons, bombings, or attempted bombings at houses of worship associated with almost all faiths and racial groups across the nation. They submitted annual findings to the president and boasted an arrest rate for church burnings that was twice as high as for other forms of arson. However, although some culprits openly admitted racist aims and ideologies, investigators were unable to trace the majority of the fires to organized white supremacist groups.[5] The investigations also exposed and exacerbated tensions between rural Black communities and federal agents, with some pastors accusing the task force of harassment, complaining that their congregations were treated as suspects and subject to lie detector tests. This lack of trust was further aggravated when two agents working on the task force were dismissed and another eight disciplined for participating in "Good Ol' Boy Roundups," annual law enforcement events in Tennessee marked by heavy drinking and the sale and display of racist paraphernalia that were eventually investigated by the federal government in 1995.[6]

The Associated Press had noted as early as June 1996 that despite the admittedly "frightening" images of burning churches, there was "little hard evidence" to suggest that "the seventy-three black church fires recorded since 1995 can be blamed on a conspiracy or a general climate of racial hatred."[7] Conservative voices took to the *Wall Street Journal* and the *New Yorker* to claim that the wave of arsons had been a hoax whipped up by left-wing activists, who had prompted more copycat crimes than they had prevented.[8] Republicans accused President Clinton of manipulating fear for political gain after he dedicated his weekly radio address to the problem on June 8, 1996.[9] But for Clinton, like many others, "the absence of any organized conspiracy [made] the phenomenon of church burning more, rather than less disturbing." As historian Jim Campbell wrote in the *Los Angeles Times*, it is "far easier to abide the idea of a tight-knit group of racist fanatics than to accept the alternative that we live in a time when a substantial number of [unconnected] individuals . . . regard burning black churches as a plausible act."[10]

While there may not have been a national conspiracy, Attorney General Janet Reno noted, "there is clear evidence of racism."[11]

This chapter explores how, in an era marked by seemingly arbitrary acts of racial terrorism, both within and without the former Confederacy, Hollywood film provided a reassuring reminder that "real" racial fanatics could still be readily identified by their white hoods and burning crosses and were largely confined to the small-town South. Films such as *Ghosts of Mississippi* and *A Time to Kill*, both from 1996, ultimately tell us nothing about civil rights or the experiences of Black people. Rather, they present competing images of post-1960s whiteness and the apparent "common sense" of secular, color-blind hegemony. Here, Hollywood liberals separated themselves from conservatives wedded to evangelical Christianity (in both the past and the present) but reflected a dominant societal acceptance of neoliberal color blindness that Justin Gomer argues had been embedded in American political and popular culture since the 1970s. If the earlier *Mississippi Burning* (1988) and *The Long Walk Home* (1990) inserted incongruous white stories into the history of the civil rights movement itself, the contemporary racial dramas of the mid-1990s reflected white frustrations with the continuing demands of a movement unfinished and presented sympathetic white characters who continued to suffer for their principles, like President Clinton seemingly did in Congress.[12] In taking such personal and professional risks, these reconstructed, underappreciated white southerners birthed yet another "New" South and, with it, the credibly color-blind nation.

"What Whites Think and Feel about Negroes": White Liberalism On-Screen

White redemption narratives, fixed on elite, usually male experiences, reduce African American characters until they simply "support and 'anoint' the protagonist as a savior," restoring white middle-class innocence by demonizing the working class "as the 'true' racists."[13] Where Atticus Finch cast himself against the white trash alcoholic Bob Ewell, Bobby DeLaughter of *Ghosts of Mississippi* has a white supremacist assassin named Byron De La Beckwith. Jake Brigance of *A Time to Kill*, meanwhile, squares off against the local Klan and a particularly zealous district attorney. Such dichotomies increase the hero's narrative power, marking him as special. As lawyers, Finch, DeLaughter, and Brigance are each afforded final summation speeches that affirm their American, rather than sectional, morality. This is especially significant in *Ghosts of Mississippi*, where DeLaughter quotes President Kennedy's June 1963 statement on civil rights. While the scene focuses on DeLaughter, frequent cuts to Myrlie Evers-Williams (played by Whoopi Goldberg) imply that

DeLaughter is speaking for her and her family, just as Atticus's final speech involves numerous cuts to the African Americans gathered in the "colored balcony" to watch Tom Robinson's trial. Indeed, Evers-Williams's admission that the assistant district attorney reminds her of her slain husband, Medgar Evers, the NAACP's Mississippi field secretary assassinated in 1963, appears as uncomfortably deferential as Harper Lee's contention that African Americans would rise to their feet in recognition of Atticus's efforts to defend Tom Robinson. Such scenes reflect the enduring legacy of what Stokely Carmichael and Charles V. Hamilton exposed as "the subtle paternalism bred into [white people] by society" that was perhaps more pervasive and harder to eliminate than overt racism. The implication of such paternalism, Carmichael and Hamilton argued in 1967, "conditioned" how white people expect others to react to their whiteness.[14]

For Allison Graham, the connections between 1990s civil rights dramas and previous waves of cinema transcended Ralph Ellison's evocation at midcentury that social problem pictures reflected only what "what whites think and feel about Negroes," or even the powerful influence of *To Kill a Mockingbird* a decade or so later. Rather, they can be traced right back to D. W. Griffith's *The Birth of a Nation* (1915), which "set out to 'heal' cultural wounds, to reunite the [white] nation by reclaiming the alienated white southerner" after the Civil War.[15] However, whereas Griffith blamed African Americans for fracturing a U.S. identity built on whiteness, the powerbrokers of late twentieth-century Hollywood often selected the poor, white, and often religious southerner as their scapegoat, always on hand to jeopardize recent racial progress. Despite developments in racial and political sensibilities, Hollywood filmmakers continued to reflect what Roopali Mukherjee calls "a myopic and enduring fascination with the American South as the mythic 'scene of the crime.'"[16]

Given the palpable divisions of the 1990s, more of which will be discussed below, it is perhaps unsurprising that sociologist Bernard Beck concluded in 1997 that contemporary white liberals were "pessimistic [and] confused," preferring to "remember a time when things made sense, when [they] were the good guys."[17] But disillusioned white liberals, many of whom came of age during the civil rights era itself, were in a position of considerable cultural power by the late twentieth century and took steps to reaffirm their moral whiteness through the media. In developing what Sharon Monteith calls "individual morality tales for a nation in which black and white individuals remain disconcertingly separate," Hollywood liberals of the Clinton era reflected an unprecedented identification with the forty-second president, whose connections with the industry were so strong that commentators assumed he would run a studio on leaving office.[18]

Just as Clinton consciously courted those with positive memories of the 1960s (and repelled those who saw the decade as the beginning of America's decline), Hollywood's 1990s liberalism was deeply rooted in the earlier era, as noted in the 1996 study *Hollywood's America*. Here, Stephen Powers, David Rothman, and Stanley Rothman argued that those who opposed the "liberal or leftist perspectives that became prominent in the 1960s" were reduced to the cinematic villains or buffoons of the 1990s. "In short," they argued, contemporary "filmmakers seek to propagate an ideology that they believe should be held by all decent people."[19] As the 1990s unfolded, Hollywood produced more television and cinema depictions of the civil rights movement of the 1950s and 1960s than filmmakers in the 1960s, 1970s, and 1980s combined. Indeed, as Jennifer Fuller notes, such representations were so plentiful that the 1990s civil rights drama became "a reference point for judging the state of contemporary race relations and for defining what constituted racial progress."[20] White liberal self-righteousness therefore became particularly apparent in the post–civil rights era depiction of religious white southerners, from the sinister Klansmen of *Mississippi Burning* (1988), to the conniving televangelists of *Fletch Lives* (Michael Ritchie, 1989), the latter a satirical approach to the numerous scandals that rocked evangelical ministries in the late 1980s.[21] Offering a ready supply of sleazy, even comedic villains and upstanding, commonsense patriarchs, southern whites found themselves dichotomized by a cinema culture desperate for morality tales with both past and present implications.

Race and the Culture Wars: The 1990s

Alongside much of Black America, the Clinton administration proved resolute in their judgment that the church burnings of the mid-1990s were racially motivated. This conclusion was not shared by most white Americans. Largely in keeping with a general divergence of public opinion along racial lines during this period, notably evident during the 1994–95 O. J. Simpson trial, differing responses to the wave of arsons nevertheless showed that despite the gains of the civil rights movement, "this nation has miles to go before its citizens feel equally at ease and at home."[22] Civil rights leaders like Reverend Jesse Jackson pointed toward a "cultural conspiracy," an atmosphere of racial animosity articulated through conservative policy and white rejection of measures like affirmative action, propelled by "neopopulists" like Pat Buchanan.[23] For Representative John Conyers, "the nation [was] in crisis"— the "symptoms" of that crisis "reflected in the church burnings in mostly African American churches."[24]

Cynicism regarding America's racial progress was evident throughout the

1990s and noted by major outlets and commentators. "After all the high hopes and genuine progress of the past 30 years, people on both sides of the color line feel they've reached an impasse," Mark Whitaker reported for *Newsweek* in 1991. Many Americans, he concluded, believe "things are getting worse." Between 1989 and 1991 alone, the number of whites who felt that African Americans were better off than they were five years ago had fallen from 49 percent to 38 percent; among African Americans asked the same question, numbers had dwindled from 33 percent to just 21 percent.[25] Although George H. W. Bush's "Willie Horton" campaign video came to represent the overt political manipulation of white fears of Black crime in the late 1980s, the internationally publicized Rodney King beating by members of the Los Angeles Police Department (LAPD) in 1991 proved a lasting, international marker of U.S. racial tensions. When King's assailants were acquitted the following year, Los Angeles erupted into six days of rioting, providing "palpable evidence of racialized police brutality, media stereotyping of African Americans, and unsanctioned racial segregation."[26] Fifty-five people were killed during the unrest and over two thousand injured.

The weight of the LA riots loomed over O. J. Simpson's murder trial, not least because the LAPD feared violence regardless of the verdict. Surveyed African Americans were three times more likely than whites to think Simpson innocent of murdering his ex-wife Nicole Brown-Simpson and her friend Ron Goldman. His acquittal therefore represented "sweet justice" for a Black man born in the projects, targeted by the racist LAPD. For Simpson's opponents, the sporting legend–turned–actor was a "murderer buying an acquittal," using his vast wealth and influence to assemble one of the most expensive legal teams in U.S. history.[27] Less than two weeks after Simpson's acquittal, Nation of Islam leader Louis Farrakhan led an all-male voter registration drive on the National Mall in Washington, D.C., deemed the Million Man March. While Farrakhan himself faced criticism for promoting anti-Semitism and misogyny, many argued that the march had achieved its goal of Black male empowerment. For many whites, it confirmed that Black militancy was on the rise.

For their part, conservative white southerners became increasingly powerful in the mid-1990s, essential to the 1994 Republican takeover of the House of Representatives headed by Georgia Congressman Newt Gingrich. All but one of the new congressional leaders appointed during the "Republican revolution" were Southern Baptists, including Gingrich himself. Some, like Strom Thurmond (South Carolina) and Trent Lott (Mississippi), were the die-hard segregationists of the civil rights era. But by 1997, Oran P. Smith argued that "the Republican party and the Southern Baptist Convention (SBC) are not only in firm alliance, they are sometimes indistinguishable from each other."[28]

The fact that President Clinton was himself a Southern Baptist only seemed to rile his conservative opponents more. "His co-religionists believed that as a Southern Baptist he should have known better," Andrew Manis writes. "Hence, eight years of a white southerner and moderate Southern Baptist in the White House, especially the two years during which the nation was embroiled in the Lewinsky scandal and the impeachment process, saw perhaps the most vigorous prosecution of the culture war since its inception."[29] A 1994 SBC booklet *Pray for the President* urged all members to pray "diligently and consistently" for Clinton, while delegates at the 1998 annual denominational convention urged Congress to overturn the president's executive order banning homophobic discrimination in the federal workforce. An amendment calling on Clinton's home church in Little Rock, Arkansas, to "discipline" the president for his support of gay rights—one of eight fielded during his presidency—was only narrowly defeated. As Gary Scott Smith notes, the SBC had not clashed so strongly with an executive since Franklin Roosevelt repealed Prohibition in 1933.[30]

The nation's largest Protestant denomination, the SBC had been overtaken by fundamentalists in 1979, following a more liberal leadership reflected in Clinton's views. The transition was solidified in 1988 when Richard Land succeeded the liberal Foy Valentine as the leader of the SBC's influential policy arm, known as the Ethics and Religious Liberty Commission (ERLC). Land, who would later argue that Valentine's "liberal antinomianism" was at least "partially responsible for producing people with the tragically flawed moral compass of a Bill Clinton," closely aligned the denomination with conservative Republican policy and would eventually resign in 2013, after accusing President Barack Obama of politicizing the murder of unarmed Black teenager Trayvon Martin.[31] Polls conducted in 1986 showed that 55 percent of SBC leaders who self-identified as "fundamentalist" disagreed or were unsure that the civil rights movement had led the nation in the right direction, as opposed to just 10 percent of moderates. However, as historian Mark Newman notes, this was not unusual among southern white protestants; "the majority of southern white Disciples of Christ, Episcopalians, Presbyterians, Southern Baptists and United Methodists believed that the federal government had no obligation to improve black living standards, and they also believed homeowners had the right to sell to whomever they chose, including the right to refuse African-American buyers."[32]

Despite orchestrating the SBC's official apology for its role in slavery and Jim Crow in 1995, as well as other drives to establish more Black churches within the denomination, Richard Land's leadership paradoxically endorsed what African American journalist Bill Maxwell called "the Republicans' cynical attack on affirmative action . . . the one federal program that modestly attempts to redress some of the wrongs of discrimination."[33] Journalists and critics derided the denomination's incredibly delayed admission that slavery was wrong and that racial divides remained a barrier in religious worship and many other aspects of American life. "Forgive me for being underwhelmed by this astonishingly belated act of contrition," Jack E. White wrote in *Time* magazine, but "I would have been more impressed if the revelation had come a generation ago, when prominent Southern Baptists like George Wallace were standing in the schoolhouse door and never-miss-a-Sunday Ku Klux Klansmen were murdering fellow Christians who believed in civil rights."[34]

"A Nuremberg Trial for America": Reopening Civil Rights Cold Cases in the 1990s

Seemingly fixated by the civil rights era and its legacies, Hollywood filmmakers in the 1990s reflected a wider cultural and political reckoning with the past, albeit through a predominantly white lens. For some white southerners, like actor and filmmaker Billy Bob Thornton, "this desire to write about all these horrible things that happened over civil rights" was both unpleasant and unnecessary, a means by which to continually disparage the South and its history.[35] As these images unfolded on-screen, millions of Americans were concurrently engrossed by the reopening of a number of real "cold cases" from the civil rights era, some of which finally brought white supremacist assassins, bombers, and murderers to justice thirty to forty years after their crimes. In a cyclical manner perhaps only possible via Hollywood, some of the real reopened cases were, to some extent, a direct consequence of the first major civil rights blockbuster, *Mississippi Burning*, which prompted investigative journalist Jerry Mitchell to revisit a range of cold cases from the 1960s. Scouring records of the Mississippi State Sovereignty Commission, a powerful state agency that worked to preserve segregation and intimidate civil rights workers between 1956 and 1977, Mitchell found that the commission had secretly screened jurors for Byron De La Beckwith's defense in 1964 despite the fact that the avowed white supremacist was being tried by the state for the murder of NAACP field secretary Medgar Evers. Working with Evers's widow, Myrlie Evers-Williams, and the NAACP, Mitchell forced the district attorney to reopen the murder case in 1990.[36] Depicted in *Ghosts of Mississippi*, Beckwith's retrial and 1994 conviction was, in the words of the movie's producer Fred Zollo, "a Nuremberg Trial for America."[37] National Public Radio (NPR) reported that listening to the former Klansman "was like listening to someone who's been locked away in a time capsule for the last three decades. . . . You have to look long and hard to find Mississippians today who express agreement with Beckwith's racist rantings."[38]

Eleven years later, preacher Edgar Ray Killen was finally convicted of planning and directing the 1964 murders that form *Mississippi Burning*'s premise. The extraordinary media attention these cases received, via outlets as diverse as *Time, Glamour, People*, and NPR, brought the history of white resistance to the civil rights movement into American homes, creating what Renee C. Romano terms "a key arena in which the American public [was] asked, even encouraged, to engage with the past."[39] However, despite the significance of these convictions, journalist Gary Younge argued that such cases "shift[ed] the burden of racist history from the institutional to the individual," proving "convenient for those who wish to claim that racism was practiced only by the poor and ended with segregation."[40]

Like Hollywood's civil rights melodramas, Romano argues, the narrative that guided these trials and their coverage in the media was rooted in three key tropes. First, that African Americans, Jews, and other minorities were hopeless victims, detached from a wider movement for human rights and political expression. Second, those committing racial terrorism were singularly responsible for their crimes and not manifestations of a wider culture of white supremacy. As such, these narratives further entrenched the image of the reconstructed white southerner, who worked to bring unruly whites to justice, enabling "southern authorities [to] showcase how they have purged themselves of racism." However, this atonement was not just afforded to contemporary white southerners of the late twentieth century. Rather, as a result of the apparent divisions within whiteness, this cultural reckoning absolved the politicians, law enforcement, and general white population of the past despite overwhelming evidence of their commitment to segregation.[41]

"All Progress Is Negotiation": *The Chamber*, John Grisham, and the Death Penalty

James Foley's 1996 film *The Chamber* foregrounded these ghosts of the southern past, as Adam Hall (Chris O'Donnell), a young Chicago lawyer, travels to Mississippi to defend his grandfather—an aging, unrepentant Klansman—from the death penalty. Following two hung juries in the late 1960s, Sam Cayhall (Gene Hackman) was reindicted and convicted in 1980 for the murder of two young Jewish boys during a bombing at their father's law office in 1967. Based on John Grisham's 1994 novel of the same name, *The Chamber* also engages with the contested political meanings of the civil rights trial in the 1990s, particularly through Governor David McAllister (David Marshall

Grant). As a prosecutor, McAllister secured Cayhall's conviction as a prosecutor before running on this success to secure the gubernatorial race. Now he acts as the state's redeemer and, "with the greatest humility," bows in deference to the verdict of the jury and refuses to grant Cayhall clemency. Rather, McAllister publicly prays "that God may grant us the strength and the courage to prevent crimes like this from ever again darkening our soil with the blood of the innocent."

The film's central attention to Mississippi State Sovereignty records show that Cayhall did not act alone when he bombed the Kramer law office but was part of a wider conspiracy in which the White Citizens Council—made up of wealthy, respectable whites, some of whom it is implied still have political careers—"told the Klan what to do." Klansmen themselves were "poor, uneducated bigots who couldn't find their butts with a map," Nora Stark (Lela Rochon), a legal aide to the governor confirms. "The Citizens Council used them to do their dirty work." Cayhall's legal defense against the death penalty is therefore rooted in the toxic history of Mississippi itself, which "raised him" to become a monster, evidenced by his face circled in the crowd at his third public lynching when he was just ten years old. While this defense ultimately fails and Cayhall is executed in the gas chamber, the implication of a wider, state-sanctioned culture of racism, evidenced by the Sovereignty Commission records, is clear.

Privately, Governor McAllister makes it clear that he plans to pursue the other names implicated with Cayhall in the next legislative session. However, he also places a courtesy call to the politicians that will seemingly be incriminated in the course of releasing the Sovereignty Commission files. Nora advises earlier in the film that McAllister's interest in Cayhall's case reflects a delicate balancing act between wanting to appear tough on crime but also avoiding any accusations that he is protecting the state's "Old Guard." Walking the tightrope of a liberal southern governor reckoning with the crimes of the past and the racial backlash of the present, McAllister is a minor character in the film but implies a Bill Clinton–esque courting of both conservative and liberal whites and a sensitivity to the concerns of Black voters. McAllister's support of the death penalty reflects Clinton's own admission that Democrats "should no longer feel guilty about protecting the innocent," evident during the 1992 presidential campaign, when then-governor Clinton returned to Arkansas to oversee the execution of Ricky Ray Rector, an African American man whom many argued was mentally incapacitated.[42]

Indeed, all of the southern white heroes of the mid-1990s civil rights drama are explicitly or implicitly pro–death penalty. Bobby DeLaughter of *Ghosts of Mississippi* is the assistant district attorney for Hinds County, Mississippi, while Jake Brigance of *A Time to Kill,* based on Grisham's debut novel, would "go back to hangings on the courthouse lawn if we could. . . . The only problem with the death penalty is that we do not use it enough." By his own admission, Jake is a liberal but does not "believe in forgiveness or in rehabilitation" and is certainly "no ACLU card-carrying radical." For Jake, the death penalty is simply a matter of assessing the crime and the criminal. He gives the example of "a crack dealer [who] guns down an undercover cop," concluding that in such a case "you strap his ass in the chair and flip the switch." When white, northern law student Ellen Roark (Sandra Bullock) encourages Jake to witness the horrors of execution before articulating such flippant acceptance of the death penalty, Brigance asks her to spare him her "northern, liberal, cry-me-a-river, we're the only enlightened ones in the northern hemisphere bullshit." At this point, Roark notes Brigance's choice to take her to a Black restaurant in a Black neighborhood, which she argues either reflects a desire to be seen as a "JFK–meets–Jesus Christ white boy," or that he is really just "another repressed hypocritical southern provincial" who does not wish to be seen with a young woman other than his wife in his own part of town. Despite this apparent impasse of values and morals, Roark and Brigance are reconciled just seconds later, when Roark admits that she can "get a little worked up." Jake admits that he does not like Roark's "politics" but that he will accept her (free) legal assistance because he and his defendant could benefit from her "passion."

An exception to Jake's defensive rhetoric, *The Chamber* questions the necessity of the death penalty altogether, an ongoing theme in author John Grisham's work and activism. The lawyer-turned-novelist, who served in the Mississippi House of Representatives from 1983 to 1990, has, according to the *New York Time*'s Janet Maslin, "fought harder for truth, justice and the American way than anyone this side of Superman."[43] Grisham, who serves on the board of the Innocence Project, which seeks exoneration for unjustly convicted people using DNA evidence, has written a number of articles and opinion pieces about the death penalty in the United States, concluding in 2017 that a decline in death penalty sentences was "not because of the courage of lawmakers or judges, but because of the compassion shown by jurors who are fully informed in trials that are fair."[44] When questioned on the enduring popularity of the death penalty among American voters in 2022, Grisham quipped that "white people love the death penalty" but "Black people know the truth" about America's criminal justice system. He has also noted that his staunch opposition to the death penalty emerged during a conversation with a prison chaplain, who asked Grisham, a practicing Christian, if God would approve of state-sanctioned killings. "That moment I switched [my opinion] and never looked back," Grisham recalled.[45]

In *The Chamber*, much of the controversy surrounding Sam Cayhall's execution revolves around the use of the gas chamber, whereas more recent convictions in Mississippi were served via lethal injection. Thus, one of Cayhall's initial appeals is filed under cruel and unusual punishment, arguing that the state had moved away from the gas chamber for a reason. He also describes in considerable detail the botched execution of one of his fellow inmates, showing his acute awareness of the fate that awaits him. Cayhall's own execution also forms the final climax of the movie, granting viewers a disturbing insight into the process and its impact on the human body.

Prior to his execution, Sam Cayhall becomes increasingly sympathetic, further exposing the political maneuvering guiding the governor's decision over his life. Granted a seemingly heartfelt moment of remorse with an African American prison guard, Cayhall is also allowed reconciliation with his remaining family members and a confrontation with his alleged coconspirator in which he denounces their brotherhood, real or symbolic. At the end of the film, following Cayhall's execution, Adam embraces his aunt Lee (Faye Dunaway), Cayhall's troubled daughter, and whispers, "Maybe the ghosts are gone." Although this may be true in the sense of their troubled family history, Adam's motives in tracking down his grandfather's coconspirator, Rollie Wedge (Raymond J. Barry), have already been exposed by Wedge himself: Adam, like so many of his counterparts in the American racial melodrama wants to "identify, quantify, and organize the concept of evil. If I did it," Wedge argues, "I can be culled from the flock. Removed, separated, destroyed. And all you good people can feel safe in the cocoon of your denial." Here, the movie addresses the central weakness identified in so many of its cinematic counterparts, the implication that racism is a solely interpersonal problem, solved by the extraction or destruction of the white trash racist.

Through its narrative of State Sovereignty complicity and the evolution of its central villain, Sam Cayhall, *The Chamber* questions the central moral impulse of the other racial melodramas of its era. But like the other white lawyers of the mid-1990s civil rights melodrama, Adam Hall is a "cinematic historian, researching the past, explaining it, and bringing it to closure."[46] Like the contemporary trials of the evil "ghosts" of the civil rights era that were unfolding in real life, late twentieth-century racial melodramas raised questions about how far the United States had come since the turbulent 1960s. Despite this reminder of the failures of the past, these narratives nevertheless encouraged audiences to put their faith in educated, secular, white liberals, just as they had thirty years earlier in *To Kill a Mockingbird*. "These films are about a certain kind of white person who came of age at a certain time," Beck concluded in 1997. "That's who makes movies."[47] As a result, while *The Chamber* is less triumphant, the enduring message of *Ghosts of Mississippi* and *A Time to Kill* is that America's abiding racial scars were smoothed out in the mid-1990s by "square-jawed white guys."[48]

Rejecting Affirmative Action in the Mid-1990s Racial Melodrama

As culturally liberal southern whites, both Jake Brigance (*A Time to Kill*) and Bobby DeLaughter (*Ghosts of Mississippi*) are horrified when they come under pressure to give up legal cases in order that Black or NAACP-affiliated lawyers might undertake them. They see themselves as the good guys: harbingers of the New South and critically removed from the racist rednecks that seemingly blight Mississippi's progress. Both fail to understand why some members of the African American community might view them with suspicion or even why a Black or movement-affiliated lawyer may be more appropriate for their cases. Like Atticus Finch at midcentury, our 1990s heroes perceive "NAACP-paid lawyers standing around like buzzards."[49] Crucially, though, in the wake of coordinated assaults on affirmative action in the post–civil rights era, it is assumed that the audience will share this understanding of a spectrum of racial attitudes among whites and root for the white protagonists to keep their cases. To push Brigance and DeLaughter aside simply for being white, these films imply, would be a violation of the nation's color-blind principles and akin to reverse discrimination.

In December 1991, journalist Tom Wicker wrote in his penultimate *New York Times* column that "a great many Americans" had bought into the existence of "a level, colorblind playing field" despite "continued documented discrimination in bank and auto loans, housing availability, education, employ-

Mississippi lawyer Jake Brigance (Matthew McConaughey) and his client, Carl Lee Hailey (Samuel L. Jackson), stand in the courtroom in *A Time to Kill* (Joel Schumacher, 1996).

ment, economic opportunities, the most vital areas of life—and not just in the South." Wicker, a *Times* reporter since the early 1960s, advocated continued government support for minority-owned businesses despite Supreme Court attacks on the constitutionality of such schemes. His argument rested on the basis that the United States was "still blatantly color-conscious."[50] But even though many white Americans disagreed with Wicker, his understanding of their attitudes proved prescient. By 1993, as Justin Gomer has shown, 60 percent of white males believed that affirmative action resulted in "less opportunity for white men." A year later, half believed that "equal rights had gone too far," an increase of 34 percent since 1987. Therefore, in the eight years between the releases of *Mississippi Burning* and *A Time to Kill*, white attitudes toward affirmative action and other remedies for persistent inequalities had hardened considerably. One study from 1995 showed that 79 percent of white Americans opposed affirmative action.[51]

In the wake of *Adarand Constructors, Inc. v. Peña* (1995) in which the Supreme Court argued that race did not warrant presumption of disadvantage and was therefore not a valid reason to put aside specific contracts for minority businesses, President Clinton signed an executive order mandating the review of all federal affirmative action policies. By the second half of 1996, as *A Time to Kill, The Chamber*, and *Ghosts of Mississippi* reached theaters, states across the country—including California, the home of Hollywood cinema—took steps to dismantle and permanently ban affirmative action. The impact was immediate. Minority enrollments at the University of California, Berkeley, dropped by 13 percent in just one year, following the state's passage of Proposition 209 in November 1996. African American enrollment at University of California law schools fell by 80 percent, while Latinx enrollment dropped to half what it had been in 1996. The NAACP opposed Proposition 209, and its key leaders, including Chairman Julian Bond and President Kweisi Mfume, committed the organization to "protecting the nation's embattled affirmative action programs."[52] Meanwhile, Republican Party advertisements urging voters to support the proposition used footage of Martin Luther King Jr.'s "I Have a Dream" speech and presented it as a "civil rights initiative."[53]

Republican tactics proved popular with white, suburban voters among whom the concept of "reverse discrimination" was deeply ingrained.[54] Only seven of California's fifty-eight counties voted against Proposition 209 in November 1996, some only by a tiny majority of 1 percent. It is therefore unsurprising that *A Time to Kill*'s cynical portrayal of the NAACP presents contemporary Black activists and politicians as hindering racial progress through an overblown sense of group identity, aggressive antiwhiteness, and a prioritization of personal profit. While civil rights dramas have faced frequent critique for their emphasis on nostalgia and interracial reconciliation, the actual agenda of the civil rights movement—legal reform, enforcement, and monitoring, alongside efforts to develop Black consciousness and solidarity—was largely ignored until Ava DuVernay's *Selma* in 2014. Generally speaking, when civil rights strategy is articulated in the contemporary context of a Hollywood movie, it is condemned.[55] In *A Time to Kill*, the local minister, Reverend Ollie Agee (Thomas Merdis), is visibly honored to be visited by NAACP representatives he recalls "marching with Dr King," making direct connection between those looking to help in a local case and the accepted national hero of the civil rights era. However, as Gomer has argued, by the time Hollywood reached its "colorblind hegemony in the mid-1990s," American audiences had absorbed over twenty years of public discourse that framed white opponents of affirmative action and school busing as the true inheritors of the civil rights movement, rather than those who continued to advocate group identities and strategies. Defenders of traditional civil rights programs, like the NAACP, were thus rendered "opponents of the movement's supposed core ideology of colorblindness."[56]

Film critic Roger Ebert surmised that *A Time to Kill*'s "awkward sequence" between Jake Brigance and the NAACP was devised "to equate the NAACP lawyers with figures like the Rev. Al Sharpton," whom conservatives frequently accused of manipulating racial discord for personal gain.[57] As such, the "sane and reasonable" groups of the 1960s, when compared to more radical Black Power advocates, were now the problem, as NAACP representatives view the case against Jake's client, Carl Lee Hailey (Samuel L. Jackson), as an opportunity for national marketing rather than a trial in the fate of an individual. "Carl Lee's acquittal for the killings of two white men would do more for the black people of Mississippi than any event since we integrated the schools," Reverend Isaiah Street (Joe Seneca) says. However, "his conviction [would be a] symbol of deep-seated racism, perhaps enough to ignite a nation." It is hard to tell which outcome Reverend Street would favor; indeed, Jake asks, "Of all your cases, how many are supposed to be lost so you can martyr the victim?" The otherwise dignified Reverend Street then loses his temper and refers to Jake as a "cracker," showing the racialized prejudice that lurks beneath his serene, progressive exterior.

Carl Lee knows from discussions with his wife, Gwen (Tonea Stewart), that Reverend Agee appealed to the common decency of the congregation to raise the money now directed to the NAACP for legal defense and that it was originally intended to help the family manage household bills in Carl Lee's absence after he was arrested for the murder of the two rednecks who raped his young daughter and left her for dead. Viewers also know from previous scenes that the NAACP representatives encouraged Reverend Agee to "take a modest administration fee" when collecting donations. Implying that the NAACP has manipulated the local church, Jake suggests that "the black community" Reverend Street claims to represent is not the *local* community but the national African American political elite. Confident that he has a better understanding of the local Black community than its pastor and the NAACP, Jake threatens to inform Reverend Agee's congregation that "Gwen and the kids can't eat because you want to get in good with the NAACP." In rewarding Jake's strategy, the film implies that local white assistance is more beneficial to local African Americans than historically significant advocates for racial equality, including the NAACP's high-flying legal team that is implicitly coded as northern and Jewish. Any legal fees raised are to go to Jake, "unless the NAACP wants to go on record as soliciting funds under false pretenses."

Although Carl Lee later deflates Jake's self-righteousness ("I ain't never seen you in my part of town. I bet you don't even know where I live"), the implication remains that Reverend Agee has overstepped his authority and that as a man of God, he should not be involved in politics. Thus, the film encourages viewers to question whether Jake, even with the best of intentions, can ever really understand Carl Lee, but not before it has offered a cynical conjecture about the continuing role and function of the nation's oldest civil rights organization and the Black church. Therefore, even though Carl Lee refuses to reward Jake with what Mukherjee calls "Uncle Tom obsequiousness," he also declines to "abide by doctrinaire racial loyalties," rejecting community organization for a "neo-liberal dicta of self-reliance."[58] Devoid of hope for systemic change, Carl Lee determines that Jake is likely to be his most effective defense against a white southern jury: "You think just like them; that's why I picked you. You my secret weapon. You're one of the bad guys. You don't mean to be, but you are. It's how you was raised. . . . You see me like the jury sees me. You are them."

True to Carl Lee's characterization, Jake secures victory in the case by appealing to the white supremacy of the jury, transforming Carl Lee from a dangerous Black assassin to a chivalrous protector of women and girls, or what Sharon Monteith calls "an African American populist hero." In court, Jake describes the brutal rape of Carl Lee's daughter in detail and then asks the jury to imagine she was white. What would any grieving father do in the circumstances, Jake asks, but avenge his daughter's innocence? Indeed, even the white police officer injured in the cross fire of Carl Lee's vigilante attack states that Carl Lee "did what I would have done. . . . Those boys raped his little girl. . . . I got a little girl. Somebody rapes her, he's a dead dog. I'll blow him away just like Carl Lee did." Deputy Looney (Chris Cooper) then implores the jury from the witness stand: "[Carl Lee]'s a hero. You turn him loose!" Jake's wife, Carla (Ashley Judd), who has previously maligned her husband for taking such a racially explosive case, finally recognizes his color-blind motivations: "You took this case because if those boys had hurt [our daughter] Hanna the way that they hurt Tonya, you would have killed them yourself." Indeed, the film works to establish this interpretation from the outset, as Carl Lee effectively tells Jake that he intends to kill the rapists before actually doing so. Although Jake admits that he tried to convince himself that Carl Lee was bluffing and therefore explain why he did not inform the sheriff of Carl Lee's intentions to murder, he also notes that deep down, "I think I really wanted him to do it." Outlining his conflicted feelings about the case with Ellen Roark, Jake discusses how he came home from that initial meeting with Carl Lee to find Hanna peacefully sleeping, which drew his mind to "all the monsters out there. Any one of them could come and steal her innocence, take her life if they wanted. Yeah, I wanted those boys dead. You're goddamn right I did. I guess I helped kill them." For Jake, then, the case is not just about Carl Lee. He is also looking to validate his own actions and opinions and the extent to which he too has taken the law into his own hands.

By the film's close, Jake and Carl Lee's victory elicits hope in a more positive future, as the Brigance and Hailey families come together for a celebratory barbecue. As the credits begin, a large choral rendition of "Take My Hand, Precious Lord" provides a triumphant musical ending, in keeping with dominant tropes of the civil rights melodrama's emphasis on reconciliation, and creates the impression that Clanton's racial turmoil has been laid to rest.[59] This self-congratulatory final message denies the need for sustained activism to secure and extend the legacy of the Black freedom struggle and implies that localized problem solving is preferable to strategic national action, reflecting the film's distinctly conservative agenda. *A Time to Kill* may direct its cynicism toward the NAACP specifically, but it reflects Hollywood's broader discomfort with Black political agitation, which has long compromised its presentation of the civil rights movement and its legacy. It also rewards Jake's self-styled status as the vehicle of justice in the community, regardless of his own personal background, politics, and biases.

Ghosts of Mississippi

Like *A Time to Kill*, *Ghosts of Mississippi*'s central drama centers on the various personal costs its white hero faces while pursuing justice for African Americans. Like Jake Brigance, Assistant District Attorney Bobby DeLaughter suffers marital discord, personal ridicule, and the threat of white supremacist violence toward him and his family, only to be undermined by "ungrateful"

Black political leaders. Publicly denigrated as "a pair of lying racists" by local community leaders, DeLaughter and his boss, Ed Peters, face scrutiny when the news emerges that the state has secured Byron De La Beckwith's murder weapon but are yet to reindict him for the 1963 murder of NAACP field secretary Medgar Evers. Accused of "putting on a show for the Black community" and with other capital cases piling up, Peters suggests that they bring Pat Bennett onto the Evers/Beckwith case, whom DeLaughter concurs is "one of the best lawyers in the state." However, despite Ms. Bennett's credentials, DeLaughter is spurned, asking, "The fact that Pat Bennett is black wouldn't have anything to do with this, would it?"

In the following scene, while watching legal drama *Presumed Innocent* (Alan Pakula, 1990) at the cinema, a distracted DeLaughter mutters to himself, "If anyone's putting on a show, they are. All they're doing is trying to stir up emotions and position themselves as the saviors of the black community. There're only two people who really care about this case, and I'm one of them." He is promptly shushed by the audience around him, the only visible member of which is a Black woman. Undeterred, DeLaughter takes his concerns to the nearest pay phone, where he calls the widowed Myrlie Evers-Williams (Whoopi Goldberg) to relieve his frustration:

> My car's been vandalized, my son's been in a fight, I've been called every ugly name you could think by every racist in the state of Mississippi—and now, just when there's a possibility of a new indictment, I gotta fight every black politician as well. . . . I've made a commitment to this case. And I'll be goddamned—pardon me—if I'm going to give this up to some special prosecutor. I don't care if he's black, green, orange, or navy blue. I've made a commitment to this case, and now I'm asking you to make a commitment to me.[60]

When Evers-Williams responds with detached courtesy rather than overwhelming gratitude, DeLaughter chastises her to his date, Peggy (Susanna Thompson): "To hell with her! She's just like the rest of them." When Peggy reminds DeLaughter that "the white world has not exactly gone out of its way to make Mrs. Evers particularly trusting," DeLaughter reveals what the case is really about for him: "We had a real chance to send a message to this country that the state of Mississippi is not just a bunch of redneck racists." Redeeming the white South is more important, it seems, than securing a murder conviction that has evaded the state for twenty-seven years.

As DeLaughter's outburst continues, he even advocates a return to racial segregation: "We should all just separate, go back to the way things were, and let the South rise again. . . . Myrlie Evers doesn't want my help. . . . She can't see the difference between me and Byron De La Beckwith." According to DeLaughter, Evers-Williams would never have questioned his decision to hide the murder weapon from her "if I were black. I would have just been a smart lawyer." At this juncture, Peggy reminds DeLaughter that he cannot expect Evers-Williams to trust him if he does not trust her; after all, he kept the discovery of the murder weapon from her because he assumed she would go to the press. Immediately after this scene, Evers-Williams returns to DeLaughter's office and provides him with her personal copy of the original trial transcript, something she has kept from three previous district attorneys. Confirming her trust in DeLaughter, Evers-Williams advises him, "I don't think you'll find any more opposition to your continuing to handle this case." The following montage documents developments in the efforts to indict Beckwith, DeLaughter's success in the case, marriage to his "symbolically progressive second wife," and an emblematic embrace from Evers herself.[61] Therefore, despite his frankly offensive outburst, DeLaughter is rewarded with renewed confidence from Myrlie Evers-Williams, a reprieve from Black complaints, and romantic success. Here, director Rob Reiner perhaps reflected on his own efforts to win over Evers-Williams, admitting that the activist was "cautious" about the project and hopeful that a project might one day emerge that foregrounded "her life with Medgar" rather than Bobby DeLaughter.

Respectful of, but ultimately unmoved by Evers-Williams's desire for a very different movie, Reiner acknowledged that his film was "not the Medgar Evers story, and it's not the civil rights story. . . . I chose to tell the story of a man who came from a racist background, who was the product of segregationist parents, and who spent 4½ years of his life working on this thing." DeLaughter, in Reiner's estimation, "is a very good prosecutor and a very principled religious man. . . . It wasn't a racial thing for him, it was more of a feeling of, 'This is just plain wrong, and I'm a prosecutor, and this is what I do for a living.'"[62] *Ghosts of Mississippi* therefore celebrates DeLaughter as an individual pragmatist, independent of the nation's various factions represented by civil rights activists, northern liberals, or southern racists. DeLaughter and Jake Brigance, like Atticus Finch before them, favor the status quo but refuse to turn a blind eye to explicit injustice. Indeed, as socially liberal white southerners, they are assumed to be all the more impressive due to the regional conditioning they have overcome. However, by the mid-1990s, these Hollywood heroes staked their claim to righteousness and entitlement in the contemporary rhetoric of white male victimhood and color blindness. Although they faced particularly regional challenges, grappling with the southern racial past, their pragmatic self-reliance in the face of sustained calls for meaningful racial and gender parity betrayed their national credentials in an age of neoliberal dismantling of the civil rights state.

Religion and the Reconstructed Southerner: Bobby DeLaughter and Jake Brigance

In *Ghosts of Mississippi*, DeLaughter's increasing commitment to racial justice strains and ultimately ends his first marriage to the appropriately named Dixie (Virginia Madsen), whose stepfather, Russell Moore, had been "perhaps the most racist judge in the history of Mississippi" and had even kept Beckwith's murder weapon as a souvenir after the original trials in the 1960s.[63] Dixie is adamant that in attempting to bring Beckwith to justice, her husband is determined to "humiliate [her] in front of [her] friends, [her] family and the state of Mississippi."[64] It is only through distancing himself from "Dixie"—both his wife and the regional captivity her name symbolizes—that DeLaughter can develop into the true American visionary the film requires. Indeed, he stops singing the song "Dixie" to comfort his young daughter, telling her that perhaps it is that very song that keeps attracting "ghosts" to her room and, by extension, Mississippi itself.[65]

Crucial to the filmic DeLaughter's gradual enlightenment, "Dixie" serves as a reminder of the prejudices this privileged white southerner has overcome. Like the scenes at the country club in which DeLaughter's father openly refers to Medgar Evers using a racial slur while being waited on by Black staff (an incident that the real DeLaughter insists never happened), the sequence in which Alec Baldwin's DeLaughter sings "Dixie" to his daughter provides an insight into the entrenched racial hierarchies the character had absorbed from birth before acknowledging Evers—another thirty-seven-year-old father of three—as a human being. According to investigative journalist Jerry Mitchell whose work, alongside the decades-long efforts of Myrlie Evers-Williams and the NAACP, was crucial in bringing about Beckwith's retrial, screenwriter Lewis Colick and producer Fred Zollo were both committed to the idea "that DeLaughter was the story: a young prosecutor, son of Ole Miss, who overcame the objections of his own racist family to join forces with Medgar Evers's widow and win the longshot case to finally put Beckwith behind bars. 'You're looking for things where you can get a movie star,' Colick says. 'This was a movie star role.'" Colick's script also granted the cinematic DeLaughter the crucial cross-examination of Beckwith's alibi, a task actually undertaken by District Attorney Ed Peters during the real 1994 retrial. In a meeting with Peters, director Rob Reiner told the former DA that it was essential that DeLaughter and Evers shared a look of understanding after the examination. "The enlightened Southern boy and the grieving widow," Peters later scoffed.[66] Reiner's own enlightenment was secured when, during a December 1996 episode of *The Oprah Winfrey Show*, Myrlie Evers-Williams presented him with her slain husband's poll tax receipt, prompting the fifty-one-year-old white director to burst into tears.[67]

Described as "one of liberal Hollywood's most courted presidential fence-sitters," Rob Reiner's personal politics have been subject to considerable discussion in Hollywood, where he has long proven a highly successful and influential fundraiser. A staunch Democrat, Reiner has often steered away from the party's left wing, taking to the campaign trail with Al Gore in 2000 and throwing his weight behind Hillary Clinton in 2008.[68] In the mid-1990s, Reiner told reporters that he had "long wanted to do a movie with a civil rights theme" and that his goal with *Ghosts of Mississippi* was "to help us remember." However, he also acknowledged that he had struggled to "find my way into [the civil rights movement] because being a white person, I felt it would be politically incorrect for me to make, let's say, a biography of Martin Luther King or Malcolm X or Medgar Evers, for that matter." When Byron De La Beckwith's case resurfaced in the early 1990s, Reiner recalled, "I couldn't believe they were going after this guy 30 years after the crime, and I thought it would make a compelling story and a good movie." Reiner also spoke of the importance of telling an "accurate and factual story," noting that "some people get their history through movies."[69]

Reflecting on his reactions to Medgar Evers's murder, Reiner, who was sixteen years old in 1963, recalled that the "very shocking and disturbing influence was discussed a lot in my household and the circles I ran in." He defined Evers as a "moderate thinking, even-keeled person, who was just working within the system to get the rights everyone is entitled to—to vote, to eat at a restaurant, to send your kids to a decent school." Reiner's implication, therefore, was that Evers was not a radical and thus particularly worthy of audience sympathy. However, despite this apparent recognition of Evers's significance, Reiner's film came under considerable criticism for the limited attention it actually paid to Evers and his grieving family. Responding to such critics, Reiner observed, "We are living in a time when people are very critical of white people doing things that have black themes in them. I think it's very unfortunate."[70]

Despite his professed emphasis on truthful remembrance, Reiner took some liberties when developing DeLaughter's character for the screen, granting him the crucial cross-examination in the courtroom scenes, for example. More generally, Reiner's film obscures the real DeLaughter's professed conservativism and its connections with his religious identity. Although Reiner acknowledged in interviews that the real DeLaughter was "a very principled, religious man," his film's constructed Beckwith-DeLaughter dichotomy could not acknowledge the real DeLaughter's admission that he drew his strengths "from the depths of [his] conservatism, under God's guidance." DeLaughter later claimed that during the period of his life documented in Reiner's movie, "there wasn't but one other alternative and that was to say a lot of prayers. And probably if I had had the authority to say, 'I want one scene to convey one thing that did not make the final cut,' it would be a scene to illustrate that in some way."[71] Despite the reality of DeLaughter's religiosity, his representation in Hollywood required him to "rise above" the deeply established confines of Mississippi, abandoning its religiosity just as he is shown to have shunned its racism.

Also in *A Time to Kill*, passionate religiosity is reserved entirely for African Americans and white supremacists, while the singular appearance of mainstream white Christianity confirms its association with older, more conservative generations. We only ever see Jake Brigance in church with his in-laws, suggesting that it is much more about maintaining pretense than spiritual involvement. Following the service, Jake's in-laws express their concern that he has taken such a high-profile case; like most southern moderates, the film suggests, they would prefer a quiet life. Jake's wife, Carla, is visibly shocked that her husband wants to talk to the press outside their church, telling him, "This isn't the time." Carla's concern, like her parents', is rooted in how much they, as a middle-class white family, have to lose from her husband's involvement in the trial. It is therefore somewhat ironic that Brigance uses his presence at a mainstream southern white church—a place where social commitment is clearly lacking—to publicly pledge himself to racial justice and Carl Lee Hailey's case. As if to further this point about the varying social commitment of religious groups, Jake's declaration of intent outside his church (and the awkwardness that preceded it) is bookended by two distinctly more enthusiastic Sunday ceremonies.

Preceded by Freddie Lee Cobb's (Kiefer Sutherland's) attempts to recruit his friends to the Klan in order that they might join "the war to protect our

Jake Brigance (Matthew McConaughey) speaks to television and newspaper reporters from the doorway of his church in *A Time to Kill* (Joel Schumacher, 1996).

Christian homes and families" and "resurrect our country from the fires of racial degradation," the scenes at Jake's church then cut to the service underway at Mount Zion Christian Methodist Episcopal (CME) Church and the rapturous response to the entrance of Carl Lee Hailey's wife and children. Reflecting continuing de facto segregation of public worship, the juxtaposed scenes of Jake's and Carl Lee's churches communicate a very different attitude toward the social purpose of religion. Indeed, John Grisham's publishers recognized that children in the fifth grade could spot the symbolic and physical differences between the two churches, as evidenced in their "Teacher's Guide" to the original novel.[72] While Mount Zion CME is actively committed to supporting the community, the mainstream white church appears more as a place to "be seen" lest your neighbors (or in-laws) think less of you.

According to Grisham's novel, Jake, who was brought up a Methodist, attends "First Presbyterian Church of Clanton," following negotiation with Carla, who had been brought up Baptist. "The Baptists had more members and more money," Grisham writes, "but the Presbyterians and Methodists adjourned earlier on a Sunday and outraced the Baptists to the restaurants for Sunday dinner." Thus, Jake and Carla's spiritual realignment does not appear to have been too taxing. On Sundays, Grisham describes, the Brigances "sat in their usual pew, with Hanna asleep between them, and ignored the sermon." Jake focuses instead on his legal cases, while Carla is "mentally redecorating the dining room."[73]

"A Searing Mad Dog Racist": The Ku Klux Klan in *A Time to Kill* and *Ghosts of Mississippi*

While Grisham's imaginary Clanton is located in a county that is 74 percent white, filming for *A Time to Kill* took place in the real town of Canton, Mississippi, which has been over 70 percent African American since the 1960s. Reaction to the election of the town's first Black mayor in 1994 prompted concerns of riots. Though they never materialized, Monteith writes, "within the year, [director Joel] Schumacher is choreographing the race riot that never happened in the same square for *A Time to Kill*," which, in line with Grisham's 1989 novel, features scenes of the Klan marching through the streets in broad daylight in full regalia, before being met by a crowd of Black counterprotesters outside the courthouse where the jury for Carl Lee's trial is being confirmed. These violent scenes, produced using a range of closeups and aerial shots to convey the scale of the disturbance, result in the death of Mississippi's Grand Dragon, Stump Sisson, and are repeated the following day when the trial actually begins. Indeed, the divisions within the town are symbolized by an entrepreneurial local selling T-shirts bearing one of two slogans: "FREE CARL LEE" or "FRY CARL LEE."

When writing such scenes, John Grisham may have been inspired by a

Klansmen march through small town Mississippi in full regalia in *A Time to Kill* (Joel Schumacher, 1996).

well-publicized Klan march in Greensboro, North Carolina, in 1987, the year he apparently finished his novel.[74] Nevertheless, public interest in the modern Klan was further bolstered by the numerous political escapades of David Duke, a former grand wizard who ran for president in 1988 and was elected to the Louisiana state senate in 1989. Far from the "stereotypical Klansman of popular imagination," Duke was middle class, educated, "handsome, well-mannered and articulate."[75] Rather than performing secret rituals under the cloak of darkness, Duke actively sought media attention, perfecting what journalist Tyler Bridges defined as "looking good and sounding reasonable." Conscious of his appeal, Duke reflected in 1978 that "the media can't resist me, [because] I don't fit the stereotype of a Klansman. I don't have hair cropped so close to my head my ears stick out. . . . I'm not chewing tobacco, and I don't have manure on the bottom of my shoes."[76] He therefore proves an interesting contrast to the poor, religious white males who swell the ranks of the Klan in Hollywood's imagination, supporting Nancy Bishop Dessommes's argument that "in contemporary film, directors seem more concerned with evoking an acceptable audience response than with adhering to historical accuracy," engendering the Klan as little more than a band of ignorant bigots. "Initiated into violence," Dessommes continues, contemporary audiences have come to expect Klan extremism in presentations of a racially volatile South, but cinema rarely probes the structural realities of white supremacy beyond fringe groups.[77]

By November 1996, four months after the release of *A Time to Kill* and a month after the release of *The Chamber*, local Klansmen admitted they were responsible for the 1995 arson attack on Mount Zion AME Church in Greeleyville, South Carolina, where President Clinton led the rededication ceremony and reflected on his administration's response to the spate of bombings and arsons. The following month, *Ghosts of Mississippi* introduced audiences to James

Woods's Oscar-nominated portrayal of Byron De La Beckwith, a figure who could easily be dismissed as a frankly ridiculous archaism, spouting no limit of racial and religious hatred, and yet was extremely real. In direct contrast to his triumphal position at the center of his 1960s trials, Beckwith was kept from the stands during the 1990s retrial, his lawyers seemingly aware of their client's limited public appeal. The tactic was politically understandable but legally risky, denying the defense's opportunity to articulate Beckwith's 1964 claim that his rifle was stolen prior to Medgar Evers's assassination.[78] *Ghosts of Mississippi*'s representation of the retrial thus provides no courtroom speech from the avowed white supremacist. However, its re-creation of a 1990 television interview between Beckwith and Ed Bryson serves as the Klansman's ideological set piece and proved central to the movie's marketing campaign despite the film's overarching focus on DeLaughter.[79]

Initial discussions between Mississippi writer Willie Morris, who served as a consultant on the film, and producer Fred Zollo show that both considered the Beckwith characterization crucial to the film's appeal and certainly its best chance at securing Oscar recognition. This was later vindicated when the film received just two Academy Award nominations: one for Woods as Best Supporting Actor and one for the makeup team responsible for his physical transformation.[80] Whereas many reviewers criticized the film's focus on DeLaughter at the expense of Medgar Evers and his family, most heaped praise on what the *New York Times* called the "wily malevolence" of Woods's Beckwith.[81] A "searing mad-dog racist," according to one reviewer, Woods's Beckwith was declared a "perfect villain," with many critics acknowledging the actor's capacity for bringing life to cinematic reprobates, from his portrayal of a pimp in Scorsese's *Casino* (1995) to another recent performance as notorious criminal Carl Panzram in *Killer: A Journal of Murder* (Tim Metcalfe, 1995).[82] And yet, although Woods's performance was widely celebrated, the specific intersections of Beckwith's extreme racial views and vengeful religious preoccupations received less attention. On close examination, they are crucial to the film's attempts to communicate his evil but also his distinctly southern, almost archaic identity.

Praised by Aryan Nations leader Richard Butler as "a great warrior for Christ," Byron De La Beckwith was ordained as a minister at the Temple Memorial Baptist Church in Knoxville, Tennessee, a congregation founded on the principles of "Christian identity," most notably anti-Semitism and racism, shortly before entering Angola State Prison in Louisiana in 1977 for illegally transporting explosives.[83] James Woods's performance is therefore of an "unregenerate hater," who "won't talk to no Jew," jokes about African American homes burning down, and is committed to his understanding that "God put the white man here to rule over all the dusky races."[84] The cinematic gaze directed toward Beckwith remains consistently public and judgmental throughout the film; unlike his prosecutor, Bobby DeLaughter, Beckwith is never seen in private moments. Rather, he seems to perform for the camera—in this case, the implied television cameras that follow him wherever he goes in constant anticipation of his next outburst.

Due to the film's omission of DeLaughter's religious identity, Beckwith's performance of a vengeful Christian committed to the protection of white supremacy forms *Ghosts of Mississippi*'s only presentation of religion, which is equated with the horrendous nature of the assassin's crimes. Beckwith's inflammatory rhetoric certainly worked to intrigue potential audiences, forming the basis of the teaser trailer that prompted the film's release in late 1996. This re-creation of Beckwith's interview with Bryson required Woods to "smile the mocking smile of a man who has gotten away with murder" before advising viewers, "I'm going to look out for my God and my family and the whole state of Christ's church and that don't encompass anybody but white Christians. All these other races, colors and creeds, sissies, whatever—they are anti-Christ." According to Morris, the trailer caused a stir in many cinemas, as audiences shouted at the screen and, in at least one recorded case, pelted it with popcorn.[85]

Refusing to meet with Beckwith "on moral grounds," Woods perfected his performance watching videos of the white supremacist, including the full Bryson interview. He also worked with a vocal coach, maintaining that Beckwith's southern accent ensured he could maintain a crucial distance from the character: "I imagined I was speaking a foreign language," he recalled.[86] By constantly reminding himself that Beckwith was a southerner, a supposed product of his environment, Woods (who grew up in Rhode Island and was educated at the Massachusetts Institute of Technology) successfully "othered" Beckwith in the context of a national culture that has continually "othered" southerners. However, in the same interview, Woods contrasted Beckwith's eventual sentencing for murder to California's failure to convict O. J. Simpson and criticized affirmative action procedures that he argued "actually [held] back progress, reducing dignity."[87]

"Playing the Race Card": The Trivialization of Race in the 1990s

George Lipsitz writes that James Woods's comparison of Byron De La Beckwith and O. J. Simpson offered "proof of the intellectual paralysis that the iconic status of Mississippi in the 1960s engenders." In noting that the state of Mississippi did eventually convict Beckwith in the 1990s, whereas the state of California had failed to convict Simpson, Woods ignored the freedom that Beckwith enjoyed for thirty-one years. Indeed, as Lipsitz continues, Beckwith was not just free between 1963 and 1994 but had the full power of law enforcement as an auxiliary police officer. His murder of Medgar Evers, unlike the allegations against Simpson, signified an attempt "to silence a political movement and disenfranchise a whole race of people" and was directly supported by the State Sovereignty Commission, which screened jurors for Beckwith's original trial. Whereas Simpson's immense wealth afforded him "the best defense money could buy," Beckwith "had only his whiteness to protect him from prison, but for thirty-one years that was enough." [88]

Like the films analyzed in this chapter, Woods "relegate[d] black grievances against whites to the past while situating white complaints about blacks in the present." Deflecting the lingering evidence of white racism through reference to the "special privileges enjoyed by O.J. Simpson and the beneficiaries of affirmative action," Woods's comments ignored the historical and structural realities that rendered affirmative action programs necessary in the first place, as well as their consistent erosion in his present day. Indeed, as Lipsitz points out, Woods referred directly to "quotas" in his tirade against affirmative action, though quotas were illegal and therefore far from a pressing issue. In doing so, Woods exhibited a common trait among defenders of white privilege, which Lipsitz defines as "an insatiable demand" for stories of "minority misbehavior." This demand, evident in the Simpson trial, was also at the root of white resentment over affirmative action, the rhetoric around which implied beneficiaries were "undeserving," just as Simpson did not "deserve" his defense team. Indeed, whereas the admission that LAPD officer Mark Fuhrman was a committed white supremacist was cited as irrelevant to the prosecution's case against Simpson, even though Fuhrman committed perjury and compromised the entire case, defense lawyer Johnnie Cochran's efforts to undermine Fuhrman's testimony were dismissed in the white media as "playing the race card." As such, whereas the LAPD and white society in general appeared content to ignore the realities of Fuhrman's actions and attitudes, or at the very least to see them as personal rather than structural issues, Cochran's defense of his client on the grounds of Fuhrman's evident racism was presented as opportunistic.[89]

Like the O. J. Simpson case, civil rights melodramas of the 1990s implied that to acknowledge white on Black racism in contemporary America was "bad taste, a violation of protocol." In his assessment of the Simpson trial, Lewis R. Gordon continued that the racism identified in the case was "trivialized," likened to "tak[ing] a position in a game for the purpose of gaining an advantage." Only in the 1990s, Gordon continued, an era "marked by such false notions as 'reverse discrimination,'" could "such an obfuscation of reality" occur. "Detective Fuhrman all but wore a white hood throughout the case, and Simpson's defense team was expected to literally ignore it." Like Mark

Fuhrman, the racist of the 1990s civil rights melodrama is easily cast aside and never assumed to speak for his community, region, or nation. Just as there was no conspiracy of racism prompting the frequent arson of Black churches, evidence of racists within the nation's law enforcement and judicial system warranted merely the purge of individuals, and a continued commitment to the color-blind hegemony. To demand anything more, Gordon implies, was perceived to stoke division—the accusation that "conveniently" emerged whenever "questions of progress for blacks [were] raised," including affirmative action and investigations into police brutality and the justice system.[90]

But while white southerners of the civil rights era were deemed "un-American" in their efforts to protect segregation, Roopali Mukherjee has written of the "reprieve" granted cinematic southern moderates like Jake Brigance and Bobby DeLaughter, who represented a "credibility and common sense on race matters" for the 1990s. Their "quintessentially Southern critiques" of racial and political practices, Mukherjee writes, implied an experienced pragmatism, "which by the nineties reflected authorized truths about multicultural excess and its mutant progeny of civil rights reforms as having overstayed their welcome."[91] Through cynical emphasis on Black group identity in the NAACP and other civil rights organizations, *A Time to Kill* and *Ghosts of Mississippi* therefore reflect a white resentment of the "undeserving" or "disruptive" African American that was prominent throughout American political culture by the 1990s but that found particular form in the civil rights melodrama due to its emphasis on white liberals as both the products and harbingers of racial progress.

However, for this strand of white liberalism to shine as brightly as possible, vital distinctions have to be drawn between the hero and his white antagonists. Such distinctions depend on simultaneous narratives of the South as both a site of evolving racial attitudes and a continuing repository for the nation's deadliest racial sins. The former designation spotlights federal intervention in pursuit of American values during the 1950s and 1960s, while the latter reflects the enduring explanatory power of southern exceptionalism in an era marked by contemporary racial tension and haunting reminders of the past triggered by a spate of reopened civil rights cases. These coinciding narratives therefore proved crucial to the rejection of affirmative action and other continued efforts to rebalance the playing field in American education and economic opportunity, documenting racism as something perpetrated only by backward individuals irrationally obsessed with color in the age of color blindness. In the face of such apparent anomalies, Hollywood's elevation of Bobby DeLaughter, Jake Brigance, and other unlikely southern liberals was no coincidence; rather, their seemingly innate propensity for justice proves the immutability of color blindness as the newly accepted national creed. Particularly in the southern context in which the civil rights melodrama takes place, African American characters must be reminded of how lucky they are to be interacting with "modern," enlightened, and implicitly secular whites instead of the lingering, recalcitrant white trash that continue to stalk the region.

As if to reinforce this threat, the 1990s produced plenty of examples of the latter white trash villain, too, from the Klansmen of *A Time to Kill* to Max Cady, the ludicrous harlequin of Martin Scorsese's *Cape Fear*. Explored in the next chapter, Cady offers perhaps the most extreme example of late twentieth-century Hollywood's perpetuation of stereotypes of southern religious depravity, rooted in a genre thriller's exploitation of extremes of class, gender, education, and politics. Through exploration of the film's characterizations and its notable deviation from the 1962 movie on which it is based, the next chapter spotlights the fragility of white liberal arrogance in the final decade of the twentieth century and the continued power of southern religious stereotypes in the midst of a culture war.

CHAPTER 4

"Jimmy Swaggart Meets Huey Long in Hell"

Cape Fear's "Monster of the South"

Released at the dawn of the 1990s, with the civil rights melodrama still in its infancy, Martin Scorsese's remake of *Cape Fear* proves a fascinating insight into the post–civil rights South of Hollywood's imagination. In its connection to and deviation from the original 1962 film of the same name, as well as the 1957 novel on which that film was based (John MacDonald's *The Executioners*), Scorsese's *Cape Fear* provides perhaps one of the most stimulating examples of how racial and religious anxieties rooted in sectional understandings of U.S. life and culture shifted in the years after the significant civil rights victories of the mid-1950s to late 1960s. Like examining *To Kill a Mockingbird* alongside its descendants, *Ghosts of Mississippi* and *A Time to Kill*, an exploration of both Thompson's and Scorsese's *Cape Fear* enables probing analysis of how the anxieties, achievements, and failures of the 1960s played out in late twentieth-century cinema.

Dismissed by many critics as a genre film thriller, Scorsese's *Cape Fear* offers a basic narrative of revenge in which Max Cady (Robert De Niro) terrorizes the defense lawyer whose actions saw Cady incarcerated for rape of an underage girl fourteen years earlier. However, its particular construction of this seemingly simple plot manages to unravel the apparent security of white middle-class American suburban identity, offering a close examination of the divisions of education, class, race, and gender that continue to shape the field of southern studies. In its reconceptualization of villain Max Cady, documented in actor Robert De Niro's papers at the Harry Ransom Center at the University of Texas, the later film engages with a much older "southern gothic" continuum, building on the racial tensions palpable in Thompson's version, while acknowledging more contemporary anxieties about the role of evangelical Christianity in the late 1980s and early 1990s. Indeed, when referring to the decision to reposition Max Cady as a pentecostal Christian, screenwriter Wesley Strick candidly admits that he envisioned the newer Cady as a "monster of the South."[1]

Whereas De Niro's physical preparation for *Cape Fear* became the stuff of legend, the expansive studies undertaken by a team of researchers for the film are less well known. These researchers investigated the most overt elements of Cady's recharacterization—serial criminality and Pentecostalism—and helped to construct an almost burlesque white "southerner."[2] Researchers contacted a host of experts—academics, filmmakers, folklorists, and medical professionals—while Strick credited *The Encyclopedia of Southern Culture* as his "main source."[3] Perhaps because of this meticulous planning, letters detailing the appointment and placement of researchers in the South often give the impression that they were navigating uncharted territory rather than documenting a highly populated region within their own nation. One researcher, Melanie Friesen, compared her experience talking to southerners to the "healthcare work [her] dad did in developing countries and growing up in places where suspicion of the outside region reigned."[4] Renowned North Carolina folklorist George Holt had apparently warned Friesen "that it's very hard to go into these communities for research cold—that someone familiar needs to accompany an outsider."[5]

Max Cady and Holiness Pentecostalism

As a result of this extensive research, the new Cady bore little resemblance to his cinematic predecessor, played by Robert Mitchum, whom Robert Casillo defines as "a fairly conventional filmic psychopath." De Niro's Cady, "less a human being than a demonic incarnation," exhibits a disturbed and misdirected Holiness Pentecostalism, the vengeful nature of which was fostered during his incarceration, when, frustrated and angry, Cady reevaluated the "old time" religion of his childhood.[6] "Hard core stuff," according to researcher Jem Cohen, Pentecostalism apparently reflected "not so much a set of customs as a world view wherein every aspect of one's life is affected by the drive towards 'Holiness' and a rejection of all things 'worldly.'" Now a celebrated independent filmmaker, Cohen argued that there is a "down home intimacy and even a renegade spirit in Pentecostalism that aligns well with the Appalachian 'mountain' people, who are fiercely independent, and frequently *very* poor" (emphasis Cohen's). Thus, as Cohen reported, "Pentecostal living would greatly increase one's sense of separation from the outside world."[7]

Although stimulated by the late nineteenth-century revival of northern

perfectionism, many southern pentecostals were already involved in the "holiness movement" that emerged from Methodism after the Civil War. They
incorporated a theology of "premillennialism," believing that the Second
Coming of Jesus Christ was imminent, and exhibited a uniquely enthusiastic worship style, including faith healing and speaking in tongues, inviting the
scorn of mainline Protestants. "Because holiness people were less bound by
prevailing social codes than members of mainline churches," Randall Stephens
writes, "their meetings were often racially integrated, wild, and loud."[8] Cohen's
interpretation of how Cady's Pentecostalism might manifest itself reflected the
work of folklorist Elaine Lawless, who argued in the 1980s that "anti-Pente-
costal sentiment from outsiders only feeds the fire of Pentecostalism" and that
this negativity is often "proof enough for [believers] that they are a special religious group." Rejection of the world, Lawless contended, becomes a "sure path
to salvation," as Pentecostals embrace their marginalized status as a reflection
of their unique relationship with God.[9]

Described as "a laboratory for the application of explanatory models,"
Appalachia has served as a petri dish for those examining the intersections
of class and religion since at least the 1880s, when Richard J. Callahan Jr. argues "'mountain whites' also came to be identified by outsiders as 'poor white
trash.'" Famously limited to three defining factors—religion, poverty, and
coalmining—Appalachia is subject to endless studies and theories about a
"culture of poverty," where "'deviant' religious practices such as serpent handling, faith healing, emotional preaching, and biblical literalism [provided a]
compensatory response to economic, social, and psychological deprivation."
A product of this environment, De Niro's Max Cady finds purpose in religion
and seeks Old Testament–style revenge on those he believes have abandoned
or undermined him. Meanwhile, his illiteracy prior to his incarceration reflects his upbringing in a community that placed no value on education or interaction with the outside world. "In short," Callahan concludes, "the religious
practices of Appalachia are either the cause or the effect of poverty."[10]

But pentecostals, like other Americans, have constantly evolved and
adapted. There were approximately eleven million pentecostals in the United
States by 2000, while the global movement was estimated to represent around
half a billion people. Mirroring many of the social, cultural, and economic
forces that shape other lives and communities, pentecostals reflected a
cross-section of southern society by the mid-twentieth century, encompassing wealthy Atlanta businessmen and Alabama sharecroppers. Many left the
region during the Depression and Great Migration, "carrying their religious
beliefs with them."[11] Like millions of other American Christians after World
War II, countless pentecostals came to embrace the "prosperity gospel" of

"pragmatism, individualism, and upward mobility."[12] Thus, as a pentecostal, Cady is by no means immune to the influence of modernity. His penchant for cigars, for example, would not be tolerated in a devout Holiness sect. A prison vice, Cady claims that he took up smoking "to remind me I was human."

The conflicting ideologies guiding the newer Cady's character prove central to his introductory scenes, as the camera pans across the images that adorn his prison wall—including Joseph Stalin, Robert E. Lee, and Christian martyrs. Whereas Thompson's 1962 film introduces Mitchum's Cady simply walking in the street, Scorsese's first shots of De Niro provide a deeply personal insight into Cady's physical and mental space. On Cady's bookshelves, Nietzsche sits alongside the Bible, legal guides, vocabulary exercises, and books on healthy eating, implying interests in "pacifism, masochism, sadism, totalitarianism, and the therapeutic."[13] Reinforced by Elmer Bernstein's reworking of Bernard Hermann's original 1962 score, itself reminiscent of Hermann's work for Alfred Hitchcock, the camera pans away from Cady's walls and bookshelf, and he appears in the foreground, stripped to the waist and doing push-ups. The bars of his prison cell also come into view. Cady's criminality, as well as his immense physical strength, is thrust on the audience, providing glimpses of his elaborate, expansive religious tattoos. Lines of biblical verse mark his arms and torso, while his back displays a huge cross that is also a set of scales, bearing the words "TRUTH" and "JUSTICE," the first signified by a Bible, the latter, a knife.

The development of Cady's tattoos is evident in De Niro's research materials, mainly through his correspondence with makeup artist Ilona Herman and several volumes of prison photography, many of which are annotated with comments that acknowledge the visible tattoos of many prisoners. Most of Herman's notes stress the need for the tattoos to be "crude," having been ap-

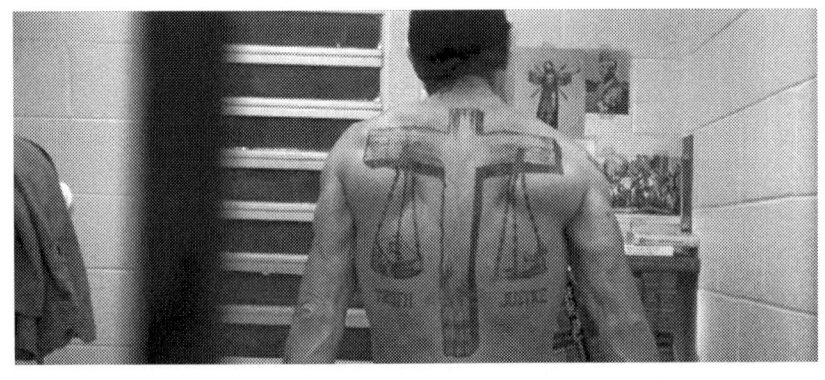

Max Cady (Robert De Niro) is introduced to viewers in his prison cell, with his large back tattoo visible, in *Cape Fear* (Martin Scorsese, 1991).

plied in prison. She also suggested that certain words be misspelt, indicative of Cady's previous illiteracy.[14] Using a Bible concordance, De Niro and Herman searched for words or passages that would best communicate Cady's sense of injustice while reflecting his faith that God's will would prevail. Passages that were finally selected include "The Lord is the Avenger," "My time is not yet at hand," and "Vengeance is mine." Suggestions were made for tattoos across the hands, "GOOD" and "EVIL," or "LOVE" and "HATE," reminiscent of Mitchum's tattooed preacher in *The Night of the Hunter*, a performance that greatly influenced De Niro. Although Cady admits "there's not a whole lot to do in prison except desecrate your flesh" and that incarceration has left him a little "coarse," his tattoos ensure that he is an active participant in the way his body is read. Despite a later strip search designed to make Cady to "feel about as welcome around here as a case of yellow fever," any attempt to render Cady physically vulnerable quickly turns in his favor, revealing his threatening physique and tattoos. Cady is never so much victimized as glorified. He consistently evades legal control, while his greatest weapon—his body—is frequently cast center stage.[15]

More than simply a physical presence, Cady's sexual threat is further communicated through his fondness for Henry Miller novels, whose vivid sexual descriptions would complicate any notion that Cady is directed entirely by fundamentalist dogma. Framed as pornography in the early 1990s, Miller's books prove vital to Cady's relationship with his nemesis Sam Bowden's fifteen-year-old daughter Danielle (Juliette Lewis). Although unfamiliar with Miller's *Rosy Crucifixion* trilogy (1949–59), Danielle admits that she has read "parts of" *Tropic of Cancer* (1934), which was banned until the 1960s. Almost thirty years later, Danielle admits that she had to "sneak it off" her parents' shelf, which Cady argues is because her parents seek to prevent her ability to "achieve adulthood." Having earlier encouraged the troubled teenager to "be yourself and be a woman" while posing as her guidance counsellor, Cady's investment in Danielle's burgeoning adulthood is distinctly sexual. Indeed, Danielle's entirely white clothing underlines her virginal status in her first meeting with Cady, where, according to screenwriter Wesley Strick, Danielle is "completely entranced by [Cady's] sophistication," failing to note his mispronunciation of "*roman à clef*."[16] "[A] literature of defilement," Miller's novels become a symbol for Cady and Danielle's illicit connection; the copy of *Sexus* that Cady leaves for Danielle on the Bowden doorstep is indicative of the sexual relationship he hopes to develop with her. That Danielle hides the book from her parents and housekeeper demonstrates her awareness of its unseemliness—both as a gift exchanged between an adult man and teenage girl and as a piece of literature.[17]

Teenager Danielle Bowden (Juliette Lewis) sucks Max Cady's (Robert De Niro's) finger in *Cape Fear* (Martin Scorsese, 1991).

Although Cady uses Miller's novels as a titillating example of the freedoms of adulthood, he launches into a more recognizably Christian sermon on the power of forgiveness and salvation once he has Danielle's attention and trust. When Danielle asks why Cady hates her father, Cady responds, "I don't hate him at all. Oh, no, I pray for him. I'm here to help him. I mean, we all make mistakes, Danielle. You and I have. At least we try to admit it. But your daddy, he don't. . . . Every man has to go through hell to reach his paradise. You know what paradise is? . . . Salvation." Implying that he and Danielle are better people than her parents, Cady asserts, "You know I think I might have found a companion, a companion for that long walk into the light." This deeply uncomfortable scene then reaches its climax, as Cady approaches Danielle and puts his thumb in her mouth before kissing her. One of the movie's pivotal scenes, this ten-minute exchange between Cady and Danielle frames one of the film's most disturbing elements: the ever-present threat of sexual violence, here rendered all the more perverse because the potential victim is a child. However, critics have failed to note the manner in which Cady shifts from overtly grooming and sexually assaulting a child to a profound discussion of the pentecostal tenets of salvation and redemption. Like many of the disgraced televangelists of the late 1980s, Cady appears to tread a fine line between the divine and the depraved.

"The Lord Told Me It's Flat None of Your Business": Televangelist Scandals in the 1980s

Screenwriter Wesley Strick appeared confident that Hollywood audiences would share his anxieties about southern evangelicals, and following the damaging sexual and financial scandals that rocked American televangelism in the late 1980s, he had considerably more reason to channel a specifically anti-evangelical feeling. From Pat Robertson's false claims about his marriage and military service during his run for the Republican Party's 1988 presidential nomination to Oral Roberts's "divinely ordained" fundraising methods, evangelical hypocrisy gripped the press. Americans were "spellbound," Michael Giuliano writes, as they glimpsed "into this sometimes seedy world of religious television, a world that many had ignored up to that point." In January 1987, Roberts announced that God told him ("in a vision") that he had to raise $4.5 million for medical missionaries by March 31, or God would "take him home." A letter was sent to supporters asking them to "come into agreement with [Roberts] concerning [his] life being extended beyond March."[18] That same March, Jim Bakker resigned his leadership of the PTL (Praise the Lord) Network amid allegations of sexual and financial impropriety.[19] Handing over control to Moral Majority founder Jerry Falwell, Bakker claimed that Falwell was a safe pair of hands in the wake of a takeover plot by Jimmy Swaggart, a fellow Assemblies of God televangelist based in Baton Rouge, Louisiana.[20]

Dubbed "the Protestant pope," Swaggart publicly condemned the actions of both Roberts and Bakker, before eventually revealing that he had, in fact, revealed the name of Bakker's mistress to church officials. Swaggart's own liaisons with prostitutes were subsequently revealed when the son of a disgruntled New Orleans preacher, against whom Swaggart had also conspired, followed Swaggart and a prostitute to a motel in the city. Photographs showing Swaggart's misdemeanors reached Assemblies of God headquarters, but the denomination supported Swaggart's emotional plea for forgiveness, subject to his enrollment in a rehabilitation program and a three-month break from preaching.[21] Swaggart's now-infamous apology sermon "was fabulous television," Quentin Schultze writes, "more compelling than most made-for-TV films and more dramatic than any evening soap opera."[22]

The inherent hypocrisy revealed by the scandals seemed to rile the secular press much more than the sexual or financial nature of the indiscretions.[23] The in-fighting between the televangelists—especially Bakker and Swaggart who belonged to the same pentecostal denomination—revealed what sociologist Joshua Gamson refers to as "a *turf war*, in which feuding preachers use scandal as a weapon in their fight for a share of the religious market." These revelations sparked further discussions about the inherent theatricality of evangelism and what Gamson calls "the workings of market-centered religious institutions."[24]

Extensively documented by the media, Swaggart's 1988 fall from grace proved fresh in the minds of Strick, De Niro, and their researchers as they began working on *Cape Fear* the following year. The televangelist's name appears frequently in their materials, and De Niro was explicitly advised to read a 1988 *Penthouse* article exposing the preacher's "secret sex life," receiving the magazine in an envelope that also contained music from professionally recorded church choirs.[25] According to researchers, the *Penthouse* piece was "an appropriate accompaniment to the enclosed cassette about fundamentalism since it includes the TV preachers," thus giving a broader picture of the movement.[26] By this point, "TV preachers" was shorthand for the fallen televangelists: ministers who had boasted huge followings and staggering church profits but had been disgraced as frauds and hypocrites. It was impossible, De Niro's researchers suggested, to understand the modern fundamentalist movement without examining these disgraced leaders. By the time *Cape Fear* premiered on November 6, 1991, Swaggart had been found in the company of a prostitute for the second time on October 11, and in contrast to his previous emotional pleas for forgiveness in 1988, had stunned his declining congregation by announcing, "The Lord told me it's flat none of your business."[27]

Given the attention these scandals received in the American media, it is hardly surprising that the Princeton Religion Research Center recorded a considerable shift in the nation's attitudes toward evangelicalism during the 1980s. Data collected in 1980 suggested that Americans were more likely to vote for a candidate who was a born-again Christian, but by 1987, voters were *less* likely to vote for an evangelical candidate and demonstrated increasing hostility toward fundamentalists and evangelists.[28] Pat Robertson stood down from his ministry during his campaign for the 1988 Republican presidential nomination after the *New York Times* reported that "large numbers of voters were opposed to a minster's running for President."[29] Robertson subsequently threatened to sue any media outlet that referred to him as a televangelist, hoping to reinvent himself as a "businessman," claiming in December 1987, "I have never been an Evangelist in my life."[30]

But while *Cape Fear*'s emphasis on "false prophets" was undoubtedly a response to the high-profile scandals of the late 1980s, it also had a long history in Hollywood.[31] Films such as *The Miracle Woman* (Frank Capra, 1931), *Night of the Hunter* (Charles Laughton, 1955), and *Elmer Gantry* (Richard Brooks, 1960) all warned of the manipulative power of persuasive, money-hungry "preachers." *Cape Fear* tapped into this tradition but also managed to participate in a specifically southern dialogue about the profound significance of Protestantism in southern life. The grotesque form of this religiosity tied contemporary concerns surrounding hypocritical televangelists to a much older, almost satirical presentation of the "gothic" South of William Faulkner, Flannery O'Connor, and Erskine Caldwell. Cady's religiosity is just one, but perhaps the most important, way in which Scorsese makes these connections. In the new Max Cady, Scorsese created an enduringly sinister "hillbilly face of horror," whose upbringing around snake handlers has made him immune to pain and empathy.[32]

"You're a VIP on Earth; I'm a VIP in Heaven": Sam Bowden and Max Cady

Inextricably linking the geographic and religious distinctions of Cady's background, the first mention of the word "Pentecostal" in *Cape Fear* is loaded with assumptions. Describing Cady to his wife, Leigh (Jessica Lange), Sam Bowden (Nick Nolte) simply states, "He's from the hills. Pentecostal crackers, y'know?" In doing so, Sam acknowledges Cady's origins and spiritual predilections in a manner afforded no other character in the film. These classifications seem to define Cady completely, while Sam's casual use of the derogatory term "crackers" implies stereotypes that enable Sam to feel culturally superior to his enemy. However, having recently inherited $30,000 from the sale of his deceased mother's farm, Cady cannot be ignored or simply "busted for vagrancy," as Sam and his friends at the police station would prefer.[33] Rather, Cady represents Pentecostalism's increasingly conspicuous presence in late twentieth-century public life. Grant Wacker points to the transformation of previously tiny Bible institutes into fully accredited colleges and universities, and the "warm welcome" that pentecostals offered Republican presidential candidates as evidence of this new visibility.[34] Cady, on the other hand, exhibits his newfound wealth through his ostentatious Cadillac and lurid clothes.

Despite their considerable visibility, mainstream pentecostal denominations remained concerned that their reputations were tarnished through common conflation with Pentecostalism's more extreme factions: the snake-handling "Signs Following" groups that boasted far fewer members but attracted considerable publicity and contributed to the consistent association of Pentecostalism with poverty. In 1983, Elaine Lawless reported that

Max Cady (Robert De Niro) holds an emergency flare as hot wax flows over his hands, proving his immunity to earthly pain in *Cape Fear* (Martin Scorsese, 1991).

"Pentecostals are associated with poor people everywhere who wear old clothes out of necessity and who do not sport fashionable hair-styles because of a lack of opportunity or sophistication."[35] Cady's fashion choices are clearly designed to render him outdated and unfashionable, but their garish colors and prints present a considerable departure from the muted styles Lawless associated with rural Appalachia. Likewise, Cady wears his hair long and slicked back, in contrast with the shorter pentecostal styles Lawless identified. Film scholar Kirsten Thompson argues that Cady's hairstyle, which he blackens with mascara, aligns him with the feminine, reflecting his oppression as a member of a white underclass and his sexual victimization in prison.[36]

As a result of this harassment and his increasing awareness of the class prejudice that cost him so many years of freedom, Cady improved himself both physically and mentally while incarcerated. Resenting his place among undisciplined criminals, Cady became a more commanding figure: "I spent fourteen years in an eight by nine cell, surrounded by people who were less than human. My mission in that time was to become more than human." Cady's Pentecostalism, as it is presented, works to reinforce many of these developing feelings of superiority. The film thus merges an intense religiosity with a criminality that is bolstered, rather than deterred, through a lengthy prison sentence. Unaffected by loneliness or other anxieties, Cady has been "neither dazed nor dulled" by prison, according to an early draft of Strick's script. Rather, on his release, Cady is extremely fit, intellectually quick, and "his eyes have a sharp glint."[37] He believes he has "a leg up, genetically speakin'," because "Granddaddy used to handle snakes in church, Granny drank strychnine." He therefore personally aligns himself with Appalachian "Signs Following" churches, known to handle snakes and fire, as well as occasionally ingesting poisons such as strychnine.[38]

More than simply clearing up Cady's denominational loyalties, this identification comes within the film's terrifying climax, as Cady makes one last attempt to baptize and redeem the Bowden family. His voice is suddenly strengthened, and as Cady booms like a preacher, the camera gradually lowers until the audience is positioned submissively beneath him. Perhaps most disturbingly, Cady appears unmoved by the hot wax that is streaming onto his hand from a lit distress flare, confirming his superior immunity to pain. Reminiscent of the "grainy black and white photographs or jerky videos of sweaty, wild-eyed worshippers, who cram into hot, rundown rural churches," this presentation of Cady reflects media fascination with Appalachian pentecostals, interest always roused following the injury or death of a believer.[39]

Despite *Cape Fear*'s preoccupation with the more extreme and esoteric strains of Pentecostalism, researcher Jem Cohen informed De Niro that "all

Pentecostals do not handle snakes—some have renounced it as demonic. Many of the more subdued church denominations have long been embarrassed by the wild behavior of some 'Holiness' branches."[40] Indeed, both the Pentecostal Holiness Church and the Church of God (Cleveland) explicitly condemned the practice by 1920, as they moved toward what psychologists Ralph Wood and W. Paul Williamson call "greater worldly success." Academics have tended to focus almost exclusively on these organized denominations, contributing to "the notion" that "fringe" or "splinter" groups "are pathological."[41] The fact that practices such as snake handling can easily be relegated to a very specific area of Appalachia only adds to the sense of both religious and cultural "otherness" that is integral to Cady's characterization.

Perhaps because of this tendency to stereotype Holiness worshippers, Cohen was keen to avoid blatant mischaracterizations of pentecostal practice and worship. In a note dated November 1, 1990, a year before the film's release, Cohen objected to the suggestion in the screenplay that snake handling and drinking strychnine were particularly associated with Easter celebrations, referencing his conversations with Dr. Tom Burton of East Tennessee State University.[42] "For a Holiness snake handler," Cohen wrote, "faith is meant to be a constant, and the handling of serpents is a proof of faith, which should come 'when the spirit moves,' rather than on a particular holiday. According to Dr. Burton . . . many of these churches have 'homecomings,' where congregations gather from near and far and snake handling would be highly likely to take place . . . but of course those days are simply chosen by the various Pentecostal churches, and would have no specific significance for the viewing public."[43]

Seemingly embarrassed at the prospect of the film containing something categorically wrong about Holiness Pentecostalism, Cohen also recognized the importance of maintaining simple allusions that could be understood by all viewers. A disconnect exists, then, between the level of research conducted in preparation for shooting Scorsese's *Cape Fear* and the depiction of Signs Following Pentecostalism in the final film. By overtly linking very distinctive worship practices with a fanatical criminal, Scorsese's film implies that Cady's misconduct and religiosity are indeed the result of a poor, rural background, reflecting the "social deprivation" theories that have been so often used by sociologists, historians, and psychologists when studying Pentecostalism. Robert Anderson's *Vision of the Disinherited* (1979), for example, argues in both title and content that "the root source of Pentecostalism was social discontent" and that association with the movement reflects personal weakness rather than genuine spiritual interest or faith.[44]

Nevertheless, Cady's behaviors and practices are often at odds with this

Max Cady's (Robert De Niro's) bumper stickers reveal his spiritual and regional loyalties in *Cape Fear* (Martin Scorsese, 1991).

supposedly destitute and devout demographic, and the film's investment in his Pentecostalism is thus twofold. Primarily, it allows the Bowdens and the audience to "understand" Cady's place within American society. His position within a marginalized group, maligned through its religious and regional allegiances, ensures that Cady is figured as "other." Second, rather than indicate Cady's vulnerability within American culture, this "otherness" ensures he is a character to be feared because his motives and preoccupations can never be preempted by the more cosmopolitan national character that the Bowdens represent. Despite Scorsese's efforts to morally compromise Sam, the lawyer remains exemplary of suburban, middle-class white existence. Indeed, the fact Sam is a practicing lawyer represents his secure and privileged place within his society: he literally interprets and implements the rules of his culture.

Ignored by society and betrayed by Sam, Cady is not remotely concerned with the preservation of his own family, reputation, or his earthly life. Even when he begins to drown, Cady shows no fear but sings "I'm Bound for the Promised Land" and speaks in tongues. His religiosity thus delivers him, he believes, from the extremely limited opportunities he has been offered on earth. If Sam has been granted earthly privilege—money, influence, and a family—Cady is sure that he will be rewarded in the next world. While Sam effectively sacrificed Cady to prison, Cady's sense of himself as God's avenging angel enables him to sentence Sam "to the kingdom of Hell," a responsibility that he takes very seriously. His power, limited on earth, is mighty in the kingdom of God, summarized in his bumper sticker: "You're a VIP on Earth; I'm a VIP in Heaven." Most important, Cady warns Bowden, "I ain't no white trash piece of shit." Rather, as Cady insists,

> I'm better than you all. I can outlearn you, I can out-read you, I can out-think you, I can out-philosophize you, and I'm gonna outlast you. You think a coupla

whacks to my good ol' boy gut's gonna get me down? It's gonna take a hell of a lot more than that counselor, to prove you're better'n me.

"I am like God and God like me.
I am as Large as God, He is as small as I.
He cannot above me, nor I beneath Him be."
Silesius, seventeenth century

In this scene, Cady again adopts the booming preacher's voice crucial to the "old-time religion" of his characterization. Cast against the Bowdens, whose professions and values suggest that they are educated liberals, Cady appears an unreconstructed southerner, wedded to the passions and distortions of the past. However, with Cady now well versed in the law and financially buffered by his recent inheritance, Scorsese conveys the horror that would ensue if the criminal underclass were suddenly able to manipulate the law in the way the privileged can. The Bowdens' apparent vulnerability at the hands of this previously illiterate, rural religious fanatic therefore delivers Scorsese's bleak message about what lies just beyond the peripheries of the "New" South's suburbia.

Despite the Bowdens' liberal credentials, including a disdain for firearms and relaxed attitude to their daughter's marijuana use, it is evident from the film's opening scenes that Sam often bends the rules to suit his own priorities and values; indeed, the audience's first introduction to Sam is of a triumphant lawyer who has just persuaded a judge to postpone a friend's daughter's alimony hearing so that the friend in question can "find out which S & L [savings and loan], in which municipality my son-in-law stashed all that money."[45] During Cady's original case, Sam buried a report that detailed Cady's teenage victim's promiscuity, hoping to alleviate the misogyny characteristic to the legal process and ensure that Cady received the maximum possible sentence. His choice is vindicated later in the film when another of Cady's victims, Lori Davis (Illeana Douglas), refuses to testify because, as a clerk at the county courthouse, Lori has seen lawyers "cross-examining people on the stands, crucifying them. I don't wanna explain why I was in a bar, why I had so much to drink, what I was wearing."

But while Bowden's decision was morally understandable, it remains professionally unacceptable: a manipulation of the privileged position he holds within the American justice system. Compromising Cady's rights under the Sixth Amendment, Bowden also violated the American Bar Association's Ethical Considerations, which require a lawyer to "represent his client zealously."[46] For Philip Wegner, Sam represents the political class of the 1980s, "whose often criminal manipulations of the economy exacerbated the growing inequities of the current economic and social arrangement." Wegner references rife insider trading and corporate buyouts and suggests that Cady's arrival in the Bowdens' fictional small town of New Essex reflects growing anxiety on the part of the middle and upper classes "about what would happen when their victims begin to come to consciousness about the crimes committed against them."[47]

Stretching from 1977 through 1991, Cady's sentence coincides with the dramatic increase in America's prison population, primarily considered to be the result of the War on Drugs. Although Elizabeth Hinton has traced the origins of the American carceral state to Lyndon Johnson's War on Crime, a response to the failures of the War on Poverty and rising urban unrest in the mid- to late 1960s, the War on Drugs—a term popularized by President Richard Nixon but most forcibly enacted by President Ronald Reagan in the 1980s—introduced mandatory minimum sentences for many previously minor drug offenses in the late twentieth century.[48] Dramatically transforming America's criminal justice system, the War on Drugs saw the prison population quadruple in less than two decades, from roughly three hundred thousand in 1980 to over two million in 2000. A significant media campaign in the 1980s and 1990s ensured public and legislative support, while most politicians strained to prove they were "tough on crime." Sweeping millions into a permanent underclass without voting, educational, or employment rights, the resulting criminal justice system has been criticized as little more than a renamed form of social, racial, and class control.[49] Although scholars such as Michelle Alexander have documented the extent to which this "war" has been disproportionately conducted in African American and Hispanic neighborhoods, "white trash" like Max Cady joined this criminal underclass in America's sprawling prison system. Illiterate and unaware of his legal entitlements, Cady had no choice but to entrust Sam Bowden with his future, a future that Bowden had already rendered worthless.

"The South Has a Fine Tradition of Savoring Fear": White Anxieties in *Cape Fear*

J. W. Williamson argues that Cady's "hillbilly face of horror" is actually a mirror, a stark reminder of the other—poorer, rural—white America.[50] An inverse of *Deliverance* (John Boorman, 1972) in which unprepared city folks invade the inhospitable mountains, *Cape Fear* suggests that the hillbilly could attack the suburban sprawl. Cady often confronts the Bowdens in public spaces: at the cinema, the ice-cream parlor, at school, and during a Fourth of July parade. However, it is his ability to enter their inner sanctum—a huge, white southern mansion that suggests antebellum fears of slave rebellion—

The Bowden family home, a white pillared mansion of the modern South surrounded by manicured gardens and Spanish moss trees, as pictured in *Cape Fear* (Martin Scorsese, 1991).

that really scares the Bowdens. Retreating into their home, which sits apart from any other building or community, the family literally seeks sanctuary within their moneyed whiteness. Using Danielle and Leigh as bait, Sam hopes to lure Cady to the house, knowing that the "white southern woman in peril" narrative will warrant any injury he subsequently inflicts on Cady. In a specific reference to white southern history, private detective Kersek (Joe Don Baker) educates Sam and the audience: "You know, the South evolved on fear—fear of the Indian, fear of the slave, fear of the damned Union. The South has a fine tradition of savoring fear." According to Kersek, Sam too must "savor that fear" if he is to defeat Cady.[51]

While Kersek's comment acknowledges the changing targets of white southern aggression, it also demonstrates a consistent paranoia. Thus, as Wegner suggests, the South's "fine tradition" may be built on fear, but it is underlined by the "deep anxiety that the violence exerted on the bodies of others will be retuned in kind—a nightmare that literally has come true with Cady's appearance."[52] Returning to terrorize the Bowdens, Cady is not simply a former client on a revenge mission but the latest manifestation of southern white anxiety. Indeed, when there is no logical explanation for how Cady entered the house, the suggestion lingers that perhaps he has been there all along. "I just had the weirdest feeling he was already in the house," Sam gasps during the stakeout.

Eventually launching a boulder at Cady's head, Sam undergoes what Kirsten Thompson recognizes as "regression to a brutal defender of his family, a man who uses rocks, not the law, as his weapons."[53] However, as Kersek reminds Sam, he is not the first white southerner to take the law into his own hands. Indeed, at this point, the film enters into a dialogue with its own cinematic predecessor, the 1962 film, in which the earlier Bowden family pondered the dangers associated with extending the rights of African Americans and "other undesirables." Here, Robert Mitchum's Cady blurs the rigidity of segregated life in the South, in part due to the actor's own criminal record, which was cited regularly by the film's promoters. The connections were especially significant given that filming took place in Savannah, Georgia, where Mitchum had been arrested for vagrancy in 1933. Sentenced to work on a chain gang, Mitchum later escaped—the length of the sentence and nature of the escape differing every time Mitchum told the story.[54] When asked by a Savannah native if he had come far from his days as a Georgia fugitive, Mitchum knowingly answered, "Not necessarily."[55] Like Norman Mailer's "White Negro," Mitchum's Cady therefore rebels against the "totalitarian tissues of American society."[56] Although he is white, Cady here represents a class of people that the Bowdens would never associate with until changes in the law render them unable to legally maintain such boundaries. Facilitating the earlier film's producers to enact what Wegner recognizes as "the nightmares of racial conflict allegorically staged," Mitchum's Cady operates on the underside of their small-town South, picking up women in jazz bars and using an entirely different vernacular (the film's first line of dialogue sees Cady greet an African American janitor with "Hey, daddy").[57]

It is surely no coincidence that Cady's 1962 pursuit of the Bowden daughter, here named Nancy (Lori Martin), occurs in her school, reflecting acute white fears of "miscegenation" following the 1954 Supreme Court decision, *Brown v. Board of Education*. By reducing Cady's sentence from fourteen years in the original novel to eight years in the 1962 film, J. Lee Thompson ensured that Cady was sentenced in 1954, the same year as *Brown*. Kirsten Thompson argues that Cady's specific targeting of Bowden's wife and young daughter "recall[s] the paranoid racist fantasies of white women in peril, from the captivity narrative to *Birth of a Nation*."[58] However, Cady's whiteness enables him to evade the Jim Crow laws that segregated downtown Savannah until 1963. He is therefore free to enter Nancy's school, Deborah Barker writes, as well as "the public, but completely segregated, leisure spaces of the white family."[59] Wearing the shirtsleeves and straw hat of many a working-class segregationist captured by photographers on the civil rights beat, Cady openly utilizes civil rights law while harassing an idealized, middle-class, nuclear white family.[60] "A man like that doesn't deserve civil rights," Sam's wife, Peggy (Polly Bergen), argues—a comment that suggests it is middle-class white people who are now unprotected by the law. "Don't the police have the right to interrogate a subject anymore?" an exasperated Sam Bowden (Gregory Peck) asks when Cady's lawyer argues that the police have "persecuted" his client. Peck's righteous indignation would be reinforced later that same year when he brought that other upstanding southern lawyer to screens in *To Kill a Mockingbird.*

The list of violations against Cady's civil rights resonated with the damning claims of police brutality and a racially biased criminal justice system that were streaming from the South by 1962. "One of them ardent types," according to police chief Mark Dutton (Martin Balsam), Cady's lawyer Grafton (Jack Kruschen) is known for "rallying the bleeding-heart squad." Wegner has argued that Grafton thus serves "as a figure for those federal civil rights agents who by the early 1960s [were present in the South] under the direction of Attorney General Robert Kennedy."[61] However, although liberal lawyers like Grafton were certainly frustrating resistant white southerners by 1962, the Justice Department was largely focused on organized crime and labor corruption during the early years of the Kennedy administration rather than civil rights. Although "the brothers Kennedy managed from the outset to project a mood of executive engagement in civil rights not apparent during the Eisenhower years," Neil McMillen writes, the administration's response to civil rights crises, including the desegregation of the Universities of Mississippi and Alabama, were often late and designed to avoid further embarrassment or fatalities.[62] They were not the executive action JFK had alluded to in his 1960 election campaign, where he had indicated that presidential action offered a unique opportunity for racial change.[63] Black activists, increasingly disappointed by limited federal efforts, developed campaigns across the country, including Mississippi, where SNCC workers filed a lawsuit against Robert Kennedy and FBI director J. Edgar Hoover for failing "to protect plaintiffs and their class from the deprivation of their constitutional rights."[64]

Nevertheless, while the Justice Department were hardly spearheading civil rights efforts in the South in 1962, the Bowdens' frustration and horror in the face of Cady's civil rights demands certainly "stands in for a whole set of entitlements that the conservative white establishment felt to be under assault by a national civil rights movement."[65] This self-righteous indignation is parodied in Scorsese's court scenes in which Gregory Peck and Martin Balsam, actors from the original 1962 film, take reverse roles. Peck, the original Sam Bowden, now plays Cady's lawyer, Lee Heller, while Balsam, who in 1962 played New Essex's police chief, Mark Dutton, a key Bowden ally, prosecutes Sam for his use of vigilante violence. "Just as God arose to judgment to save all the meek of the earth," Balsam's judge grants Cady a restraining order against Sam Bowden, concluding, "This court does not condone feuds, vendettas or vigilantism. Let me quote our great Negro educator, Mr. Booker T. Washington: 'I will let no man drag me down so low as to make me hate him.' Yes. I will grant the restraining order not to validate the malice between you but in the interest of . . . er, Christian harmony." The irony of this scene is undeniable. Kirsten Thompson points out "the dissonance between the words of a former slave espousing a Christian demand for equality and justice, and their enunciation by a representative of the Southern judiciary known for its racist opposition to desegregation in the sixties."[66] Cady, whose poor white heritage aligns him with thousands of other southerners effectively "blamed" for the violence of the civil rights era, can now manipulate the color-blind logic of civil rights legislation to suit his own agenda, endorsed by a pompous southern judiciary. The judge's plea for "Christian harmony" suggests a conservative and sanctimoniously religious white South that speaks to Cady's understanding of divine justice, best exemplified by Heller's assurance to the judge that "King Solomon could not have adjudicated more wisely." Continuing his elevated, religious rhetoric, Heller concludes that he is "so offended at the philistine tactics of Mr. Bowden, I petition the ABA [American Bar Association] for his disbarment on the grounds of moral turpitude."

"He Ain't Ever Gonna Forget It": Women as Property in *Cape Fear*

Scorsese's deliberate and ironic use of stereotypes about white southern manipulation of the legal system reflects continued understandings of the region as ideologically removed from the rest of the nation. Little has changed, this scene suggests, since the early 1960s. Similarly, despite Sam's morally upstanding decision to protect Cady's victim back in 1977, reflecting the contemporaneous adoption of rape shield laws across the United States, the second *Cape Fear* suggests that sexual politics is also no more sophisticated than in the 1960s.[67] Despite the passage of thirty years, Lori repeats Diane Taylor's (Barrie Chase) refusal to testify when raped by Cady.

Cady's initial seduction of Diane in the jazz bar in the 1962 version of *Cape Fear* reveals the true root of white fears of miscegenation: that white women would actively seek or willingly succumb to African American sexual partners. Cady's later attempt to draw up a sexual contract with Sam's wife, Peggy, reflects this anxiety, as he specifically requires her "consent." However, more important than Peggy's bodily autonomy, or lack thereof, is the perceived impact on her husband. According to Cady, Sam may appreciate Peggy's "noble gesture," offering herself to protect their daughter, but "he ain't ever gonna forget it." Similarly, when Sam suggests that he would never put his daughter through the "ordeal" of testifying in a rape trial, one wonders whether it is actually he who would struggle in the courtroom. When Diane refuses to press charges against Cady, she reminds the police that she is "somebody's daughter too." The law, the film suggests, is therefore balanced in the favor of the degenerate, who knows that even the most brutalized (white) girl or woman would never face the indignity of a rape trial or, more important, drag her father through it. In both versions of the film, Sam's descent into vigilantism reflects his reactionary adoption of traditional southern honor codes around gender, jealously protecting "his" women from Cady's sexual threat.

The fact that all of *Cape Fear*'s sexual crimes seem to be constructed to test Sam rather than as violations and even mutilations of individual women's bodies demonstrates a complete disavowal of women's experiences in Scorsese's film. Perhaps a symbolic representation of the South's history of denying women full agency, it is more likely that this marginalization of women is a result of the film's inherently masculine outlook. De Niro's annotations on the original 1962 script imply that he was most intrigued by Cady's violent manipulation of women when it was likely to encourage an emotional response from another man. For example, when Mitchum's Cady describes abducting and raping his ex-wife, he mentions that he made her "sit down and write me a love note . . . askin' me to invite her on a second honeymoon," a tactic clearly designed to torment her new husband. According to De Niro's annotations, Cady's ex-wife's new husband would "always think she might a liked it *just a little* [*sic*]." De Niro also suggested that Cady might "tie [Sam] up to watch Max fuck Nancy & then kill Sam [sic]."[68] Thus, De Niro presents male sexual jealousy and violence as a more powerful narrative construct than the rape of a woman or girl. Whether Scorsese himself is comfortable with the appalling treatment of women in so many of his films or whether, as Annette Wernblad argues, their mistreatment reflects "the emotional state of his male characters, which is often unhealthy and infantile," is hotly debated by critics. However, Scorsese's more recent releases *The Wolf of Wall Street* (2013), *Silence* (2016), and *The Irishman* (2019) have done little to redeem him among feminists, with the first glamorizing the degradation of women and the last affording its most prominent female character just six words of dialogue.[69]

Without Sam's protection, the women of Scorsese's *Cape Fear* appear vulnerable and easily duped. Although they are all initially drawn to Cady as a result of their own disappointment with Sam—Lori as a jilted lover, Leigh as the sexually unsatisfied victim of marital infidelity, and Danielle as a bored teenager resentful of her father's attempts to police her behavior—they are each punished for their attempts to understand Cady on their own terms. However, their penalties are merely collateral damage from the real battle between Sam and Cady. Cady plans to teach *Sam* a lesson by raping Lori, Leigh,

and Danielle. Unlike in the previous *Cape Fear*, all of Cady's victims are connected to Sam, thus expanding the film's emphasis on women as property or
the spoils of war. Reflecting Eve Sedgwick's thesis of "male homosocial desire,"
Stoddart has noted that women exist in *Cape Fear* "insofar as they may be mobilized as the conduits of male/male fear and desire."[70]

Max Cady and the "Christ-Haunted South"

Even though the suggestion of sexual peril was central to Thompson's original movie, it is only in Scorsese's remake that it is conflated with spiritual preoccupations and therefore rendered even more sinister. De Niro's Cady's behavior evokes a psychopathic desire to rape women and girls in the name of
divine justice. As Cady moves toward Leigh on the houseboat, he asks her,
"Ready to be born again, Miz Bowden? A few moments alone with me and
you'll be speaking in tongues." Seeing himself as an avenging angel, Cady's religious inspirations encourage him to violate and dispose of human life that
does not fit his vision of a God-fearing world. By conflating evangelicalism
with sexual violence, Scorsese's film reinforces a host of southern stereotypes
developed around the charismatic nature of many southern faith traditions,
perhaps most prominently seen in *The Night of the Hunter,* based on Davis
Grubb's novel of the same name.

An unsettling vision of rural, Depression-era Appalachia, Charles
Laughton's 1955 adaptation of *Night of the Hunter* sees "Preacher" Harry Powell
(Mitchum) stalking the landscape, marrying, and then murdering women
in the name of the "religion the Almighty and me worked out betwixt us."
Committed to the belief that God hates "perfume-smelling things, lacy things,
things with curly hair," Powell displays an irrational, fanatical disdain for female sexuality despite, or perhaps because, he is drawn to it. Early in the 1955
film, we see Powell at a burlesque club, watching a dancer with a disgusted yet
fixated stare. As his expression develops into a grimace, he clenches his tattooed left hand, which bears the word "HATE," before reaching into his pocket
and releasing his pocketknife, which tears through the fabric of his jacket, providing phallic release. "There's too many of them," he sighs, looking toward
the sky. "Can't kill a world."

When Powell marries Willa Harper (Shelley Winters), he refuses to con-
summate the marriage and chastises his new wife for her sexual advances
while he was praying. "You thought, Willa, that the moment you walked in
that door that I'd start to paw at you in that abominable way that men are supposed to do on their wedding night," he goads her. Forcing her to look in the

Willa Harper (Shelley Winters) preaches of her new life of Christian sacrifice in *The Night of the Hunter* (Charles Laughton, 1955), as Preacher Harry Powell (Robert Mitchum) looks on.

mirror and see herself for what she truly is, "the flesh of Eve that man since Adam has profaned," Powell shames Willa until she looks up, as in prayer, and implores God: "Help me get clean, so I can be what Harry wants me to be." Denied sex, Willa redirects her passion into evangelicalism, hysterically testifying at Harry's tent revivals, repenting her former "sins" of lust and greed.

Stuck between two paradigms, both De Niro's Cady and Mitchum's Powell seem to crave total isolation from a fallen world while paradoxically feeling compelled to "redeem" it. Both are happy to enact violence and even murder in the name of religion: "Not that you mind the killins," Powell prays. "Your book is full of killins." Many religious organizations found Powell's characterization offensive, especially his haunting renditions of the hymn "Leaning on the Everlasting Arms" and direct assertions that he is "a man of God."[71] Ultimately, though, Powell is defeated by the angelic Rachel Cooper (Lillian Gish), whose own rendition of "Leaning" will triumph over Powell's more sinister intonation and reclaim the hymn for its true purpose, inserting the refrain "Leaning on Jesus." Rachel passes on this pure faith to Willa's children, enabling John (Billy Chapin) to overcome his understandable mistrust of religion.

Scorsese's *Cape Fear* offers no such alternative to Cady's religious vision, and the viewer eventually witnesses his appropriately violent death at Sam's hand. According to screenwriter Wesley Strick, "Cady has planned for 14 years to make Sam Bowden suffer acutely, but he truly believes that Bowden's suffering will end in salvation."[72] Like the Misfit in Flannery O'Connor's short story "A Good Man Is Hard to Find," Cady will "shoot [Sam] every minute of [his] life" until he reaches his salvation, his moment of grace.[73] "Remember this," Cady warns Sam in Strick's first draft of the script: "I'm the best thing that ever happened to you. I bring meaning to your spiritless life. What's the New South, anyway? It's the Old South with air conditioning instead of religion. Well you need a baptism! Not that polite sprinkling you Episcopalian-types call a baptism. I'm talking total immersion! Or you'll never get to heaven, counselor."[74] Cady's embodiment of an "Old South" is explicit here, as he chastises the Bowdens for neglecting their spiritual obligations and for their embrace of a consumerist "New" South. "A fine hamlet of the New South," according to Strick, New Essex "has become like the rest of the country: gentrified, yuppified, and concerned only with wealth and comfort. The Bowdens, for [Cady], exemplify that change in their complacency and happiness, in their nice house with their nice daughter in their nice town."[75] Intruding on this world, Cady's presence alerts viewers to the enduring power of the white South's religious culture, as does the crude roadside sign the Bowdens pass on route to the Cape Fear River ("WHERE WILL YOU SPEND ETERNITY?"). Yet, like Cady's message, this sign goes unnoticed by the Bowdens as they speed toward their escape: their houseboat. However, Cady has penetrated their ranks; attached to the underneath of the car, he rides with them to the river, where he will make his final attempt to baptize them.

Cady's grotesque efforts to enact salvation reflect his disturbed religiosity, a faith that permeates Scorsese's southern landscape, perpetuating O'Connor's description of the South as "Christ-haunted."[76] Thus, Cady is both cause and effect: fashioned by his rural pentecostal upbringing but determined to de-

A crude road sign the Bowdens pass en route to their houseboat in *Cape Fear* (Martin Scorsese, 1991), shaped like a cross, reads "WHERE WILL YOU SPEND ETERNITY?"

liver that message to a broader southern audience. Cady's almost supernatural ubiquity thus contributes to *Cape Fear*'s regional aesthetic, echoing tropes of the southern gothic to render Cady "a monster of the South."

"Religious enthusiasm is accepted as one of the South's more grotesque features," O'Connor once wrote. It is thus unsurprising that Cady's "evangelical fervor" consistently terrifies the secular Bowdens.[77] Long before Cady actually descends into glossolalia at the end of the film, his religious rhetoric has proven indecipherable to his victims. Despite his incarnation of an unfettered, politically powerful, and culturally influential Evangelicalism, Cady invokes fear because the Bowdens, and by extension the audience, view him as a grotesque, overblown personification of some of the South's most distinctive tropes, terrifyingly removed from American norms and values. This fear of the unknown, of the repressed identity that lies beyond the city limits, is a cinematic trope as old as Hollywood itself, constantly adapting to reflect the social issues of the day. Channeling Fredric Jameson, Wegner notes that Scorsese's adaptation of an earlier film "creates a narrative space" for the exploration of "current anxieties and contradictions."[78] Whereas the previous Bowdens' anxieties offered a white middle-class response to the civil rights gains of the 1950s and 1960s, Scorsese's Bowdens see something different but not completely removed in the new Cady. His ability to manipulate divisions already at work within the family shows the extent to which the perception of suburban family existence had changed since 1962.

Like their predecessors, Scorsese's Bowdens succeed in killing the Cady that haunts them, but unable or unwilling to recognize their own prejudices and anxieties, they suppress rather than acknowledge the reasons they fear him in the first place. Throughout the film, Danielle is constantly told "Don't look" or "Go to your room" by her parents. They encourage her to avoid that which scares her, a process confirmed at both the beginning and the end of the film in Danielle's monologues. As the film begins, she reminisces about her idyllic childhood, reflecting, "the only thing to fear on those enchanted summer nights was that the magic would end and real life would come crashing in." As soon as this line is delivered, the music shifts to the menacing horns of Bernstein's score that will so often accompany Cady's appearance. The camera shifts immediately to our first shot of Cady, and it is clear that he represents "real life" about to "come crashing in." However, at the film's end, Danielle confirms that the family "never spoke about what happened [with Cady], at least not to each other. Fear, I suppose, that to remember his name and what he did would mean letting him in to our dreams . . . if you hang onto the past, you die a little every day," she concludes. Denial allows the Bowdens to "live."

Cady's religious devotion, constructed in lewd, unrestrained terms, has presented the Bowdens with existential questions that they choose to ignore, allowing Scorsese to leave the lingering sense that their issues—individually, as a family, and even as a nation—have not been fully confronted, let alone resolved. A morally compromised, yet in many ways archetypal American family, the Bowdens are tormented by the inheritance of their ancestors' repressions. That a southern religious zealot should act as agent and focus for their anxieties betrays the film's links to the social and political milieu of the 1980s and 1990s. For Strick, the presentation of Cady's "Pentecostalism" reflected years of liberal outcry about the dominant political position of evangelical Christians in American political culture, having entered the public consciousness in the late 1970s. Regardless of qualifications between fundamentalist Protestants and more culturally liberal evangelical groups, historian George Marsden writes, "the news in the decades since the 1960s is that a wide variety of evangelical traditions that earlier would have been thought of as culturally marginal . . . have been mobilized into a significant mainstream national political force" with a "conspicuously southern leadership best exemplified by Jerry Falwell, Pat Robertson and James Robison." Southern white prejudice, it seemed, extended beyond African Americans, as the religious right publicly defended their moral crusade in the name of the nuclear "American family" and proved strong opponents to campaigns for gay rights, abortion, and a host of other issues that apparently compromised "family values." Transplanted southerners who had left the region both before and after World War II added to this sense of a southern-led movement and contributed to evangelical success across the Midwest and in Southern California.[79]

It is likely that Strick had these conservative religious groups in mind when he described Cady's Pentecostalism as "the most kind of primitive, and to me, as a New York Jew, the most terrifying."[80] To Strick, rural southern evangelicals symbolized excessive intolerance, racism, and ignorance and represented a unique threat to his personal liberty. That Cady is a "pentecostal" does not simply indicate denominational preference but suggests zealous fanaticism. As Thomas Long has argued, "'Evangelism,' a broader term, is for many people a frankly nose wrinkling word, a term they hold in approximately the same regard as 'professional wrestling.' Both are considered to be activities that draw large uncritical crowds, involve a measure of sham, work on irrational emotions and could end up hurting somebody." Indeed, Long suggests that the suffix "-ism" probably produced some of these image problems, as "ism words [often] refer to social movements and have about them the aroma of ideological strife and party politics," as well as "cells of true believers who devotedly practice the ism, such as anarchists, Maoists, terrorists, or fundamentalists." It is not surprising, then, Long concludes, that even "many church people come to think of evangelism as a kind of partisan activity practiced only by a cadre of special zealots called evangelists."[81]

"A Six-Foot Palmetto Bug": Cady as Southern Demagogue

In an early draft of his screenplay, Strick describes Cady's passionate verbal deliveries as "Jimmy Swaggart meets Huey Long in hell," a description that fuses the disgraced pentecostal evangelist with a charismatic, populist politician of the early twentieth century.[82] According to this characterization, there is little distinction between how a southern preacher might deliver his sermon and the overt revanchism of some of the white South's most notorious politicians. This similarity, as least as it is represented in popular culture, reflects a more symbolic manifestation of the constructed "southern demagogue," whose assumed origins in racial politics have become conflated with the urgency and passion of the fundamentalist preacher, forming a deeply gendered and class-based understanding of how white southerners have used rhetoric to influence public life in the region. The power of the southern racial demagogue archetype has ensured that even southern populists whose contribution to racial tensions are much more ambiguous, most notably Huey Long himself, have been absorbed into a characterization that continues to contribute to the constructions of southern race, gender, class, and religiosity. Dubbed "the Messiah of the rednecks" by Arthur Schlesinger, Long's appeal among the lower classes has ensured his longevity as "the poster child for an especially insidious brand of demagoguery."[83]

Serving as governor and then senator for Louisiana in the late 1920s and early 1930s, Long divided political opinion. He claimed that his wealth-distribution policies came directly from God and regularly read biblical passages aloud. Despite never descending into the incendiary racial rhetoric of many of his contemporaries, Long and his supporters have been chastised and even ridiculed by historians and rhetoricians: terms such as "peasants," "peanut-fed people," and "hillbillies," all indicative of a class-based rather than ideological disdain for Long's populism.[84] Cady's characterization reflects this cultural bias. Although Cady is a criminal, the Bowdens judge him long before they know his history. They are repelled by his garish clothes, crude tattoos, and his general demeanor, all of which they consider vulgar. Long was famous for adopting styles and behaviors considered entirely inappropriate in politics, from wearing pajamas in diplomatic meetings to his central role in a 1931 national debate over corn pone and pot likker.[85] But like the politician, Cady is acutely self-aware. He takes the very insults he knows will be thrown at him—white trash, hillbilly, cracker—and actually amplifies those aspects of his appearance and behavior. When the Bowdens first encounter Cady in the cinema, he is loud and obnoxious, actively courting their revulsion without revealing his actual identity. In an early draft of the script, Cady describes his prison sentence among the "rednecks": "Comic books and cornpone music all day," he remembers. "And I don't wanna say what at night."[86]

In Strick's original screenplay, Cady shows an apparent pride in the South, a place he defines as "slow" but where "anything can happen." More specifically, and in a comment omitted from the final script, Cady celebrates the region's simultaneous histories of racial violence and consumer innovation, arguing that "Confederate folk invented supermarkets, Coca-Cola, lynchings." Similarly removed from the final script, Danielle's designation of Cady as a "revolting redneck" after he disturbs the family in the cinema with his raucous laughter demonstrates the teenager's assumptions about Cady's intelligence: "I wanted to say, 'Even if [the film] was that funny, *you* wouldn't get it.'" The family's understanding of the word "redneck" is clarified moments later when Danielle and Sam belt out Johnny Russell's 1973 country hit "Rednecks, White Socks, and Blue Ribbon Beer."[87] It is not clear whether Strick decided to remove these passages himself or whether he faced pressure from other people working on the film, but there is a consistent pattern of Strick's more overt characterizations disappearing as the script developed.

The Cady evident in the final screenplay is far too self-aware to associate himself with racial violence of any kind. Yet, despite his intelligence, Cady's conversation remains colloquial and at times ungrammatical, echoing that of Huey Long. Just as historians have argued Long's public persona was surely cultivated, Cady shows that he can adopt alternate personas if and when it aids his mission. Ben Tillman, governor and later senator for South Carolina at the turn of the twentieth century, admitted that he "acted the demagogue at times . . . because I was opposed so unscrupulously I had to defend myself and fight the devil with fire."[88] Similarly, there is no reason to believe Cady's "natural," criminal white-trash identity is any less consciously constructed than the other roles he fulfills while terrorizing the Bowdens. Indeed, as Kirsten Thompson recognizes, "Cady is a master impersonator of class, race, and gender, and as part of his dramaturgy of terror, he performs multiple roles: innocent citizen, accident victim, pot-smoking drama teacher, nuclear power protestor, Danny's father, sympathetic guidance counselor, and in literal drag, Graciella, the Bowdens' maid."[89] By drawing attention to, rather than attempting to hide, his rural roots, Cady is able to take pride in the progress he believes he has made, both physically and intellectually. When he rapes and tortures Lori, he is not only attempting to punish Sam but to showcase his "superiority" over an educated woman who has patronized and mocked him.[90]

Indeed, rather than resent the existence of the term "white trash," Cady re-purposes it to abuse others. In an attempt to validate his newly acquired education and money, Cady demeans those who rape him in prison as "hairy hillbillies": an image that Wegner argues "brings to mind the infamous rape scene in John Boorman's *Deliverance* and one of the classic American fantasies about the menace of the white rural South. But here, Cady identifies himself with the earlier film's urban victims, rather than with its mountain-men perpetrators."[91]

Cady also takes extra pleasure in murdering private detective Kersek, who has previously referred to him as a "white trash piece of shit" and a "six-foot Palmetto bug." When Cady murders Kersek, he relishes in returning the insult; standing over his latest victim, he asks, "How do you like that, you white trash piece of shit?" At this point, Cady is disguised as the Bowdens' Latina maid, Graciella (Zully Montero), adding a further complexity to the racial and class-based significance of this epithet. If Cady's threat is mostly communicated through religious and class distinctions, Kirsten Thompson argues that his impersonation of the maid suggests that figuratively it is also Graciella who "rises up and tries to slaughter her class oppressors."[92]

Whereas the original film was cast in purely Black and white racial terms, the addition of Graciella to the story, and indeed the fact that Cady can literally become her and dispose of her, helps reflect the evolving demographics of the modern South. Between 1970 and 2010, African Americans maintained a remarkably stable percentage of the southern population, constituting 19–20 percent. However, while the southern Hispanic community grew from 7 percent to 17.6 percent in the same period, white populations declined from 79.3 percent to 58.3 percent.[93] Thus, although the anxieties evident in the later *Cape Fear* reflect an increasingly complex response to the political and social climate of the late 1980s and early 1990s, they perhaps reflect a "new" source of white racial anxiety. Cady never expresses any racial prejudice, but the suggestion is always there because the film encourages viewers to connect him to other white southern archetypes whose racial intolerance has become legendary. Through Cady's construction, Scorsese is able to communicate a white southerner whose intersecting poverty, religiosity, and criminality can suggest traditional Black-white southern racial anxieties in a film that contains no African American characters.

Remembering the 1960s

Cady's manipulation of the law in the later *Cape Fear* suggests that many "ordinary," white middle-class Americans in the late 1980s and early 1990s were as concerned about immigration and the political rise of evangelicals as their predecessors had been about the dismantling of racial segregation. Acknowledging the 1960s as a period of immense cultural change, Scorsese's *Cape Fear*, like so many other cultural products, divides Americans over their interpretation of and commitment to the legacy of the 1960s. Despite being overtly repackaged and manipulated by capitalism, as Thomas Frank has argued, the popular understanding of "the sixties" is "as the decade of the big change, the birthplace of our own culture, the homeland of hip, an era of which the tastes and discoveries and passions, however obscure their origins, have somehow determined the world in which we are condemned to live."[94] For many conservatives, however, the sixties, counterculture, and the New Left are often interchangeably responsible for the decline of traditional "American identity."

Engaged in an intertextual dialogue with Thompson's original film, Scorsese's *Cape Fear* uses these debates over the legacy of the 1960s to explore social, racial, gender, and religious change in the United States. The film's references to Henry Miller contribute to this dialogue; after all, the book is only available to Cady, and by extension Danielle, because of the anticensorship hearings of the 1960s. Although Sam and Leigh would undoubtedly have welcomed such decisions, the consequences of the liberalizing forces of the 1960s seemingly make it harder for them to protect their daughter. In the film's conservative outlook, the legacy of the 1960s has come back to haunt the Bowdens.

This difference of opinion when remembering—or imagining—the 1960s is crucial to understanding the liberal-conservative divide in the late twentieth-century United States, a gulf that was consistently reinforced by both sides and implied the absence of a middle ground. We know "what goes with what" in American politics, Thomas Carsey and Geoffrey Layman argued in 2014, noting that "opposition to tax increases and opposition to abortion go together as 'conservative' positions in our current politics because the Republican Party put them together." Broader cultural divisions are easily built on these foundations, especially given the moral, or highly emotive, charge with which so many issues are discussed and presented to the electorate. Carsey and Layman provide the example of abortion, which they argue is "a fairly complex issue about which many people have rather ambivalent feelings." However, the fact that it "is nearly always presented as a pro-life versus pro-choice dichotomy" ensures "overheated rhetoric," often with "moral and religious underpinnings."[95]

This amplified sense of polarization helps to explain the very clear distinctions at the beginning of Scorsese's *Cape Fear*. The Bowdens appear secular, liberal, and educated. We can quite easily assume their political leanings even before they are pitted against a rural, religious fanatic. Like the white southerners who murder the counterculture bikers at the end of *Easy Rider* (Dennis Hopper, 1969), Cady is a grotesque manifestation of the conservative backlash against supposedly decadent, irresponsible liberalism, constantly reminding the Bowdens that their smug complicity with contemporary consumerism contributes to an illusion of social change that has left millions of Americans in the cold. "You think you're better than me," Cady observes before forcing them to face the hypocrisy he sees in their lifestyle.

The film's burlesque, overblown presentation of an exceptional South often renders Cady's professed religious concerns absurd, just as *Night of the Hunter* works to discredit its tattooed, demonic "preacher." The overt influence of this earlier film on Scorsese's *Cape Fear* provides an interesting insight into the particularly southern and religious aspects of the project. Extrapolating his own concerns about the rise of the religious right, screenwriter Wesley Strick presented a contemporary indictment of evangelical Christians within a timeless southern landscape scarred by racial terrorism and religious extremism: a land of demagogues and vigilantism. Despite the considerable research undertaken, the film offers little nuance in its presentation of Pentecostalism or Appalachia. Indeed, both of these things, irreparably linked through the narrative, exist entirely within Cady: their wider geographic and cultural significance denied. Pentecostalism serves as an indicator of a world the film's producers did not wish to understand, and yet it offers visual and rhetorical tropes used to indicate the rural horrors of unknown America. Thus, the film manages to discredit Pentecostalism without ever engaging in a theological or even political debate, offering an enduring indictment of distinctly southern religious cultures rooted in the past and yet distinctly shaped by the culture wars of the present.

CHAPTER 5

"You Don't See Billy Graham Walking Any Picket Lines"

Redefining the Civil Rights Genre in the "Age of Obama"

Since the release of Alan Parker's *Mississippi Burning* in 1988, Hollywood film-makers have returned to the civil rights movement and its legacy numerous times, with cinematic interpretations of the civil rights struggles of the 1950s and 1960s a proven and marketable way to wrestle with more contemporary racial issues too. These films helped to construct and uphold dominant ideas of the movement and its legacy, often distorting public memory with depictions of passive Black martyrs unable to organize and liberate themselves. This is especially evident in the civil rights melodrama, which encompasses a range of white-centric civil rights narratives produced between 1988 and the late 1990s. As a result of this trend, scholarly criticism has tended to focus on the white savior complex evident in but not exclusive to the civil rights drama.[1]

However, as this book has shown, in pitting dignified Black Protestants and their white secular allies against zealous Klansmen in a simplified battle of good versus evil, cinematic constructions of the civil rights movement and its legacies frequently rely on popular preconceptions about Protestantism in the American South to further entrench conceptualizations of the civil rights movement and its legacies as a battle within, rather than as a result of, white-ness. Because Hollywood requires clearly delineated divisions when it wrestles with any period of social change, it simplifies ideologies and personalities in pursuit of streamlined narratives. Its portrayals of southern religion therefore often magnify regional, racial, class, and educational distinctions, implying a united African American quest toward freedom curtailed due to irreconcilable divisions of educational attainment, income, and racial attitudes among southern whites. This fanatically violent, segregationist South is best exemplified by the Ku Klux Klan, which Hollywood seldom contrasts alongside other, more moderate supporters of Jim Crow. The result is a continued conflation of white southern evangelicalism with reactionary, even racist, politics, the complete omission of the moderate segregationist, and a consistent failure to acknowledge white Americans who were compelled by their faith to join the civil rights movement.

Hollywood's foregrounding of white secular righteousness is therefore rooted in popular ideas of poor white southerners as irrationally religious as well as racist. *Mississippi Burning*, for example, offers no local theological, social, or political alternative to the Klan, which is pitted solely against the secular, federal power of the FBI, ensuring that the film's heroes and villains are starkly opposed. In *Ghosts of Mississippi*, the intersection of Byron De La Beckwith's extreme racial views with his vengeful religious preoccupations proved central to the film's communication of his distinctly southern, almost archaic identity. However, it is in its portrayal of its white savior, Assistant District Attorney Bobby DeLaughter, that the film manipulates the religious leanings of its characters, omitting the faith that DeLaughter openly admitted guided his actions when bringing Beckwith to justice. Like most civil rights dramas, *Ghosts of Mississippi* reserves white religiosity only for fringe extremists.

By way of contrast, Ava DuVernay's *Selma* (2014) exposes and expands the limited projection of religion in previous films and highlights a broad landscape of religious thought in the freedom struggle, as Martin Luther King Jr. (David Oyelowo) urges people of all faiths to march in pursuit of African American voting rights in Selma, Alabama, in 1965. In the film, as in reality, the response was both "rapid and astonishing," christened "The Charge of the Bible Brigade" by *Ramparts* magazine. "Never in the history of the United States has organized religion collaborated to such an extent on an issue of social justice," Warren Hinckle and David Welsh wrote at the time. "The clergymen did not merely exhort—they led the way."[2] Thus, although *Selma* undoubtedly centralizes the role of Black activists in the campaign, it acknowledges the ecumenical and racial solidarity crucial to its eventual legislative success, making an essential narrative point about the universal morality of King's message, directed in the film to "men and women of God and goodwill everywhere." In so doing, *Selma* is the first mainstream civil rights drama that uses religion to unite rather than divide its characters.

In response to the film, critics and journalists have explored *Selma*'s use of spiritual music and raised questions about its omission of Rabbi Abraham

Joshua Heschel.[3] Conservative evangelicals questioned the visible absence of their forebearers in King's "beloved community," including "America's Pastor," Billy Graham. This chapter examines these debates, alongside the film's inspired use of religious and secular music, which marks another break with the traditions of the white-centric civil rights drama. By focusing on what makes *Selma* so different from its predecessors, we can remind ourselves of the predominant tropes when exploring issues of race and religion in Hollywood's South.

Of course, *Selma*'s divergence from its predecessors encompasses more than simply its presentation of religion, and this chapter will also explore the broader historical significance of civil rights cinema as produced during the early twenty-first century. Directed by an African American woman in time for the fiftieth anniversary of the 1965 Voting Rights Act (which was gutted by the Supreme Court eighteen months earlier in June 2013), *Selma* remains the closest Hollywood has come to a biopic of Martin Luther King Jr. However, Ava DuVernay intentionally focused on a specific period in King's life and the wider movement rather than stretching her narrative across decades.[4]

Selma was also released during the second term of the nation's first Black president, who screened it at the White House, and amid the first wave of the Black Lives Matter movement, which developed in response to a series of Black killings at the hands and weapons of law enforcement officers and white citizens. Indeed, *Selma*'s cast and crew wore T-shirts saying "I Can't Breathe" to their December 2014 New York City premiere, following the July 17, 2014, death of Eric Garner, who was placed in a prohibited chokehold by a New York Police Department officer during an attempted arrest for allegedly selling individual cigarettes without a license. When promoting *Selma*, DuVernay, Oyelowo, and other cast members also drew connections between the film and the recent uprisings in Ferguson, Missouri, prompted by the fatal shooting of eighteen-year-old Michael Brown by local officers on August 9, 2014. The initial wave of unrest in Ferguson lasted for around two weeks following the shooting but erupted again in November 2014 when a grand jury failed to indict the officer who had shot Brown. "Ferguson is a mirror of the past. And Selma is a mirror of now," DuVernay wrote. "We are in a sad, distorted continuum. It's time to really look in that mirror."[5] Despite the significance of this historical moment, debates about *Selma* in the mainstream press implied that its depiction of President Lyndon B. Johnson was its most significant contribution to the memory of the civil rights movement, reflecting a continued prioritization of whiteness within national discourse, despite or perhaps because of DuVernay's efforts to depart from such preoccupations in her vision of 1965.

"You Will Hate *Selma* but Should Watch It Anyway": White Evangelical Responses to *Selma*

Historians have long debated the roles—and absences—of various white religious congregations during the civil rights era, but *Selma* is the first mainstream drama to do so.[6] Unprecedented among civil rights cinema, *Selma* highlights mainstream white religious responsibility, as King chastises hypocritical white ministers who quote the Bible but "remain silent before their white congregations." He equates these clergymen with politicians and law enforcement officers who blindly accept and enforce segregation and brutality. Following the horrific violence inflicted on marchers at the Edmund Pettus Bridge on March 7, 1965, King uses the media to appeal directly to white clergy. Yet, in highlighting the later murders of Boston minister James Reeb (Jeremy Strong) and Detroit activist Viola Liuzzo (Tara Ochs)—both Unitarian Universalists—*Selma* suggests that the enlightened whites that heeded King's call were likely to be northern and certainly not from the evangelical denominations that dominated the southern religious landscape.

As evangelicals questioned the conspicuous absence of their denominations in *Selma*'s depiction of King's beloved community, Southern Baptist pastor Jon Speed titled his review of the film "You Will Hate Selma but Should Watch It Anyway." Reflecting on King's message "to men and women of God and goodwill everywhere," Speed was faced with the invisibility of his own denominational forebearers among the mainline Protestants or the Eastern Orthodox. "Where were the conservative evangelicals?" Speed wrote. "It makes me cringe to type it, but I suspect they were on the other side of the bridge. They were standing with the Alabama State Troopers. If they weren't standing with them in body, perhaps they were in spirit. Maybe they were watching it on television with 70 million other viewers cheering on the police."[7]

Sharing Speed's anxieties about *Selma*, the Gospel Coalition (TGC), a network of evangelical and Reformed churches, looked to religious historians for answers, publishing a series of specially commissioned articles from scholars working on segregation and religion in the twentieth-century South. One such historian, J. Russell Hawkins, reiterated the National Association of Evangelicals' blunt response to King's 1965 call to clergy: the association "has a policy of not becoming involved in political or sociological affairs that do not affect the function of the church or those involved in the propagation of the gospel."[8] In another post, Carolyn Dupont argued that "any suggestion that the religion of southern whites aided the civil rights struggle grossly perverts the past." While "every major denomination in the United States embraced the Supreme Court's *Brown v Board of Education* decision that declared segregated schools unconstitutional. . . the picture looks very different at the local level, where southern evangelicals more often fought ferociously against any effort to dismantle the system of white supremacy."[9] The fact that such a conversation occurred on TGC's website is testament to the skill with which *Selma* forces audiences to acknowledge those present at the marches but also ask questions of those who were not, prompting a long-overdue reflection, within Hollywood cinema at least, of the place of so-called white moderates during the civil rights era.

Billy Graham

A decade before *Selma*'s release, Billy Graham, the most prominent American evangelist of the mid-twentieth century, lamented his own absence from the 1965 marches, calling it "a mistake."[10] In the mid-1960s, Graham had called for all parties to come together "in a spirit of Christian love, understanding and brotherhood" but released a statement arguing that it was "wrong for people in other parts of the country to point an accusing self-righteous finger at Alabama." Deeming the state "a whipping boy," Graham argued, "the [race] problem is just as acute" elsewhere. This language of "finger-pointing" was classic Graham; he had previously argued that "few parts of the world can point a self-righteous finger at Little Rock," during the 1957 desegregation crisis at Central High School, or "convict Philadelphia [Mississippi]," following the murder of three civil rights workers in 1964.[11] In the wake of the September 1963 Sixteenth Street Church bombing that killed four young girls in Birmingham, Alabama, which DuVernay powerfully evokes in the opening minutes of *Selma*, Graham parroted "growing suspicion that the bombings may be from professionals outside Alabama who want to keep the racial problem at fever pitch in the South."[12]

As Michael Long has argued, Graham was far from wrong in recognizing that racism was more than a southern problem. However, Graham failed to appreciate the tactics of the civil rights movement, which consciously foregrounded specific towns, cities, and individuals, "personalizing the system of racism" in order that it might inspire outrage and direct action. Although Graham bailed Martin Luther King Jr. out of jail in Albany, Georgia, in 1962, he was wary of the movement's increased emphasis on direct action campaigns and largely avoided the Deep South during some of the most significant years of racial turbulence. Much of this was the result of a grueling international schedule, but it left civil rights leaders disappointed.[13] Graham had famously integrated his revivals in 1953—leading to some southern states' first officially interracial mass gatherings—and shared a stage with King in 1957. But he also shared platforms with segregationists, which King warned him "can well be interpreted as your endorsement of racial segregation and discrimination."[14]

A native of North Carolina, Billy Graham rose to prominence against a backdrop of rising evangelical power, reflected through the development of a large umbrella organization, the National Association of Evangelicals (NAE), in 1942. This movement, which boasted over a million members by 1960, was overwhelmingly white, just as it had been at its founding. In the immediate postwar era, the NAE rose to meet the acutely perceived threat to American life and Christianity: communism. A staunch Cold Warrior, Graham's immense popularity developed in the late 1940s and early 1950s, the result of some prominent revivals in Los Angeles and a subsequently relentless cross-country schedule. Here, Graham preached what Anthea D. Butler calls "the dual importance of personal salvation and resistance to communism," when many in the evangelical movement cited civil rights activity as a communist front. Graham acknowledged racism as a sin "but was unwilling to break ranks with the white status quo."[15] He offered counsel to Black and white ministers and politicians and was commonly asked by presidents to act as something as a go-between when tensions became particularly pronounced or direct-action campaigns seemed imminent. By the early 1960s, Graham's caution with regard to direct action had evolved into outright rejection. Meanwhile, he sought to remind Americans that racial equality was impossible before the Second Coming of Christ. Thus, although King did not name Graham in his April 1963 "Letter from Birmingham Jail," many assumed that Graham was included in King's conceptualization of "the white moderate, who is more devoted to 'order' than to justice . . . who constantly says: 'I agree with you in the goal you seek, but I cannot agree with your methods of direct action.'" Like the Alabama clergymen whose indictment of King's "extreme" actions prompted the letter in the first place, Graham publicly encouraged his "good personal friend" King to "put the brakes on a little bit," as protests in Birmingham, Alabama, confronted brutal segregation and political apathy. "What I would like to see," Graham continued, "is a period of quietness, in which moderation prevails."[16]

Morality would ultimately prevail in Birmingham, as President John F. Kennedy later told the nation that events there "and elsewhere have so increased the cries for equality that no city or State or legislative body can prudently choose to ignore them." Images of city police violently confronting student and child protesters contributed to a growing geography of unrest in the South and ultimately forced Kennedy to finally acknowledge that the United States was "confronted primarily with a moral issue. It is as old as the scriptures and is as clear as the American Constitution." He would use this speech, on June 11, 1963, to propose federal civil rights legislation.[17] Twelve days later, a triumphant King offered an emboldened defense of direct action to those who told him "to put on brakes" in Birmingham: "the motor's now cranked up and we're moving up the highway of freedom toward the city of equality, and we can't afford to stop now because our nation has a date with destiny. We must keep moving."[18]

The following summer, the prolific African American journalist Chuck Stone lamented Graham's inability to "come out and unqualifiedly denounce racial segregation and those who practice it." Writing in the *Chicago Defender*, Stone argued that "in an era which nurtures middle-class mediocrity and phony religious values, Rev. Billy Graham is exactly what we Americans deserve," noting that Graham had never "walk[ed] any picket lines or even admit[ted] they have a spiritual redemption for the sinner." According to Stone, Graham's "attitude and pronouncements on the racial crisis in America attained soiled apotheosis" when the esteemed evangelist "pontificated that the racial crisis would be solved at 'the foot of the cross of Jesus Christ.'" Stone compared this "vapid and silly declaration" to a recent statement from Reverend John Cronin of the Catholic Welfare Conference in which Cronin argued that clergymen "should be in the forefront of demonstrations to show our support for the civil rights movement."[19]

Half a century later, Jon Speed turned to his evangelical blog, *Gospel Spam*, to process his reflections on the newly released *Selma*, Hollywood's latest foray into the civil rights era. "When Martin Luther King, Jr. called for men of faith to come to *Selma* to march with him," Speed wrote, "Billy Graham wasn't there."[20] And yet, despite this visible absence among King's "people of God and goodwill" and Graham's own acknowledgment that avoiding Selma had been a mistake, America's Pastor's legacy remains largely intact, supported by politicians, the popular media, and scholars unable to subdue their admiration for the man who led interracial revivals but who, by his own admission, failed to support direct action in word or deed. Criticizing Graham in the twenty-first century can still provoke "the thundering wrath of his devoted partisans" that Chuck Stone noted in 1964.[21]

On Graham's death at age ninety-nine, historian Matthew Avery Sutton offered a conclusive break with the dominant narrative: "Graham was on the wrong side of history."[22] But Graham's legacy was not merely his own, as Jemar Tisby notes. Coming less than four years after *Selma*'s release, Graham's death prompted considerable soul-searching on the role of evangelical churches in the fight for racial justice, past and present. The first faith leader to lie in honor in the U.S. Capitol Rotunda, Graham profoundly shaped U.S. evangelical culture "into one that is prone to looking at personal sin while failing to consider how society's sins are upheld by unjust structures."[23] Like the majority of white evangelicals of his era, Graham favored evangelizing over the Social Gospel, writing in 1964 that "some men have made the race question their gospel. That is not the Gospel."[24] On Graham's advice, President Johnson advocated a Day of Prayer in response to the 1965 Watts uprisings. But Martin Luther King's response was damning: "I take prayer too seriously to use it as an excuse for avoiding work and responsibility."[25] "Prayer is a marvellous supplement of our feeble efforts," King preached, "but it is a dangerous and callous substitute." Here, King recalled a man who, like Graham, advised that "Negroes should stop protesting and start praying."[26] With such differing views on the intersections of religion and political power, it is therefore unsurprising that Graham was not compelled to Selma by King's call to clergy, but his absence, as documented in DuVernay's film, proved an enduring symbol of the failure of white moderates of his generation.

Selma and the Black Church

Positioning its Black churches as both religious and political sites, Ava DuVernay's representation of African American clergy and religiosity is central to *Selma*'s diversion from the white-centric narratives of previous civil rights melodramas, demonstrating the regularity with which King and others skillfully intertwined Black and white evangelical traditions with contempo-

Martin Luther King Jr. (David Oyelowo) demands the right to vote from a pulpit in Selma, Alabama, in *Selma* (Ava DuVernay, 2014).

rary political concerns within the walls of Black Protestant institutions. All too often, Eddie Glaude has written, "the prophetic energies of black churches are represented as something inherent to the institution" rather than the result of the concerted effort of individuals.[27] Not so in *Selma*, where King's first speech on arrival in Alabama is met with a rapturous reception in a Black Methodist church, the congregation united, not in a meek rendition of a hymn akin to the presentation of Black churches in *Mississippi Burning* but in their vocal, political demand: "Give us the vote! Give us the vote!"

Where other films have downplayed or even degraded Black political activity within the walls of the church in favor of a more uniformed, unthreatening spirituality, *Selma* does not shy from it. When eulogizing Jimmie Lee Jackson, murdered by an Alabama state trooper during a peaceful protest, King does not just implicate the man who pulled the trigger but "every negro man and woman who stands by without joining this fight as their brothers and sisters are humiliated, brutalized and ripped from this earth." In the final words of his eulogy, King speaks directly to the murdered Jackson: "We will vote. We will put these men out of office. We will take their power; we will win what you were slaughtered for. We're going back to Washington. We're going to demand to see the President. . . . If he does not act, we will!" Suzanne E. Smith recognizes this as "a type of political theater to dramatize the cause of the movement and energize its followers." Determined to incite rather than soothe, the civil rights funeral had become a "direct catalyst for activism."[28]

In *Selma*, King is visibly distressed following his eulogy for Jackson, but the scene cuts quickly to his discussions with other movement leaders about the demands and priorities of their voting rights campaign: "We know [President] Johnson can't see the full picture, so let's paint it for him." The deftness with which the film moves from the pulpit to this political debate shows how, unlike previous white-centric Hollywood representations of the civil rights movement, DuVernay's vision draws little distinction between religious and political gatherings. Many of the same people, and certainly many of the same ideas, are found at both. However, in its commitment to King's leadership, *Selma* obscures the fact that it was SCLC director of direct action James Bevel who actually used Jackson's death to inspire the march from Selma to Montgomery, perhaps due to crimes and controversies in his later life, including convictions for incest.[29] In 1965, Bevel publicly likened Governor George Wallace to King Herod, who "laid violent hands" on Jesus's followers. Speaking just hours after Jimmie Lee Jackson's death, Bevel then shifted his biblical focus to the Old Testament story of Esther, who sought counsel with the king and protection for her people. "We must go to Montgomery and see the king!" Bevel advocated. "The blood of Jackson will be on our hands if we don't march. Be prepared to walk to Montgomery. Be prepared to sleep on the highways."[30]

Music in *Selma*

Constantly evolving and adapting, the civil rights movement depicted in *Selma* exists within a broad cultural and political landscape. Music is crucial to this sense of dynamic individuals and the movements they created, balancing the contemporary with the historical to replicate a range of voices, tactics, and legacies rather than a static image of the Selma campaign. Just as Martin Luther King Jr. remains contextualized among a range of other figures, the film does not pursue a particular historical sound to the exclusion of others. Rather, music supervisor Morgan Rhodes was clear that her musical choices were intended to link *Selma*'s protesters to their collective history, reflecting the power of African American music across generations of struggle. From the release of the film's first trailer, commentators noted an audible shift from the patterns of Hollywood's historical dramas as well as the civil rights genre itself. Rather than foregrounding "period-appropriate music about racial equality," Mark Blankenship noted in November 2014, *Selma*'s first trailer featured Public Enemy's "Say It like It Really Is," described as "a furious, modern hip-hop song, pounding us with beats and the promise of a revolution."[31] The trailer thus reflected *Selma*'s commitment to an unflinching examination of the legacy of the civil rights movement and signaled its capacity to provoke deeper, more probing questions than its cinematic forebearers in the civil rights genre. It also linked the film with bold explorations of African American identity like Spike Lee's *Do the Right Thing* (1989), which prominently featured Public Enemy's "Fight the Power."

Celebrating rather than obscuring the political will displayed in the voting rights campaign, Morgan Rhodes selected Martha Bass's rendition of the spiritual "Walk with Me" for *Selma* in an effort to communicate "generations of freedom fighters and generations of struggle."[32] Backed by full choir, Bass's powerful delivery of the spiritual provides a composed yet mournful soundtrack to the chaos of the visual scene as marchers are assaulted at the hands of Alabama law enforcement on what is now known as Bloody Sunday. While the original footage seen by millions in news reports offers a clear view of the initial confrontation between law enforcement officers and marchers, this optimal camera angle was lost once the marchers were pushed further and further back toward the Edmund Pettus Bridge. Obstructed by police cars and tear gas, the main scenes of violence and altercation soon became unclear to viewers, who, as media historian Aniko Bodroghkozy writes, "had to imagine,

In *Selma*, Ava DuVernay re-creates the violent attack that Alabama law enforcement inflicted on civil rights protesters on the Edmund Pettus Bridge on Bloody Sunday, March 7, 1965.

with the audio assistance of disembodied shrieks and screams, what was going on behind the car and inside the clouds of tear gas."[33] In contrast, "DuVernay's film puts viewers right in the center of the violence as marchers choke on the gas, their bodies bludgeoned by state troopers' clubs."[34] Kenn Rabin, *Selma's* archive producer, agreed that filming this sequence anew in color—rather than relying on the archival footage he knew so well from researching *Eyes on the Prize*—proved crucial to the scene's power. "Seeing the actors that we'd gotten to know throughout the film take on that devastating punishment, rather than their historical counterparts in black and white archival, struck me as exactly the right way to handle that very emotional and galvanizing sequence,"

Rabin argued.[35] *Selma* "asks viewers to be with the marchers," Bodroghkozy concurs, "sharing and participating in their brutalization."[36]

Supplementing DuVernay's camera angles, which put audiences in the midst of the action, "Walk with Me" becomes more than just a plea for God's grace and deliverance.[37] It forces viewers to acknowledge their position among the marchers and the violence they are witnessing. Rhodes claims that she was attracted to the words "tedious journey" in the song, which she equated to the journey across the Edmund Pettus Bridge.[38] Even though "tedious" may seem an unlikely description for an event that was surely terrifying, Rhodes understands the word here as synonymous with "wearisome," a reference to the sheer length of the journey: both physically, as it is over fifty miles from Selma to Montgomery, but also historically.[39] Selma's activists were building on an African American struggle that began with the arrival of the first enslaved Africans. As a spiritual, the song "had travelled over the generations," Rhodes advocated, "from slaves singing it to now, this critical moment in civil rights history."[40]

With its specific references to the book of Revelation, Sister Gertrude Morgan's up-tempo "I've Got the New World in My View" was another important religious choice for Rhodes, heard as protesters march to demand their right to register to vote at the Dallas County courthouse. Advised by King that they "have clear avenues of approach to a defined battle zone," the marchers descend on "a citadel defended by fanatics . . . the perfect stage." As King's words fade into Sister Morgan's vocals, her lyrics reflect the desire for change: "I got the new world in my view / On my journey I pursue / Said I'm running / Running for the city / I got the new world in my view."[41] "People were marching for rights that they did not yet enjoy," Rhodes explained, but they "had a vision of the world that they wanted."[42] This emphasis on agency reflects a key distinction between *Selma* and its predecessors in the civil rights genre. Where previous films have relied on muted hymns offering the promise of eventual deliverance to soundtrack scenes of African American suffering, *Selma* articulates the movement's commitment to earthly change through bold political action and profound religious witness, accompanied by a diverse musical selection that encompasses gospel, soul, and contemporary R & B/rap.

Rhodes largely avoids movement classics such as "We Shall Overcome," though an audio recording of activists singing a medley of "This Little Light of Mine/Come by Here" at Jimmie Lee Jackson's funeral follows plays toward the end of the closing credits.[43] "I thought it was a good way to end," Rhodes recalls, "so that you remember that there was a time, a significant time in 1965 . . . [when] the core of this movement was also faith. It gets into your spirit and it just gives you chills, because you're transported back to that time."[44] For

Robert Darden, who has written extensively on the religious music of the civil rights movement, the inclusion of the gospel medley at the very end of *Selma*'s credits was simply not enough; indeed, it is unlikely that many audience members are still in their seats by the time the medley begins. Although Darden praised the writing, directing, and acting evident in *Selma*, he lamented the exclusion of "the real sounds of its story."[45] Sung during protests and meetings, in jail cells, and in churches, songs like "Oh Freedom" and "Keep Your Eyes on the Prize" were powerful rhetorical actions designed to invoke racial pride and collectiveness, as well as practical information about how current obstacles (sometimes specific politicians or law enforcement officers) could be overcome. But as others have noted, *Selma*'s understated presentation of King and his followers in some of their most private moments meant it was unlikely that DuVernay would focus on the "big group sing-alongs and celebrity sightings weighing down our memories of King's crusades."[46] Indeed, DuVernay's instructions that Rhodes "focus on using B-sides and underground hits" imply that Rhodes may have deliberately avoided them.[47] Instead, King's interaction with spiritual music, like so many of his experiences in *Selma*, occurs privately, when he calls Mahalia Jackson (played by Ledisi Young) in the middle of the night, fearful of what awaits him and his friends in Alabama. "I need to hear the Lord's voice," King tells Jackson, who responds with a heartfelt, unaccompanied rendition of "Take My Hand, Precious Lord." Like the scenes in *Selma*'s jail, where Ralph Abernathy (Colman Domingo) reminds his weary friend of biblical teachings on the ineffectuality of worrying, this moving evocation of King's personal spirituality is vital to the film's capacity to highlight King both as a powerful orator and leader but also as a man who looked to his friends and his faith for guidance and inspiration.

Shannon M. Houston notes that the scene with Mahalia Jackson "could have made for an incredible, musical film moment on a much grander scale," evoking the song's hallowed place within King's legacy. Performed at King's funeral by Jackson herself and at a later memorial by Aretha Franklin, "Take My Hand, Precious Lord" conveys weariness and longing. King had implored Ben Branch, the musical director of SCLC's Operation Breadbasket, to play the song "real pretty" at an upcoming rally just moments before he was assassinated on April 4, 1968.[48] Thus, it is through this song, Powers argues, that "King lived, died, and was spiritually resurrected."[49] Despite all this, DuVernay enshrines the song within a private moment, enabling the audience to hear the song as King would have heard it, without the symbolism it acquired on his death. King may have needed "the headlines and the big names at the protests," Houston continues, but "in the midnight hour, so to speak, it's 'the voice of the Lord' (the voice of a woman) that allows him to keep his eyes on the prize."[50]

Even in her use of more mainstream popular music, Rhodes upholds the sense that the Selma campaign was a spiritual mission. Immediately following King's first speech in Brown AME, the scene transition is accompanied by the Impressions' 1964 hit "Keep on Pushing," which echoes biblical ideas of transcendence in Curtis Mayfield's lyrics, "Hallelujah, hallelujah / Keep on pushing / Now maybe someday / I'll reach that higher goal."[51] Born and bred in the Chicago projects, Mayfield's gospel roots lent "lyrical and spiritual support to the civil rights movement."[52] But "Keep on Pushing" reflects the transition of African American political thought in the mid-1960s, chronicling what Tammy Kernodle calls the "growing anger that exploded in 1964 and '65." Musically, "Keep on Pushing" is just one example of how "the freedom song [developed from] its beginnings as revamped spiritual and gospel song performed in call-and-response format to a secular individually performed song that reflected the feelings and aspirations of the larger community."[53]

In the film's final scenes, "Yesterday Was Hard on All of Us" by British singer-songwriter Fink soundtracks archive footage of the actual Selma to Montgomery march. Its opening lyric, "Where do we go from here?" seems to reference the fact that the movement was at a crossroads.[54] More specifically, though perhaps coincidentally, the song borrows these words from the figurehead of the movement, Martin Luther King Jr., who titled his 1967 book *Where Do We Go from Here: Chaos or Community?* the last he published before his assassination. *Where Do We Go from Here* begins where Selma leaves off, with the signing of the 1965 Voting Rights Act. Reflecting on the movement's victories, King pondered the urban riots that nevertheless rocked major cities that summer and concluded that Americans of all races needed to work together to combat poverty.[55]

Selma's ending—like King's book—encourages viewers to recognize the conclusion of the Selma to Montgomery marches as the final high point of a movement that has continuing relevance and unfulfilled promise. Befitting this sentiment, the film ends with "Glory," the Academy Award–winning duet between John Legend and rapper Common. Connecting mid-twentieth-century gospel with contemporary R & B and rap, it features a powerful, gospel-inspired chorus, while Common's verses are delivered like a sermon.[56] Reinforced by his role in the film as SCLC leader and preacher James Bevel, Common—an artist renowned for his social commentary and political activism—exemplifies the film's attempts to make links between the past and the present. Referencing contemporary racial injustices as well as the high points of the civil rights movement of the 1950s and 1960s, "Glory" plays over the film's end credits, transporting audiences from the periodization of *Selma* back into the twenty-first century by encouraging them to examine more recent events and the limitations of America's racial progress.[57] "Glory" urges continued political action, contributing to a very different cinematic ending than those of earlier, white-centric civil rights dramas such as *Mississippi Burning* and *A Time to Kill* in which the triumphant use of gospel music over closing credits often suggests that American racism has been overcome. When compared with what Anthony Puccinelli calls *A Time to Kill*'s "rows of 'good, churchgoing black folk' . . . praising the Lord as gospel music swells on the sound track," *Selma*'s use of both spirituals and religiously influenced popular music ensures the film is rooted in a much more complex understanding of Black activism and religion and their expression through music.[58]

Cinema in the Age of Obama

It is probably too early to fully comprehend what has already been touted as "Cinema in the Age of Obama," but few scholars, critics, and cinemagoers could fail to notice the increased visibility of Black filmmaking and Black stories in the early twenty-first century, which continued to develop in line with the crucial and largely unprecedented racial awakening prompted by the second wave of Black Lives Matter protests following the murder of George Floyd in 2020. Indeed, although Obama left office in January 2017, the election of Donald Trump constituted a forceful rejection of America's "post-racial" present and future, as celebrated eight years earlier amid Obama's presidential campaign. The symbolic importance of Obama's presidency is therefore impossible to omit from any assessment of Black-centered cinema in the early twenty-first century. However, the political, social, and cultural realities of recent American history have hardened all but the most optimistic believers in a future without racial prejudice and division.

In reality, the writing was on the wall long before Trump succeeded Obama at the White House. The opposition Obama faced in many aspects of his presidency often reflected a thinly veiled racial hostility, whether in response to his policies and associations or simply his birth, heritage, personal conduct, and demeanor. Although many supporters were initially disappointed by Obama's tendency to reflect rather than challenge status quo politics, by his second term, the killings of unarmed Black men and boys sharply focused the nation and the world on the ongoing reality of racist violence in the United States and the complicity of law enforcement in protecting and upholding that reality. Obama spoke publicly and unprecedentedly about the 2012 killing of Trayvon

Martin the following year, when George Zimmerman was found not guilty of second-degree murder, remarking that "if I had a son, he'd look like Trayvon." But Obama's remarkable personal response obscured the political response of his administration, which rendered Martin's killing a local matter and a range of what Michael Eric Dyson deems "dispiriting speeches" in which Obama, touting a popular rhetoric of personal responsibility, had previously and publicly "flogged black people for poor moral habits and for making excuses for their failure."[59]

By the final years of his presidency, Obama adopted an increasingly honest and personal approach to racial issues, evoking his own stories of being racially profiled, followed around stores, and his proximity to the violence that stalks so many Black men. In 2015, the slaughter of nine African Americans at the Emanuel African Methodist Episcopal Church in Charleston, South Carolina, one of the oldest Black churches in America, proved a frightening reminder of the realities of white nationalist extremism, prompting renewed conversations about the Confederate flag, which still flew on state capitol grounds in South Carolina. Delivering a televised eulogy for Clementa C. Pinckney, the slain pastor of Emanuel AME, Obama seemed at home in the Black church and discussed its significance to the civil rights movement. His contribution to the service in Charleston, including a seemingly impromptu rendition of "Amazing Grace," generated further discussion of the president's "Blackness" and the significance of his being president at such a critical moment in U.S. race relations, when the power of white supremacist attitudes and violence in American life proved undoubtable.[60]

This context reflects just some of the issues scholars must reckon with when deciphering the cinematic output during the age of Obama, an intellectual process that began almost as early as the presidency itself due to the noticeable increase in productions engaging with racial themes on the big and small screens. Several Hollywood films made in the early years of the Obama administration reflected an apparent faith in the postracial nation. However, as Douglas Thomas Woodhouse has written, "the mainstream filmic depiction of 'blackness' evolved over the years of Obama's presidency [as] the issues raised by Black Lives Matter have inflected Hollywood cinema." Despite ostensibly engaging with racial themes and prejudices, a number of early Obama-era films like *The Blind Side* (John Lee Hancock, 2009) and *The Help* (Tate Taylor, 2011) prioritized white-centric narratives that evoked the civil rights melodrama of previous decades. Meanwhile a "second wave" of Obama-era Black-themed films, including *Selma*, "eschewed the conventional racial tropes of Hollywood—the 'master's tools,' if you will," and centered Black experiences and Black perspectives instead.[61] Nevertheless, a consistent lack of

diversity among industry award nominations contextualizes the limited acclaim Hollywood bestowed on productions like *Selma*.

Released a year before *Selma, 12 Years a Slave*, Steve McQueen's unflinching
adaptation of Solomon Northrup's 1853 memoir, proved highly popular at the
2014 Oscars, receiving nine nominations and three wins. Just two years earlier,
the *Los Angeles Times* had reported that 94 percent of the Academy's almost six
thousand voting members were white, and 77 percent were male. The median
age was sixty-two. Unfortunately, *12 Years a Slave* proved an outlier, prompting commentators to question if the Academy was showing signs of "racial fatigue" as early as 2015.[62] When the nominees for that year's Academy Awards
were announced, the #OscarsSoWhite hashtag quickly spread across social
media, as users reacted to the first all-white shortlist across all acting catego-
ries since 1998. When the Academy again selected all-white nominees in 2016,
African American stars including director Spike Lee and actress Jada Pinkett-
Smith called for a boycott. The Academy's first Black president, Cheryl Boone
Isaacs, subsequently fast-tracked an initiative already in development to diver-
sify Academy membership, recruiting new members and phasing out voting
privileges for those no longer active in the industry. The new rules prompted
some disgruntled members to accuse Boone Isaacs of "exchanging purported
racism with ageism" and point the finger at a lack of diversity among the studios. In total, the planned changes affected only around seventy people.[63]

In 2015, *Selma* was tapped for Best Picture and Best Original Song but failed
to secure nominations for Best Director, Best Actor, and Best Screenplay. As
David Sims recorded in the *Atlantic*, high-profile Oscar snubs were not new,
but "the 2015 list feels all the more galling because David Oyelowo's performance and Ava DuVernay's direction were not just extraordinarily good,
but also very Oscar-friendly."[64] Indeed, the Academy has a tendency to reward historical films and biopics, and even films that allude to racial themes,
but often side-steps this predisposition when presented with films that explicitly engage with civil rights history. On this contradiction, Lamont
H. Yeakey contrasts the manner with which the Oscars rewarded white-
centric, fictionalized "social problem pictures" like Stanley Kramer's *The
Defiant Ones* (1958), *Guess Who's Coming to Dinner?* (1967), and the 1962 adaptation of *To Kill a Mockingbird*, but largely overlooked films that explicitly
re-created moments in America's racial history, such as *The Long Walk Home,
Glory* (Edward Zwick, 1989) and *Amistad* (Steven Spielberg, 1997) in the latter decades of the twentieth century. *Mississippi Burning*, it should be noted,
was nominated for seven Academy Awards but secured only one win (for
Best Cinematography). But one might make similar comparisons in the early
decades of the twenty-first century, with *The Help* and *Green Book* highly suc-

cessful at the Academy Awards, while *Selma* and *Detroit* (Kathryn Bigelow, 2017) were largely or completely overlooked. Yeakey also argues that this latter category of films, while considered historically important, rarely secure high box office returns.[65]

It is hard to disagree with Sims that *Selma* is "a stirring biopic about one of the most famous Americans in history, filled with brassy supporting performances from Oscar veterans like Tom Wilkinson and Tim Roth."[66] David Oyelowo has since argued that the Academy rejected *Selma* because of the direct connections its cast and crew exposed between the nation's racial past and present and, in particular, their choice to wear T-shirts marked "I Can't Breathe" to the New York premiere. "Members of the Academy called in to the studio and our producers saying, 'How dare they do that? Why are they stirring S-H-I-T?'" Oyelowo recalled in 2020. Citing the cast's activism as a reason not to vote for *Selma*, the Academy members in question, according to Oyelowo, "used their privilege to deny a film on the basis of what they valued in the world."[67]

Selma and Lyndon Johnson

Meanwhile, DuVernay's portrayal of President Lyndon Johnson prompted Joseph A. Califano Jr., a key Johnson adviser in the 1960s, to call for *Selma* to "ruled out" of the 2015 awards season. Califano's argument, and the countless others raised in support of and against DuVernay's representation of Johnson, provoked fascinating questions about the image of the presidency during the Obama era, especially when a range of politicians, journalists, and prominent civil rights figures, including Julian Bond, threw their weight behind Califano's critique.[68]

Although many commentators questioned DuVernay's presentation of Johnson, they found much to praise in the film's central characters, performances, and depiction of key events like Bloody Sunday, when protesters were brutalized on the Edmund Pettus Bridge on March 7, 1965. Califano, however, associated the film's entire worth with its depiction of a white politician, arguing that far from an obstacle to King's campaign for federal voting rights protections, Johnson developed the whole idea himself. "Selma was LBJ's idea," Califano wrote in the *Washington Post*. "He considered the Voting Rights Act his greatest legislative achievement, he viewed King as an essential partner in getting it enacted—and he didn't use the FBI to disparage him."[69] The film's screenwriter, Paul Webb, was similarly critical of DuVernay's edits to his work, arguing that "Ava reduced Johnson in her depiction to a racist."[70]

First seen in private dialogue with an aide, Tom Wilkinson's Lyndon

Johnson certainly appears exasperated with King at the film's opening and, although not uninterested in voting rights, is cautious to push forward with another civil rights bill less than a year after the passage of the Civil Rights Act of 1964 and before the rollout of his War on Poverty. When he and King meet for the first time in the film, Johnson is much more pleasant than behind closed doors. He congratulates King on his recent Nobel Prize, informs him that "ending segregation [was] the proudest moment of my life," and that "civil rights is a priority of this administration." Johnson alludes to the fact that King has turned down an offer to work at the White House in an official capacity but makes it clear that he wants King to remain at the forefront of the movement, "not one of these militant Malcolm X types." However, in response to King's request for federal voting protections, Johnson notes that "most of the South is still not desegregating. Let's not start another battle when we haven't even won the first."

As King outlines in response, the protected registration of southern Black voters would not only fulfill their constitutional right as American citizens but would help bring an end to all-white juries in the region, which so often allowed white vigilantes to walk free despite their violent crimes, murders, and bombings. He makes specific mention of the 1963 attack on Birmingham's Sixteenth Street Baptist Church that killed four young girls and that DuVernay dramatically re-creates earlier in the film. When this fails to convince Johnson of the immediate necessity of voting rights, King returns to his colleagues and states, "Selma it is," meaning direct action. It is true, then, that Johnson's resistance to immediate voting rights reform proves a catalyst for the film's main story, but this is hardly the egregious divergence from history that some have suggested. Rather, it is directly in keeping with King's own account of the events, published in his autobiographical collection of writings edited by Clayborne Carson. Here, King recalled Johnson's reluctance to offend the congressional "Southern bloc" by pushing a voting rights bill so soon after the Civil Rights Act, arguing that he was dependent on them for the passage of bills related to his War on Poverty. "The President said nothing could be done," King wrote; however, three months later, Johnson was "on television singing in speaking terms, 'We Shall Overcome,' and calling for the passage of a voting rights bill in Congress."[71] Johnson is therefore far from unsympathetic in DuVernay's initial rendering but rather a politician with a range of issues on his mind and a delicately balanced legislative strategy. "As black and white lives hung in the balance," Yeakey writes, Johnson "waited until he had a 'critical mass' of support." He was a pragmatic politician, but this earned him "no kudos from civil rights activists," especially when he extended personal sympathy to the family of murdered white minister James Reeb but not the

Martin Luther King Jr. (David Oyelowo) and President Lyndon Johnson (Tom Wilkinson) meet for the second time in *Selma* (Ava DuVernay, 2014), standing underneath a large portrait of George Washington. Johnson's body language conveys his frustration as he points accusingly at King.

relatives of Jimmie Lee Jackson. Eventually, after weeks of protests and violent, sometimes lethal, repression, "Johnson rose to the occasion."[72]

When King and Johnson meet for the second time, later in the film, both are angrier, more frustrated with each other. But Johnson remains conscious of the situation, observing, "You're an activist and I'm a politician. You've got one big issue; I've got a hundred and one. Now you demand more and more and put me on the spot; that's okay, that's your job, that's what you do." Johnson then demands that King meet him halfway, but King insists that voting rights cannot wait, that "people are dying in the street for this." In the subsequent scene, an angry-looking Johnson asks to speak to FBI director J. Edgar Hoover (Dylan Baker), who has previously suggested that federal agencies target King's wife: "weaken the dynamic, dismantle the family." Although we do not see or hear Johnson's and Hoover's latest meeting, the implication in the next scene is that Johnson has approved Hoover's plan, as the Kings listen to an infamous tape apparently evidencing King's extramarital affairs. In reality, this tape was sent to the SCLC in late 1964 and without input or orders from Johnson. It had nothing to do with the Selma campaign. Although the film does not explicitly hold Johnson responsible for the tape, it strongly implies that his frustrations with King's demands led him to approve Hoover's plan. Undoubtedly, this is an ahistorical representation of the truth and unfair to Johnson's legacy.

However, Johnson is granted his redemption, after King reminds him that although he is "just a preacher from Atlanta, [Johnson] won the presidency of the world's most powerful nation by the greatest landslide in history four months ago." Seemingly convinced by King's warning that his legacy is at stake, Johnson goes head-to-head with Alabama governor George Wallace (Tim Roth), imploring him to take control of the situation in Selma. Like the FBI agents of *Mississippi Burning*, Johnson finds himself in the gutter with the enemy. He uses a racial slur, alongside other offensive language as if to communicate on Wallace's level. But his overall message is similar to the one King gave him minutes earlier: "In 1985, what do you want looking back? You want people remembering you sayin' 'Wait,' or 'I can't,' or, uh, 'It's too hard'?" When Wallace responds that he does not care what the historians of the future think and that the president should not care either, Johnson rallies for his final blow: "I'll be damned if I'm gonna let history put me in the same place as the likes of you." The scene then cuts from Wallace's smirking face to Johnson's congressional speech in support of voting rights, securing his status on the right side of history and as the redeemed white southerner.

In pitting Wallace and Johnson against each other late in her film, DuVernay reflects a key trope of the civil rights melodrama in which a white character undergoes the personal growth needed to rise above his or her upbringing and help to deliver American, national values of freedom and equality. That Johnson does this from the nation's seat of political power, with a

President Lyndon Johnson (Tom Wilkinson) calls on congressional representatives to support the proposed Voting Rights Act of 1965 in *Selma* (Ava DuVernay, 2014), flanked by a large American flag.

large American flag behind him further enhances this symbolism and implies that he has risen to meet the demands of his office. Nevertheless, in response to hyperbolic criticisms from Califano and others, DuVernay designated herself "a storyteller" rather than "a historian" and defended her right to interpret and present Johnson as a "reluctant hero." DuVernay therefore sought to remind critics that Johnson was not the center of her story and exposed the white-centric gaze that rendered Johnson's presentation the most important part of the movie. "The real problem people have with this movie," historian Peniel Joseph surmised, "was that it was too black and too strong," especially when compared to mainstream Hollywood's previous civil rights narratives.[73] Johnathan Holloway agreed that "using the black past to reckon with and redraft memories of national exceptionalism remains fundamentally destabilizing," especially for white men who had previously considered such political history "theirs." In Holloway's estimation, "that an African American woman should be the person crafting this narrative seems only to have intensified the reflexive anxiety of those who feel a loss when they watch *Selma*."[74]

However, as discussed in relation to the FBI tapes, the film is not above historical scrutiny. As Holloway implies, DuVernay's representation of SNCC is not as well developed as it could be and implies a particularly youthful petulance to SNCC executive secretary James Forman (Trai Byers), who was actually three months older than Martin Luther King Jr. Others have criticized the film's limited attention to the murders of white protesters James Reeb and Viola Liuzzo and its underwhelming mobilization of women such as Diane Nash and Coretta Scott King, who are granted only minor roles. Whereas Nash is largely forgotten after bringing King and his team to Alabama, Scott King, Barbara Reynolds argues, is portrayed as little more than a "tormented victim," frustrated by her husband's frequent absences and his implied infidelity as well as her family's modest finances.[75]

The Butler

Released a year before *Selma*, Lee Daniels's *The Butler*'s most controversial contribution to debates on the modern presidency concerned its depiction of Ronald Reagan's complicity in South African apartheid. Its representation of Lyndon Johnson was hardly flattering, though, and mostly limited LBJ to his toilet habits and crude racist epithets. But *The Butler* never evoked the same outcry as *Selma* prompted, limiting its presidents to "minor supporting characters" and often simply a "sideshow attraction."[76] Depicting presidents Eisenhower to Reagan, with the exception of Ford and Carter, as part of its dramatic representation of the civil rights era and its legacies, *The Butler* failed to score a single nomination at the 2014 Oscars, exactly a year before *Selma's* disappointing awards season. *The Butler* was extremely popular at the box office (much more so than *Selma*) and with many critics.[77] Indeed, the majority of criticism *The Butler* endured centered on its obvious posturing for awards, with some likening it to *Forrest Gump* due to its anthology approach to postwar U.S. history in which the central character's life serves as a catalyst for exploration of a range of historical agents and events.

However, *Forrest Gump*—a narrative centered on what Allison Graham calls "the befuddled homilies of [a white] Alabama idiot"—proved much more successful at the 1995 Oscars than *The Butler* nineteen years later, earning thirteen Oscar nominations and six awards, including Best Picture, Best Actor in a Leading Role, Best Screenplay, and Best Director. Despite placing the titular character (Tom Hanks) in news footage of, among other things, the desegregation crisis at the University of Alabama, the Vietnam War, and the Watergate scandal, *Forrest Gump* offers "an apologia for southern racism" in which Forrest, the newly prosperous and redeemed white southerner, is revealed to have "[led] the Klan in silly bedsheets, [before] following Vivian Malone through the schoolhouse door in Tuscaloosa like a guardian angel."[78]

But whereas *Forrest Gump* is invited to the White House on a number of occasions, as evidence of the extent to which he holds "the tapestry of American history" together, *The Butler* takes place largely within those hallowed walls, as its titular character becomes a witness to history and, the narrative implies, America's redemption from its racist past.[79] Based on the life of Eugene Allen, an African American butler who served eight administrations at the White House, from 1952 to 1986, *The Butler* was adapted from a *Washington Post* article published just days after Barack Obama's election in November 2008.[80] The film uses that election as both start and end point, with the protagonist, here named Cecil Gaines (played by Forest Whitaker), reflecting on his life and all that African Americans have overcome on the occasion of Obama's inauguration. In the film's final scene, following the depiction of his life, Cecil is invited to enter the Oval Office to meet President Obama, crossing a literal threshold into the central office of American political power. However, despite the political significance of Obama's Oval Office, the film elevates the quiet dignity of older generations like Cecil, implying the importance of legacy— symbolized here by Cecil's choice of tie pin: "LBJ for the USA." Like *Selma*, then, *The Butler* presents Johnson as a callous and crude man but ultimately elevates him to redeemed status by the film's end and cements his place in civil rights history.

After applying the LBJ pin to his meticulously ironed tie, Cecil recites to himself the advice his old mentor, Maynard, gave him as a teenager in North Carolina: "You gotta look 'em in their eyes. See what it is that they want. See what it is that they need. Anticipate." Following Maynard's advice that "to get up in the world, you have to make [white people] feel nonthreatened," Cecil spends most of the film at odds with his son Louis's involvement in the civil rights movement, from student activism in Nashville to the Freedom Rides, King's assassination, and the Black Panthers. Indeed, on some occasions, Lee Daniels juxtaposes the chaos of the white violence inflicted on Louis and his comrades with the decorum and order of the White House, a technique put to particular effect during the film's reconstruction of the Nashville lunch counter sit-ins. Soundtracked by organizer James Lawson's articulation of Gandhian philosophies of nonviolence and specific strategies for the sit-ins, these scenes are also interposed with images of Cecil and his fellow butlers setting up a particularly elaborate White House dinner. Back in the kitchen, the butlers raise a toast ("To serving our country"), as scenes of the Nashville students flicker on a nearby television, with Louis visibly led away by police. He is later sentenced to thirty days in jail.

Cecil and his son eventually reconcile when Louis's attentions turn to South African apartheid in the 1980s and in particular the efforts to free Nelson Mandela, a topic that sees the film and the family move beyond the issue of race in the United States, implying that the fight for equality is now elsewhere. However, the issue of U.S. complicity in racial hierarchies remains, as Cecil overhears President Ronald Reagan's intention to veto congressional sanctions in response to apartheid, prompting a flashback to the cotton fields of the Jim Crow South. Although Reagan is the first president to secure equal pay for White House staff regardless of race and to invite Cecil and his wife to a state dinner, Cecil struggles with the contradictions of the president's personal generosity and his political actions. Although Reagan deems Cecil to be "like family" to him, the president "has attacked or dismantled every civil rights bill program that has ever been put in place," as Louis informs crowds gathering outside the South African embassy. "Aiding the oppression of black South Africans," Louis continues, "is absolutely consistent with [Reagan's] policies on race issues." Meanwhile, Cecil is moved by the wave of civil rights histories published in the 1980s and finally accepts that "Louis was never a criminal. He was a hero fighting to save the soul of our country." He takes his first trip south since leaving as a teenager, and on returning to the old plantation he grew up on, Cecil compares the scene and its history to that of Europe's concentration camps.

Fittingly, father and son are together for a particularly emotional moment in November 2008, when Obama's election is confirmed. Here, for the first time, Louis stands behind his father, both physically and symbolically, as the reality of Obama's election washes over the older man. At the end of the film, when the elderly Cecil informs the chief usher that he knows the way to the Oval Office and does not require chaperoning, the audience is reminded of his three decades of working in the White House, diligently serving generations of presidents, politicians, and dignitaries, but also witnessing key decisions on civil rights, from Eisenhower's decision to send the National Guard to Little Rock in 1957 to Lyndon Johnson's efforts in pursuit of the Voting Rights Act. As Cecil moves through the halls, stirring speeches on civil rights from John F. Kennedy, Johnson, and Obama can be heard over the swelling music before a final screen of text announces that the film is dedicated to "the brave men and women who fought for our freedom in the civil rights movement."

The Butler and Southern Exceptionalism

In 1953, the year after Eugene Allen joined the White House, Washington, D.C., began to desegregate, when the Supreme Court upheld local post–Civil War laws that had previously been "lost." Several scholars have written of the Cold War imperative of desegregating the nation's capital, which was— by most stretches of the imagination—a southern city, especially as the U.S. government played host to a range of African leaders from newly indepen- dent nations at the dawn of the 1960s. However, it would be another twenty years before Congress granted District of Columbia residents the right to gov- ern local affairs. Visitors to the capital during the civil rights era therefore experienced a city "suspended between legal segregation—with its often- lethargic, contentious enforcement—and the nominal political independence of home rule."[81] However, although *The Butler* never engages with the reality of race and politics in the District of Columbia specifically, it strongly implies that Cecil has traveled a long way from his childhood on a Georgia planta- tion, where his mother was raped by a white overseer and his father murdered for looking the rapist in the eye in 1926. Although Cecil was born in the early twentieth century, the implication is that the former Confederacy had not evolved past the racial and economic chokehold of slavery and that escape northward was Cecil's only hope of survival. When he leaves North Carolina for the Excelsior Hotel in Washington, D.C., Maynard advises him that "white folks up north like some uppity coloreds," reflecting the film's presentation of Washington as "North." However, the first customer seeking Cecil's input to a conversation offers a stereotypically southern interpretation of the *Brown v. Board of Education* decision, arguing that Chief Justice Earl Warren "should be shot and hanged [for] trying to integrate our schools." Ever the apolitical professional, Cecil politely responds, "I think Judge Warren is going to find that quite a challenge."

Because of his past, Cecil feels no sentimentality toward the South and "made sure that [his two sons] never laid eyes on a cotton field." He cannot understand why Louis would sacrifice this privileged position to endure the inhumanity that he purposely left behind, especially in the shadow of Emmett Till's lynching, which Cecil chalks up to "crazy white folks down South." The family's discussion of the murder reveals that Louis and Till are the same age, placing Louis within the "Emmett Till generation," traumatized but mobilized by their peer's murder into future civil rights action. Indeed, Louis and Cecil's first disagreement in the narrative occurs when Cecil forbids Louis from attending one of Mamie Till's speeches, and he later cites Eisenhower's use of federal troops in Little Rock as evidence of the president's intention "to make things better for us."

After graduating from his all-Black high school, Louis opts to attend Fisk University in Tennessee, rather than the nearby Howard, with the distinct intention of attending James Lawson's seminars on nonviolent protest. The decision to go south for college prompts Cecil's anxiety for his son's safety: "I can't protect him in the South." Despite his wife's protestation that "the South has changed," Cecil implies that it is the South, not the United States, that is unsafe for young Black men, perpetuating stereotypes of the recalcitrant South, geographically and culturally removed from the rest of the nation. This sectionalism is reinforced by the fact that the majority of the film's narrative takes place in the White House, where Cecil overhears consecutive presidents acknowledge and occasionally intervene in specifically southern civil rights activity that is contained within, and apparently indicative of, the troublesome region. When watching scenes from Birmingham, Alabama, in the spring of 1963, a frustrated President Kennedy (James Marsden) mutters, "I don't know what country I'm looking at."

Because Cecil cannot see the need for a civil rights movement outside of the South, the film offers a distinctly regional understanding of America's racist history and therefore fails to always interrogate the reality of its past and present. Rather than presenting the evidence of sustained racial degradation in the North, and even in Washington, D.C., itself, the film is committed to the "dividing line" that Jeanne Theoharis argues has been constructed between "the heroic southern freedom struggle and the civil rights movement's militant and northward turn."[82] As a result of this logic, the deeply shocking reality of the Freedom Rides, in which a bus of integrated passengers was firebombed outside Anniston, Alabama, and another met by violent mobs in their Sunday best in downtown Birmingham, is dialed up several notches to encompass a nighttime attack complete with a burning cross and Klansmen in full regalia. What happened during the Freedom Rides was surely shocking enough to evoke an emotional reaction from the audience, and Lee Daniels juxtaposes his scenes with images of the actual firebombed bus from 1961. But in casting his scenes at night and with the visible presence of Klansmen in full regalia, Lee Daniels's depiction spoke more forcefully to Hollywood audiences accustomed to seeing white supremacists attacking under cover of darkness and white hoods. In doing so, his film evokes the common Hollywood myth that racial violence comes at the hand of the individual, rather than the system, and that those individuals offer no resemblance to the average white viewer.

Cecil is later informed of the bus explosion by a four-year-old Caroline Kennedy and does not learn for weeks whether Louis is alive or dead. He will later learn from President Kennedy that Louis has been arrested sixteen times in two years but that "these kids" have changed the president's heart and that of his brother, Attorney General Robert Kennedy. The scene then cuts to a re-creation of President Kennedy's June 11, 1963, speech committing Congress to civil rights legislation, which Louis reads about in jail. A close-up of Kennedy's eyes then fades to white, as a gunshot is heard and Walter Cronkite is seen reacting to the news of the president's assassination five months later.

As the history of the African American freedom struggle plays out through Louis's life and television coverage beamed into the White House, Louis begins to resent his father's apolitical nature and his job. To Louis, both exemplify servility. Through these family disagreements, including a notable discussion of Sidney Poitier, the film presents Black Power advocates as spoiled, disrespectful youngsters incapable of building on the sacrifices of their hardworking, patriotic elders. Indeed, Louis's usually sympathetic mother, Gloria (Oprah Winfrey), strikes her son for disrespecting Cecil, arguing, "Everything you are, everything you have, is because of that butler." These scenes, during Louis's brief stint as a Black Panther, are particularly evocative of "the declension narratives of the 1960s" in which the destructiveness of the Black Power movement—specifically what Peniel Joseph calls its periodic embrace of "violent rhetoric, misogyny, and bravado"—is seen to have squandered decades of racial progress, corrupted a new generation of potential leaders, and "seemingly destroyed the potential of the civil rights movement to establish new democratic frontiers."[83]

Even though Louis and Cecil have disagreed on civil rights strategies before, Louis's demeanor is noticeably different as a Panther and distinctly hostile, even aggressive, toward his parents. While Louis's girlfriend Carol (Yaya

DaCosta) outlines the Panthers' community work—breakfast clubs, free clothing, medical centers—she is otherwise presented as ill-mannered, disrespectful, and distinctly unladylike—a marker of the influences leading Louis astray from the "true" movement. Indeed, while Carol later admits she is ready to kill, if necessary, in retaliation for the murder of Panthers by police officers, Louis admits that he is not, prompting the breakdown of their relationship and his departure from the Panthers. In many ways, this is not a surprise; Louis had previously expressed discomfort with Malcolm X's views on self-defense back in 1965, and Carol's reluctant commitment to their relationship is emphasized on a number of occasions.[84] Meanwhile, Cecil overhears President Richard Nixon describe the Panthers as "God damned terrifying," informing his advisers that he has given J. Edgar Hoover of the FBI "the green light to gut those sons of bitches. . . . Round them all up and throw them down an elevator shaft." As news reports detail the brutal repression of the Panthers, the camera pans in on an image of a very young child in Panther attire, before cutting to a chalkboard list displaying the first four points of Chairman Mao's "Eight Points for Attention" at the Panther headquarters in Oakland, California:

1. Speak politely.
2. Pay fairly for what you buy.
3. Return everything you borrow.
4. Pay for anything you need.

This lingering shot complicates the film's representation of the Panthers. On the one hand, the film implies that the Panther ideology breeds resentment and generational disrespect, while the Panther headquarters is decorated with highly sexualized images of Black women. Panthers speak openly of retaliatory violence, which alienates Louis and ends his relationship with Carol, a relationship that originally developed after meeting at James Lawson's nonviolent workshops in Nashville and has seen the couple working together at every civil rights milestone to date. However, in this lingering shot of the Points for Attention, Daniels draws particular attention to the governing principles of the Panthers, which seem far from the violent image usually evoked in the media. The viewer is left with a sense of tragedy and loss, as Louis walks away from Carol and the audio news reports tell of numerous Panthers dead at the hands of police. Shortly afterward, Cecil and Gloria learn that their younger son Charlie has been killed in Vietnam. Louis fulfills his earlier promise not to attend his brother's funeral should he be killed in action, his absence marked by an empty chair next to his parents at the graveside. Reflecting on the death, Cecil admits, "Vietnam took my boy. And I didn't understand why we were there in the first place." In subsequent scenes with President Nixon, Cecil is colder than he has been with any other president, implying a loss of faith in the office and a weight of grief and anger.

Earlier in the film, Louis discusses his parents' assumed support of the Vietnam War with Martin Luther King Jr., making Cecil's later disillusionment all the more significant. Along with the Panthers, Charlie's death further reinforces the film's depiction of the demise of the 1960s and its promise, contributing to a Nixon-era malaise that challenges even Cecil's patriotism. It further reinforces *The Butler*'s declension narrative that King is the only character, other than Gloria, who explicitly encourages Louis to see value in his father's work, firmly establishing King as a figure who had the power and potential to unite generations and heal divisions between Black and white America. In his last words before he is assassinated, King advises Louis that "the black domestic defies racial stereotypes by being hardworking and trustworthy. He slowly breaks down racial hatred with the example of his strong work ethic and dignified character." Danny Strong's script states that in this moment, Louis "stares at [King, having] never thought about his dad in this way." King continues, "Now while we perceive the butler or the maid as being subservient, in many ways they are subversive without even knowing it." The scene then immediately cuts to Cecil at the White House, attempting to negotiate a pay raise for Black staff that would put them in line with white employees, and support for promotions. He is promptly informed by the chief usher that those unhappy with their salary or position should seek work elsewhere and not to let "that Martin Luther King shit fill your britches out." As Cecil moves to open the doors to leave the usher's office, his silhouette blends into that of King smoking a cigarette on his balcony at the Lorraine Motel, as reports of his assassination become audible. With the implication that both King and Cecil are not so different after all or at least fighting for the same principles of equality and justice, King's world violently crashes into Cecil's as the nationwide unrest prompted by King's assassination forces Cecil to abandon his car on his way home from work: "I wasn't sure if I would get home alive. It was the first time I felt that I didn't belong in my own neighborhood. The whole world was changing and I didn't know how to fit in."

"I Didn't Want to Make *Mississippi Burning*"

Although Ava DuVernay faced a range of criticism for her depiction of civil rights history in *Selma*, the concern raised with the most consistency and intensity reflected a continued assumption that America's racial history be depicted and told in a manner tolerable and even complimentary to white actors.

And yet, as David G. Holmes has argued, "the question for DuVernay, as the film makes clear, is not whether [Lyndon] Johnson backed the Selma movement but when and how forcefully."[85] Inheriting the film from Lee Daniels, no less, DuVernay felt that Paul Webb's script was too slanted toward Johnson and that it reflected a conventional political biopic style. "I didn't want to make *Mississippi Burning*," DuVernay asserted, indicating the 1988 movie's archetypal hold over Hollywood's civil rights genre:

> [*Mississippi Burning*] had its place; it was among the first that dealt with African-American-centered history and the only way to get people into the theaters then was to have a "white savior." But we're past that point. If in 2014 we're still making "white savior movies" then it's just lazy and unfortunate. We've grown up as a country and cinema should be able to reflect what's true. And what's true is that black people are the center of their own lives and should tell their own stories from their own perspectives. That was my first order of business.[86]

Although DuVernay does not have a screenwriting credit for *Selma*, her first major studio film, the director removed composite characters, meaning that all featured in the film are based on real figures. This had a particular impact on the number of women in the film, including Diane Nash, Amelia Boynton, and Annie Lee Cooper, but also ensures that the film does not shy from the internal tensions—particularly between the SNCC and the SCLC—that, by 1965, threatened the movement's cohesiveness. Rather than hiding from this reality, the film confidently displays moments of division as part of a wider visualization of the African American freedom struggle as one of personalities with distinctive and sometimes opposing views. In doing so, DuVernay demythologizes King, showing him to be a powerful leader, yes, but also a man with flaws and whose colleagues and loved ones often disagreed with. DuVernay's King is bold, committed, and radical, refusing to take no for an answer from a president who had already done more for civil rights than any in modern history.

However, when *Selma* shows King leading the protesters in a silent prayer on the Edmund Pettus Bridge before abandoning the second attempt to reach Montgomery, it implies a deeply spiritual preoccupation, which although not untrue, works to deny the shrewd political maneuvering that actually produced this "symbolic" march. Evidence shows that King had already negotiated this outcome, promising to lead the marchers to the bridge and then back to Selma in return for peaceful restraint from the police and Alabama state troopers.[87] Although *Selma* presents King in conversations with John Doar (Alessandro Nivola), the assistant attorney general for civil rights, these discussions are inconclusive. DuVernay portrays the dissatisfaction many in the movement felt at the turnaround; she never provides the viewer with the evidence or even the suggestion of King's deal. In DuVernay's vision, James Reeb (Jeremy Strong) goes to his death in the film trusting that King was "tapped into what's higher, what's true." King had "prayed to God and got an answer," Reeb believes.

Although these scenes actually overemphasize the place of religion in King's decision-making, DuVernay's film conveys religion as a powerful force that can unite people across racial and regional divides but also provide political, even radical, inspiration. This is a dramatic departure from Hollywood's usual emphasis on progressive, secular whites, which so often pushes white religious expression to the margins of segregationist society, overlooking what Carolyn Dupont recognizes as "the racial hierarchy's powerful but often subtle articulation by more polished religious leaders and prominent laymen."[88] *Selma*, by contrast, confidently presents a range of white involvement in the voting rights campaign, disrupting the popular assumption that no religious whites supported the civil rights movement without simply rewriting history to alleviate white guilt. In doing so, it has raised powerful discussion on the place of religion in the civil rights movement and questions from those unable to see themselves in the beloved community. Whereas *Selma* ends with Common and John Legend's song "Glory," which equates the struggles of the civil rights movement with contemporary racial injustices in the United States, the more conventional civil rights dramas of the late twentieth century often gave the impression that America's racial turmoil had been laid to rest by resolutely secular white heroes. In this and many other respects, *Selma* diverged from its predecessors in the civil rights genre, which appeared much more concerned with eliciting positive responses from white audiences than engaging in any meaningful debate about the experience and legacy of the civil rights movement for African Americans.

"Why There's This Desire to Write about All These Horrible Things That Happened over Civil Rights, I Don't Know"

Southern Authenticity in the Age of the
Civil Rights Melodrama

In 1998, Robert Duvall's independently financed movie *The Apostle* gained numerous awards and accolades, including three Independent Spirit Awards and the Un Certain Regard Award at the Cannes Film Festival. Duvall, who starred in the film as well as writing and directing it, was nominated for Best Actor at the Oscars and the Screen Actors Guild Awards. Bill and Hillary Clinton hosted a White House dinner and preview screening of the film on January 24, 1998, just three days after the Monica Lewinsky scandal broke in the mainstream press and in the run-up to the president's State of the Union address on January 27. Janet Maslin of the *New York Times* rendered the film the third-best release of 1997, behind James Cameron's mega blockbuster *Titanic* and the neo-noir *L.A. Confidential* (Curtis Hanson).[1]

Duvall's film, which probably has the most references to southern religiosity of any major picture since John Huston's 1979 adaptation of Flannery O'Connor's *Wise Blood*, told the story of Sonny Dewey, a white pentecostal preacher who finds solace preaching in a predominantly African American church in a Louisiana bayou. Religious scholars and journalists were "stunned" by Duvall's performance, rendering it "the first picture in modern times that accurately portrays a holiness-style white preacher without making him an object of ridicule or evil personified."[2] Indeed, a deep faith permeates everything that Sonny does, and he spends much of the film speaking aloud to the Lord, constantly seeking guidance, conveying anger, or offering praise. After attacking his wife's new lover at his son's Little League game, Sonny flees Texas and rebaptizes himself as The Apostle E. F. Over time, he raises money to build a new church in Louisiana, where slots preaching on a local radio station ensure a swelling interracial congregation. He is even able to convert Billy Bob Thornton's racist troublemaker, who appears at a church picnic determined to destroy the church. Eventually, though, Sonny's violent past catches up with him and he is arrested. In the film's final scenes, Sonny preaches to other inmates on a chain gang.

Patton Dodd has argued that Sonny's narrative, particularly his "psychology and personal history remains basic, unexplored," positing that Duvall's "fiction is just the frame for capturing some textures of truth about a peculiar American religious phenomenon." Indeed, Duvall deemed Pentecostalism "a distinct American art-form" and spoke of his decades-long effort to secure financing for *The Apostle*, which he was first inspired to make in the 1960s, before deciding to fund it himself. The actor, who is not a practicing pentecostal, recorded the film's church scenes by simply informing existing congregations to conduct worship while the cameras rolled—a technique that Dodd calls "qualified realism." In documenting these moments with a rare verisimilitude, Duvall "does not perform Pentecostalism for the camera so much as he recreates it." Where other films have played such religious devotion for laughs or to incite fear, *The Apostle* offers merely quiet observation.[3]

Mainstream Hollywood's apparent disdain for religion, Duvall argued, was rooted in a broader tendency to ridicule "the interior of the United States of America, the heartland" rather than simply a discomfort with evangelicalism.[4] As this book has shown, religion intersects with tropes of race, class, and gender to further distance poor whites in particular from "American norms." Yet, even though they are often mocked or disdained for their violent ignorance and intolerance, such characters were increasingly sensationalized in late twentieth-century film, whether through visible association with the Ku Klux Klan in *A Time to Kill* or through the tropes of psychological thrillers like Scorsese's *Cape Fear* in which the lunatic on the periphery of society subscribes to a celestial set of rules and so is unlikely to be disheartened by the threat of penal justice. The tendency with which mainstream Hollywood filmmakers represented white supremacists as religious as well as racial zealots during the latter decades of the twentieth century implied a shared concern about the intersections of intolerance and fundamentalist Christian belief. In some cases, like *Cape Fear*, these intersections ran so deep that they alluded to racial tensions within an exclusively white narrative.

Debates in the 1980s and 1990s about affirmative action, along with the rising tide of civil rights genre films, reflected this apparent failure to deal with the American past. Mounting racial tensions were exacerbated by church burnings targeting African American communities across the South, while the civil rights melodrama became an arena in which to discuss competing political ideologies, refracting the present through the memories of the past. Reducing historical events and legacies to personal histories, films such as *Ghosts of Mississippi* and *A Time to Kill* used religious language and iconography to communicate and contest the meaning of the 1960s in the 1990s. They fashioned a simplistic binary of good versus evil that, although designed to alleviate white guilt for the racial sins of the past, actually contributed to a much older scapegoating of the southern rural poor, whose apparent ignorance and zealous religiosity rendered them convenient actors of racial violence. As the following concluding case studies suggest, the defensiveness of filmmakers like Billy Bob Thornton demonstrates the discomfort many white southerners felt at being represented in such narrow and unflattering confines, opening up age-old debates about southern racial exceptionalism and northern hypocrisy. Such defensiveness, however, exhibited little concern for the tendency with which the civil rights melodrama excised Black southerners from their own stories but rather focused exclusively on the psychological burden white southerners were consistently expected to carry for the nation's racial sins. In return, Thornton constructed narratives that ironically served many of the same aims as the maligned civil rights melodrama, primarily restoring the white southern male to a position of morality through redemptive narratives centered on family, regional loyalties, and a "common sense" approach to racial egalitarianism.

Sling Blade

Dubbed "the hillbilly Orson Welles" by his frequent costar Robert Duvall, Thornton admitted that his home region had influenced him "completely and totally."[5] Happy to discuss his favorite southern writers, the Arkansan actor, writer, and director welcomed seemingly endless questions about the southerner's propensity for storytelling while promoting his film *Sling Blade* in 1996. "The South is a rich place," he told *Creative Screenwriting*. "There are ghosts in the South. The atmosphere's different, the air's heavier. It's an area where stories are a staple. The South is all about stories. I loved growing up there. I loved hearing the stories."[6] In these interviews, Thornton indulged journalists determined to emphasize *Sling Blade*'s "southern-ness," contributing to an exoticized mythology about southern authenticity. Drawing comparisons with William Faulkner, some critics have argued that Thornton's work is "as distinctly Southern as anything produced by the author of *As I Lay Dying*," while Rita Kempley of the *Washington Post* wrote that *Sling Blade*, in particular, was "rich in the rhythms and peculiarities of a vanishing Southern dialect. [Its] antique locutions recall humid Southern evenings alive with stars and fireflies."[7]

The film tells the story of Karl Childers (Thornton), an intellectually disabled man released from the Arkansas state "nervous hospital" twenty-five years after murdering his mother and her lover. Finding a new family with twelve-year-old Frank (Lucas Black) and his strict Baptist mother, Linda (Natalie Canerday), Karl eventually sacrifices himself on the day of his immersive baptism, returning to the "nervous hospital" after murdering Linda's abusive boyfriend, Doyle (Dwight Yoakam). Described in the film as a "closed-minded redneck," Doyle, like *To Kill a Mockingbird*'s Bob Ewell, poses a threat to the narrative's innocent white child. As such, Karl, "a cross between Frankenstein's monster and Boo Radley," according to Thornton, becomes *Sling Blade*'s "fading specter of southern gentility." As "a cinematic cousin of [Forrest] Gump's," Karl's actions also reflect Gump's determination to bulldoze the Alabama shack in which his adored Jenny was systematically abused by her father as a child.[8]

Much has been written about Karl as a "Christ figure": an outsider who can be both tender and violent, serving as both redeemer and punisher.[9] Thornton admitted that "there's definitely a whole lot of underlying stuff" to Karl's characterization, drawing attention to the fact that Karl's only possessions are books: "the Bible, a book about carpentry and another about Christmas."[10] But while the Christ figure has been identified in southern films as varied as *Cool Hand Luke* (Stuart Rosenberg, 1967) and *The Green Mile* (Frank Darabont, 1999), the trope is not confined to films about the region alone. As such, Thornton does not simply rely on it to imbue his film with religious meaning.[11] Rather, he depicts Karl within a distinctly southern vision of a violent and all-encompassing faith that reinforces it as a region set apart from the rest of the nation. "Karl was reared on the Ten Commandments. And little else," Rita Kempley wrote on the film's release. "His parents, both religious fanatics, considered him a punishment from God, and kept him in the shed behind the house. He was waiting for his Bible lesson the night he caught his mother in the act with her young lover and killed them both with a sling blade."[12]

When Karl visits his reclusive father (Duvall, i.e., Boo Radley himself), their interaction confirms the abuse that the film has until now merely suggested. Yet, despite the older man's ungodly acts, Mr. Childers's living room contains at least thirty images of Christian iconography. In another region, the framing of such imagery might provide visual evidence of a man's deep religious preoccupations. However, there is little in word or deed to suggest that Karl's father is concerned about the fate of his soul. Rather, the religious iconography is "just there," according to Bradley Shaw, "part of the fabric of [Karl's] southern reality."[13] Indeed, Karl contends that his parents gave him false information about the Bible, telling his father, "I learned to read some. I read the Bible quite a bit. . . . Those stories you and Momma told me, they ain't in there. You ought not done that to your boy [*sic*]." It is implied that the stories the Childers told Karl justified their abuse of him and their murder of their other, younger son.[14] Now older and more spiritually aware, Karl, who admits he cannot understand all of the Bible, uses it to pass judgment on his father, criticizing his abuse of both his children and drawing attention to his false theology.

Despite its depiction of deceitful, manipulative religious practice, *Sling Blade*'s rural Arkansas setting nevertheless serves as a theological backdrop, with Thornton personally identifying religion "as a good thing."[15] Adherence to religious norms helps an otherwise marginalized Karl understand and navigate southern life before eventually developing his own moral code. Like Scout Finch, it seems, Karl must understand the Bible before he can move on to any other book. But like Scout's neighbor, Miss Maudie, Thornton recognizes that the Bible can be dangerous, "worse than a whiskey bottle," for some men.[16] As such, Karl not only criticizes his father's theological hypocrisy but anoints Vaughan Cunningham (John Ritter), a gay man, to be his successor in caring for Frank: "I don't reckon that you have to go with women to be a good daddy to a boy. . . . Bible says two men ought not to lay together. But I'll bet you the good Lord wouldn't send nobody like you to Hades." Presumably, Karl makes a similar concession regarding his own morality, knowing that as a multiple murderer, he too could face eternal damnation.

"A lot of people might think the movie is a slam on religion, but in fact it's very much in support of religion," Thornton told the *Washington Post* on *Sling Blade*'s release. "The problem is people who take it into their own hands and use it for their own purposes, the guys that wear white shoes and have their own TV shows." Here, Thornton presumably referred to the televangelists rocked by scandals in the late 1980s, many of whom brought southern religiosity into disrepute and further ridicule. But Thornton continued that he was "suspicious of anyone who starts telling me that God told 'em to do something," arguing that one was supposed to simply "believe in God, God's not supposed to be running our lives and giving us advice."[17]

By focusing on Thornton's upbringing in Arkansas, film critics touted the star as a genuine southerner, thus qualified to make value judgments about southern religion as well other films set in the region. As such, Thornton's attention was often drawn to the contemporaneous civil rights drama: "these things they make like *Ghosts of Mississippi* or *Mississippi Burning*. I can't even discuss those. . . . Why there's this desire to write about all these horrible things that happened over civil rights, I don't know." Such films achieve little more than "reminding people of our horrible past," Thornton continued, creating the impression that "everyone's supposed to be racist—it's just a bunch of poor fuckin' people eating cornbread down there. It makes people think that everyone from Mississippi is like Byron De La Beckwith or something." Making specific reference to *Ghosts of Mississippi*, released in the same year as *Sling Blade*, Thornton contended that James Woods—"a terrific actor"—had "no business playing" Beckwith, "just like I've got no business playing a yuppie lawyer from Manhattan."[18] However, although nonsouthern audiences may have made some presumptions about white Mississippians as a result of figures like Beckwith, Thornton did not acknowledge the lengths that civil rights melodramas went to portray a white liberal alternative to overt white supremacists. Nor did his concern for the representation of southerners appear to extend to African Americans. As such, Thornton's revealingly white conceptualization of southern identity perhaps explained his defensiveness, as poor white southerners absorbed a nation's racial guilt once again. That African Americans remained secondary players in what should have been their own stories did not appear to contribute to Thornton's indictment of the civil rights melodrama.

A Family Thing

Simultaneously lamenting and claiming ownership over Hollywood's repeated portrayal of the South's bitter racial history, Thornton's sensitivity reflects the fact that the civil rights drama had become a recognizable Hollywood preoccupation by the mid-1990s, shaping popular opinion about the South and the legacy of its racial progress. "There's more and more of those movies," interviewer Erik Bauer concurred when Thornton mentioned *Mississippi Burning* and *Ghosts of Mississippi*. "They're like their own genre now."[19] For Thornton, this was an unnecessary reminder of a turbulent past, and it was diverting attention from tales of racial reconciliation, like *A Family Thing* (Richard Pearce, 1996), which he cowrote with fellow white Arkansan Tom Epperson. "A specifically southern myth," *A Family Thing* centered on what Johnathan Rosenbaum called "the everyday intimacy among black and white people in the deep south that persists in spite of all the taboos against recognizing and acknowledging it."[20] The *Los Angeles Times* concluded that "if there were more films that explored America's racial divides with this much sense and sensitivity, maybe they wouldn't seem as broad and deep as they currently do."[21]

A Family Thing's plot revolves around Earl Pilcher Jr., a white Arkansan in his sixties who discovers his birth mother was actually African American and travels to Chicago to meet his surviving Black relatives. The story evolved from discussions with actor Robert Duvall, "who with his fair skin and blue eyes is about as Anglo as you get, [but] wanted to play a man who was half black."[22] Yet, when the final picture was released, its director Richard Pearce (who had also directed *The Long Walk Home*) claimed that the film was "not about race." Given the film's premise, *Variety* pondered, "why would any sentient viewer want to see it if it's not about [race]?"[23] Centered on Duvall's Earl, the film is less about experiencing life as a Black man in America and more about a white man coming to terms with his own "impure" bloodline. As a result, Earl's use of racial slurs is a key barrier in his early relationship with his newly discovered half brother Ray (James Earl Jones), while his attempt to engage a reluctant group of African Americans in a tired debate on affirmative action begins with tedious complaints of qualified white men being overlooked as the result of quotas. Despite the fact that he has known about his African American heritage for a matter of only days, Earl presents himself as a victim, arguing that "with me it's even worse, because I'm black as a coalminer's drawers, but still can't get on the quota wagon because I look like a white man."

In reaching Chicago, Earl follows in the footsteps of many a Black southerner hoping to leave Jim Crow behind. But once there, as Steven G. Kellman notes, Earl assumes the role of the tragic "born-again mulatto," or as he calls himself, a "blue-eyed n****r."[24] Little more than an out-of-town white cracker to the local toughs, Earl is goaded, beaten, and carjacked in broad daylight at a busy intersection. Here and later when he is thrown out of a bar, the camera moves in a deliberately disorienting fashion as a sea of Black faces watch Earl with suspicion and hostility. Ignored by these anonymous Black Chicagoans, he is nevertheless nursed back to health at the insistence of his birth mother's sister, Aunt T (Irma P. Hall). The only living person who truly knows the circumstances around Earl's birth, Aunt T's physical blindness renders her a color-blind prophet, further symbolized during the film's final credits as she walks through Chicago's West Side to the tune of Aretha Franklin's "Spirit in the Dark."

As a result of Aunt T's persistence, Earl begins to make in-roads with Ray, bonding over their shared experiences in the U.S. military and as fathers. Eventually, they return to Arkansas together to visit their mother's grave. Here, Earl makes plans to introduce Ray to his family, though we never actually see this happen on-screen or how Earl's family respond. Therefore, although the narrative is ostensibly about two brothers finding each other, it is more about Earl's experiences in a fetishized Black Chicago—"I might as well be on Mars than be up here with y'all people." Indeed, Earl is supported to come to terms with his African American heritage within a Black space, but Ray is not afforded the same emotional development when confronted with whiteness. Although Ray has always known about his white half brother, having been present at his birth, they have been separated for approximately sixty years. Ray admits that his only thoughts of his half brother up until this point were of killing him and his father. However, in centering southern whiteness as neutral and nonthreatening, as opposed to a racially exclusive urban Blackness, it is nevertheless implied that it will be much easier for Ray to return to white, working-class Arkansas and find himself face-to-face with the man who raped his mother (Earl's father) than it was for Earl to survive Black Chicago. Indeed, the rural South remains the most logical place for their reunion to culminate—as native Arkansans, they are both now "home."

This emphasis on the healing powers of the rural South also marks *Down in the Delta* (1998), Maya Angelou's only directorial venture, as Loretta (Alfre Woodard), a poorly educated, alcohol- and drug-addicted Chicago mother, finds solace and inspiration among forgotten extended relatives in the Mississippi Delta. In its focus on multiple generations of the same African American family, the film forces viewers to consider the history of slavery and its lasting implications for inherited wealth and Black opportunity. Also explored are the false promises of the urban North and the ease with which those failed by the education system can slip into a life of poverty and/ or substance abuse. As such, *Down in the Delta* does not flinch from the enduring and unsettling legacies of slavery and Jim Crow on African American life in the 1990s, causing one unsympathetic reviewer on the Christian site *Movieguide* to lament its "politically correct and socialist implications of minority entitlements."[25]

For his part, Billy Bob Thornton made no explicit comment on contemporary race relations—in the South or nationally—when criticizing the civil rights melodrama in the mid-1990s. Rather, his comments reflected an assumption that racial tension was confined to "our horrible past" and that stories of reconciliation were more important in late twentieth-century America, where the races remained unnervingly separate. Indeed, what Thornton seemed to resent the most was the image of poor whites that was circulating through the civil rights melodrama, or at least the image of "poor fuckin' people eating cornbread." But even though Earl Pilcher leaves the region on a voyage of self-discovery, before returning—enlightened and reconciled—to Arkansas with his Black brother in tow, our image of the South itself is effectively limited to the first twenty minutes of the film and a few key visu-

Half brothers Earl (Robert Duvall) and Ray (James Earl Jones) climb the hill to the Arkansas churchyard where their mother is buried in the final scenes of *A Family Thing* (Richard Pearce, 1996).

als: African American men playing dominoes under a looming Confederate statue in the town square, Earl's father's disdain at a "damn Yankee" customer from Wisconsin, the white-columned house with a wraparound porch where Earl's parents live, and an isolated statue of an angel as a propeller plane flies overhead.

A Family Thing's engagement with religion is subtle but evident. Both Ray and Earl frequently make reference to "the Good Lord," while Ray in particular is certain that he has been "blessed." Scenes of the two men climbing a country lane in rural Arkansas, the white-painted church where their mother is buried looming ahead of them, were used frequently in promotional materials, symbolizing the spiritual journey they are undertaking together in search of family and identity. Such emphasis reflects Thornton's general sympathy for religion, which stood in direct contrast to the ambivalence exhibited by the white directors of civil rights melodramas, whose representations of the South tended to malign white religiosity while celebrating an apparently static, monolithic Black faith.

Reinforcing the divisions of whiteness arguably first evidenced in *To Kill a Mockingbird*, religion proved crucial to late twentieth-century Hollywood's attempts to make sense of both the backlash to civil rights legislation in the 1960s as well as the rising surge of conservatism in its present day. As a result, civil rights melodramas flattened the diversity of white responses to the civil rights movement, ignoring those Christians inspired by their faith to protest alongside African Americans as well as those who expressed their commitment to segregation in a more refined manner than demagogic preachers committed to the supposedly biblically sanctioned separation of the races. In reality, social passivity was common among white southerners of all convictions.

As white redemption narratives, few civil rights dramas contain any reference to mainstream Christianity, where religious preoccupations would seemingly obscure the white hero's and indeed the film's claims to secular righteousness. *Selma* has complicated the notion that white religious southerners were alone in their resistance to the legislative changes of the civil rights era or that white Christians were not compelled by Martin Luther King Jr.'s message of ecumenical solidarity in the pursuit of human rights. However, celebrating secular whiteness remains a powerful convention in mainstream Hollywood. This often comes at the expense of screentime for Black activism and empowerment but creates prominent divisions of whiteness along regional, class, and religious fault lines too.

Religion is crucial to the continued representation of the South as a region apart from the rest of the nation. Accordingly, its specific manifestations in films that examine the civil rights era and its legacy have lasting implications for popular understandings of the movement, the region, and its religious culture. Analyzing how religion intersects with other key coordinates of the white South in mainstream cinema provides fresh perspectives on the region's place in American cinema as well as new methodologies through which to examine the enduring inferences of the 1960s and the resulting culture wars.

NOTES

Introduction. The Divine and the Depraved

1. Wesley Strick interviewed in "The Making of the 1991 *Cape Fear*," DVD Special Features, *Cape Fear* Boxset, J. Lee Thompson, Martin Scorsese (dir.), Universal Pictures UK, 2001.

2. Throughout this book, religious movements such as Evangelicalism or Pentecostalism are capitalized, while references to individual adherents or rhetoric are lowercase—"evangelical" or "pentecostal." Exceptions occur when quoting other authors who prefer to capitalize any reference to religious movements and groups.

3. Beth Barton Schweiger, "Max Weber in Mount Airy; or, Revivals and Social Theory in the Early South," in *Religion in the American South: Protestants and Others in History and Culture*, ed. Beth Barton Schweiger and Donald G. Mathews (Chapel Hill: University of North Carolina Press, 2004), 32.

4. Rama Allen, interview conducted by Remco Vlaanderen, March 2009, for "Watch the Titles," accessed March 18, 2019, https://www.watchthetitles.com/titlesequence/true-blood/.

5. "Making of, Featurette," Digital Kitchen website, accessed February 1, 2019, https://www.thisisdk.com/trueblood.

6. Matt Mulder quoted in "Making of, Featurette."

7. Allen, "Watch the Titles."

8. Allison Graham, *Framing the South: Hollywood, Television, and Race during the Civil Rights Struggle* (Baltimore: Johns Hopkins University Press, 2001).

9. Leigh Anne Duck, *The Nation's Region: Southern Modernism, Segregation, and U.S. Nationalism* (Athens: University of Georgia Press, 2006), 9.

10. Justin Gomer, *White Balance: How Hollywood Shaped Colorblind Ideology and Undermined Civil Rights* (Chapel Hill: University of North Carolina Press, 2020).

11. David R. Jansson, "Internal Orientalism in America: W. J. Cash's The Mind of the South and the Spatial Construction of American National Identity," *Political Geography* 22, no. 3 (March 2003): 293, 296–98; Edward Said, *Orientalism* (New York: Vintage, 1979). For the original "southernization" hypothesis, see Howard Zinn, *The Southern Mystique* (New York: Knopf, 1964); John Egerton, *The Americanization of Dixie: The Southernization of America* (New York: Harper's Magazine Press, 1974). For its specific development later in the century, see Peter Applebome, *Dixie Rising: How the South Is Shaping American Values, Politics and Culture* (New York: Harcourt Brace, 1996); Dan Carter, *The Politics of Rage: George Wallace, the Origins of the New Conservatism, and the Transformation of American Politics*, 2nd ed. (Baton Rouge: Louisiana State University Press, 2000).

12. Gomer, *White Balance*, 145. Sharon Monteith writes that prior to the 1980s, civil rights analogies "could turn up in any popular genre from westerns to courtroom dramas, and even comedies." Sharon Monteith, "The Movie-Made Movement: Civil Rites of Passage," in *Memory and Popular Film*, ed. Paul Grainge (Manchester, UK: Manchester University Press, 2003), 121. See also Sharon Monteith, "Exploitation

Movies and the Freedom Struggle of the 1960s," in *American Cinema and the Southern Imaginary*, ed. Deborah E. Barker and Kathryn McKee (Athens: University of Georgia Press, 2011), 196.

13. Jennifer Fuller, "Debating the Present through the Past: Representations of the Civil Rights Movement in the 1990s," in *The Civil Rights Movement in American Memory*, ed. Leigh Raiford and Renee C. Romano (Athens: University of Georgia Press, 2006), 176.

14. James Snead, *White Screens, Black Images: Hollywood from the Dark Side*, ed. Colin McCabe and Cornel West (New York: Routledge, 1994), 3; Judith Weisenfeld, *Hollywood Be Thy Name: African American Religion in American Film, 1929–1949* (Berkeley: University of California Press, 2007), 236.

15. Ralph J. Poole and Ilka Saal, eds., "Passionate Politics: An Introduction," in *Passionate Politics: The Cultural Work of American Melodrama from the Early Republic to the Present* (Newcastle, UK: Cambridge Scholars Publishing, 2008), 2; Graham, *Framing of the South*, 154.

16. Robert Jackson, *Fade In, Crossroads: A History of the Southern Cinema* (New York: Oxford University Press, 2017).

17. See, for example, Matthew D. Lassiter, *The Silent Majority: Suburban Politics in the Sunbelt South* (Princeton: Princeton University Press, 2006); Lisa McGirr, *Suburban Warriors: The Origins of the New American Right* (Princeton: Princeton University Press, 2001); and E. J. Dionne Jr., *Souled Out: Reclaiming Faith and Politics after the Religious Right* (Princeton: Princeton University Press, 2009), 54.

18. Ralph C. Wood, *Flannery O'Connor and the Christ-Haunted South* (Grand Rapids: Eerdmans, 2005), 52.

19. W. Fitzhugh Brundage, review of *Flashes of a Southern Spirit*, by Charles Reagan Wilson, *Church History* 81, no. 3 (September 2012): 731.

20. Wood, *Flannery O'Connor and the Christ-Haunted South*, 34.

21. Colleen McDannell, *Picturing Faith: Photography and the Great Depression* (New Haven: Yale University Press, 2005), 83.

22. Charles Angoff and H. L. Mencken, "The Worst American State: Part III," *The American Mercury*, November 1931, 371.

23. Fred Hobson, "'This Hellawful South': Mencken and the Late Confederacy," in *A Southern Enigma: Essays on the U.S. South* (Valencia, Spain: Publicacions de la Universitat de Valencia, 2008), 38. Hobson also notes that until the Scopes trial, Mencken had never been farther south than Virginia (46).

24. John B. Boles, "The Discovery of Southern Religious History," in *Interpreting Southern History: Historiographical Essays in Honor of Sanford W. Higginbotham*, ed. John B. Boles and Evelyn Thomas Nolen (Baton Rouge: Louisiana State University Press, 1987), 511.

25. Edward L. Ayers, "W. J. Cash, the New South, and the Rhetoric of History," in *The Mind of the South: Fifty Years Later*, ed. Charles W. Eagles (Jackson,: University Press of Mississippi, 1992), 125. See C. Vann Woodward, *The Burden of Southern History*, 1960 (Baton Rouge: Louisiana State University Press, 2008).

26. Ayers, "W. J. Cash," 126.

27. C. Van Woodward, letter to Hunter D. Farish, February 5, 1940, published in *The Letters of C. Vann Woodward*, ed. Michael O'Brien (New Haven: Yale University Press, 2013), 76.

28. Charles Reagan Wilson, *Flashes of a Southern Spirit: Meanings of the Spirit in the U.S. South* (Athens: University of Georgia Press, 2011), 51.

29. Graham, *Framing the South*, 154. Others suggest that the scholarly neglect of religion is not unique to the study of the South. See Jon Butler, "Jack-in-the-Box Faith: The Religion Problem in Modern American History," *Journal of American History* 90, no. 4 (March 2004): 1357; Kevin M. Schultz and Paul Harvey, "Everywhere and Nowhere: Recent Trends in American Religious History and Historiography," *Journal of the American Academy of Religion* 78, no.1 (March 2010): 129–62.

30. Notable exceptions include Arthur Remillard, *Southern Civil Religions: Imagining the Good Society in the Post-Reconstruction Era* (Athens: University of Georgia Press, 2011); and John Hayes, *Hard, Hard Religion: Interracial Faith in the Poor South* (Chapel Hill: University of North Carolina Press, 2017).

31. "Pew Religious Landscape Study 2014, Chapter 3: Demographic Profiles of Religious Groups, Regional Distribution of Religious Groups," accessed November 30, 2019, http://www.pewforum.org/2015/05/12/chapter-3-demographic-profiles-of-religious-groups/.

32. "The American Religious Landscape in 2020," *PRRI*, July 8, 2021, accessed August 11, 2022, https://www.prri.org/research/2020-census-of-american-religion/.

33. Frank Newport, "Mississippi Retains Standing as Most Religious State," February 8, 2017, https://news.gallup.com/poll/203747/mississippi-retains-standing-religious-state.aspx; Frank Newport, "Mississippi Most Religious State, Vermont Least Religious," February 3 2014, http://www.gallup.com/poll/167267/mississippi-religious-vermont-least-religious-state.aspx.

34. "Pew Religious Landscape Study," accessed May 27, 2019, http://www.pewforum.org/religious-landscape-study/; Map: "Percentage of U.S. Adults Who Are affiliated with the Evangelical Protestant Tradition," accessed May 27, 2019, http://www.pewforum.org/religious-landscape-study/religious-tradition/evangelical-protestant/.

35. As of the 2014 Pew Religious Landscape Study, Southern Baptists make up 5.3 percent of the American population. Kate Shellnutt, "Southern Baptists Drop 1.1 Million Members in Three Years," *Christianity Today*, May 12, 2022, https://www.christianitytoday.com/news/2022/may/southern-baptist-membership-decline-covid-pandemic-baptisms.html.

36. "Pew Religious Landscape Study, Geography," accessed March 11, 2019, http://www.pewforum.org/religious-landscape-study/#geography.

37. Ted Ownby, "Evangelical but Differentiated: Religion by the Numbers," in *Religion and Public Life in the South: In the Evangelical Mode*, ed. Charles Reagan Wilson and Mark Silk (Walnut Creek, Calif.: AltaMira, 2005), 39.

38. James R. Shortridge, Philip Barlow, and Roger Stump, "Geography of Southern Religion," in *Encyclopedia of Religion in the South*, ed. Samuel Hill, Charles H. Lippy, and Charles Reagan Wilson (Macon, Ga.: Mercer University Press, 2005), 345.

39. Samuel Hill, ed., "Florida," in *Religion in the Southern States: A Historical Study* (Macon, Ga.: Mercer University Press, 1983), 70, 57.

40. "Pew Religious Landscape Study, Adults in Louisiana," accessed November 25, 2019, http://www.pewforum.org/religious-landscape-study/state/louisiana/.

41. Schweiger, "Max Weber in Mount Airy," 36–37.

42. Wilson, *Flashes of a Southern Spirit*, 95.

43. Charles Reagan Wilson, "Conclusion: Mobilized for the New Millennium,"

Religion and Public Life in the South: In the Evangelical Mode, ed. Charles Reagan Wilson and Mark Silk (Walnut Creek, Calif.: AltaMira, 2005), 197.

44. Carole Emberton, *Beyond Redemption: Race, Violence, and the American South after the Civil War* (Chicago: University of Chicago Press, 2013), 4.

45. Paul Harvey, *Freedom's Coming: Religious Culture and the Shaping of the South from the Civil War through the Civil Rights Era* (Chapel Hill: University of North Carolina Press, 2005), 230.

46. Edward J. Blum and Paul Harvey, *The Color of Christ: The Son of God and the Saga of Race in America* (Chapel Hill: University of North Carolina Press, 2012), 215.

47. Harvey, *Freedom's Coming*, 229.

48. On white Christian nationalism, see Robert P. Jones, *The End of White Christian America* (New York: Simon and Schuster, 2016); Philip S. Gorski and Samuel L. Perry, *The Flag and the Cross: White Christian Nationalism and the Threat to American Democracy* (New York: Oxford University Press, 2022); Anthea D. Butler, *White Evangelical Racism: The Politics of Morality in America* (Chapel Hill: University of North Carolina Press, 2021); and Robert P. Jones, *White Too Long: The Legacy of White Supremacy in American Christianity* (New York: Simon and Schuster, 2020).

49. Jane Dailey, "Sex, Segregation, and the Sacred after Brown," *Journal of American History* 91, no. 1 (June 2004): 120.

50. David Chappell, *Stone of Hope: Prophetic Religion and the Death of Jim Crow* (Chapel Hill: University of North Carolina Press, 2004), 8.

51. Dailey, "Sex, Segregation, and the Sacred," 120.

52. Schultz and Harvey, "Everywhere and Nowhere," 150.

53. Weisenfeld, *Hollywood Be Thy Name*, 235.

54. Ryan Jay Friedman, *Hollywood's African American Films: The Transition to Sound* (New Brunswick, N.J.: Rutgers University Press, 2011), 145.

55. Richard Corliss, "Fire This Time," *Time*, January 9, 1989, http://content.time.com/time/magazine/article/0,9171,956683,00.html.

56. Monteith, "The Movie-Made Movement," 121. Rick Altman has argued that genre "provides a specific set of intertexts (the other films identified by the film industry as belonging to the same genre)" and thus links filmmakers and audiences in "a self-contained equivalent of an interpretive community." Over time, genres "control the audience's reaction to any specific film by providing the context in which that film must be interpreted." Rick Altman, *The American Film Musical* (Bloomington: Indiana University Press, 1987), 4.

57. Laurie Schulze, "The Made-for-TV Movie: Industrial Practice, Cultural Form, Popular Reception," in *Hollywood in the Age of Television*, ed. Tino Balio (Cambridge, Mass.: Unwin Hyman, 1990), 364. See also Elayne Rapping, "Made for TV Movies: The Domestication of Social Issues," *Cineaste* 14, no. 2 (1985): 30.

58. See Richard Levinson and William Link, *Stay Tuned: An Inside Look at the Making of Prime-Time Television* (New York: St. Martin's, 1981), 46, 27.

59. Gary Edgerton, *The Columbia History of American Television* (New York: Columbia University Press, 2010), 246. "Gail Fisher Only Black TV Star to Win an Emmy," *Jet*, June 25, 1970, 57. Fisher won Best Supporting Actress in a Dramatic Series for her role in another Levinson and Link production: the detective series *Mannix* (CBS, 1967–75).

60. Ruth Feldstein, *How It Feels to Be Free: Black Women Entertainers and the Civil Rights Movement* (New York: Oxford University Press, 2013), 159; Pauline Kael, "The Current Cinema: Cicely Tyson Goes to the Fountain," *New Yorker*, January 28, 1974, 74. Quotations from Kael's review were used to promote the film.

61. Allison Graham and Sharon Monteith, eds., "Southern Media Cultures," *The New Encyclopedia of Southern Culture*, vol. 18: Media (Chapel Hill: University of North Carolina Press, 2011), 7.

62. "Says Lonne Elder: 'Sounder' Movie Is Not like the Book," *New York Amsterdam News,* September 23, 1972, 2.

63. See Henry Bourgeois, "Hollywood and the Civil Rights Movement: The Case of *Mississippi Burning*," *Howard Journal of Communications* 4, no. 1–2 (1992): 157–63; Robert Brent Toplin, "*Mississippi Burning*: 'A Standard to Which We Couldn't Live Up,'" in *History by Hollywood: The Use and Abuse of the American Past* (Champaign: University of Illinois Press, 1996), 25–44; David R. Jansson, "'A Geography of Racism': Internal Orientalism and the Construction of American National Identity in the Film *Mississippi Burning*," *National Identities* 7, no. 3 (September 2005): 265–85.

64. Although my emphasis here is on Faulkner's presentation of intra-white conflict, it should be noted that his novel and Clarence Brown's subsequent film adaptation feature a strong Black male character in Lucas Beauchamp. In 1973, Donald Bogle praised Juano Hernandez's "performance and extraordinary presence" in the role of Lucas, which Bogle argued "still rank[ed] above that of almost any other black actor to appear in an American movie." See Donald Bogle, *Toms, Coons, Mulattoes, Mammies, and Bucks: An Interpretive History of Blacks in American Films* (New York: Continuum, 2001), 154.

65. Thornton quoted in Erik Bauer, "'I'm Pretty Anti-violence. I Don't Want to Do More Movies about Violence'—Billy Bob Thornton," interview for *Creative Screenwriting*, accessed January 3, 2023, http://creativescreenwriting.com /im-pretty-anti-violence-i-dont-want-to-do-more-movies-about-violence-bill -bob-thornton/.

Chapter 1. "They Take the Bible Literally You Know"

1. Janet Maslin, "For a True Story, Dipping into the Classics," *New York Times*, December 20, 1996, https://www.nytimes.com/1996/12/20/movies/for-a-true-story -dipping-into-the-classics.html?rref=collection%2Fcollection%2Fmovie-guide.

2. Ty Burr, "A Time to Kill; To Kill a Mockingbird," *Entertainment Weekly*, January 10, 1997, http://www.ew.com/article/1997/01/10/time-kill-kill-mockingbird. Other reviews that specifically compare the two films include Hal Hinson, "'Time to Kill': Justice Gets a Make-Over," *Washington Post*, July 24, 1996, http://www .washingtonpost.com/wp-srv/style/longterm/review96/timetokillhin.htm; and Rob Dreher, "Time to Star: Moral Tale, Memorable Performances," *Sun Sentinel*, July 24, 1996, http://articles.sun-sentinel.com/1996-07-24/lifestyle/9607230183_1_carl-lee -hailey-jake-brigance-gas-chamber.

3. Random House, "Teacher's Guide: A Time to Kill," accessed December 14, 2019, https://www.randomhouse.com/catalog/teachers_guides/9780440245919.pdf, 1.

4. Burr, "A Time to Kill." Peck was forty-six years old when he played Finch.

5. Jennifer L. Pierce, *Racing for Innocence: Whiteness, Gender, and the Backlash against Affirmative Action* (Stanford: Stanford University Press, 2012), 49.

6. Donald Bogle, *Toms, Coons, Mulattoes, Mammies, and Bucks: An Interpretive History of Blacks in American Films* (New York: Continuum, 2001), 418.

7. Rob Atkinson, "Liberating Lawyers: Divergent Parallels in *Intruder in the Dust* and *To Kill a Mockingbird*," *Duke Law Journal* 49, no. 3 (December 1999): 601.

8. Ralph Ellison, "The Shadow and the Act," *The Reporter*, December 6, 1949, reprinted in Ralph Ellison, *Shadow and Act* (New York: Vintage, 1973), 281.

9. Maureen E. Markey, "Natural Law, Positive Law, and Conflicting Social Norms in Harper Lee's *To Kill a Mockingbird*," *North Carolina Central Law Review* 32 (2009): 221–22.

10. Although the chronology of Lee's writing remains somewhat unclear, the dominant understanding is that *Go Set a Watchman* (London: William Heinemann, 2015) reflects her first manuscript about the adult Scout (now known by her real name Jean Louise) returning to Maycomb from New York to visit her ailing father, Atticus. *To Kill a Mockingbird* (1960; New York: Grand Central Publishing /Hachette Book Group, 2010) resituated the narrative to Scout's childhood and was released to huge success in 1960.

11. *To Kill a Mockingbird* has not been sheltered entirely from controversy. Sporadic lawsuits occurred across the South in the mid-1960s as the novel became entrenched in school curricula and emerged again from the late 1970s onward. Yet, whereas objections in the 1960s usually arose from concerned white parents critical of the book's integrationist message and derogatory depictions of whites, more recent concerns have been raised by liberals, who argue that the book uses racial slurs and fails to critique institutionalized racism. See Jill May, "In Defense of *To Kill a Mockingbird*," in *Social Issues in Literature: Racism in Harper Lee's To Kill a Mockingbird*, ed. Candice Mancini (Farmington Hills, Mich.: Greenhaven Press, 2008), 56–58.

12. Rebecca H. Best, "Panopticism and the Use of 'the Other' in *To Kill a Mockingbird*," *Mississippi Quarterly* 63, no. 3–4 (Summer 2009): 541–43. See also Michel Foucault, *Discipline and Punish: The Birth of the Prison* (London: Penguin, 1991); Lee, *To Kill a Mockingbird*, 7. Hereafter referenced as *TKAM*.

13. Cleanth Brooks, *The Hidden God: Studies in Hemingway, Faulkner, Yeats, Eliot, and Warren* (New Haven: Yale University Press, 1963), 22–23; TKAM, 9, 213.

14. Sam Hodges, "Harper Lee Was United Methodist in Word, Deed," United Methodist Church News, February 19, 2016, http://www.umc.org /news-and-media/harper-lee-was-united-methodist-in-word-deed.

15. *TKAM*, 139. John Stevens offers a similar, if not overtly religious, moral insight in the film adaptation of *Intruder in the Dust*, informing Lucas Beauchamp that "I'm trying to save your life. Not for your sake, since you're bent on throwing it away, but for my own sake, so I won't have to carry it on my conscience."

16. *TKAM*, 11.

17. *TKAM*, 59–60.

18. *TKAM*, 22, 33.

19. *TKAM*, 285, 194, 157–58.

20. See Robert Butler, "The Religious Vision of *To Kill a Mockingbird*," in *On Harper Lee: Essays and Reflections*, ed. Alice Hall Petry (Knoxville: University of Tennessee Press, 2007), 131. *Go Set a Watchman* offers a considerably differ-

ent take on this scene as the grown Scout (now known by her given name Jean Louise) visits Calpurnia's home. She is horrified to find Calpurnia detached and "wearing her company manners," treating Jean Louise like any other white visitor. "Why are you shutting me out? What are you doing to me?" Jean Louise demands of her former carer, who responds simply, "What are you all doing to us?" See Lee, *Go Set a Watchman*, 160–61.

21. *TKAM*, 157; Teresa Godwin Phelps, "The Margins of Maycomb: A Rereading of *To Kill a Mockingbird*," *Alabama Law Review* 45, no. 2 (Winter 1994): 528.

22. *TKAM*, 158–59.

23. It was at Christmas 1956, as the Montgomery bus boycott came to an end, that songwriter and composer Michael Brown gifted Lee enough money to quit her job and dedicate herself to writing what would become *Go Set a Watchman* and later *To Kill a Mockingbird* full time. Lee never revealed the names of her benefactors, but they spoke of their gift during interviews for Mary McDonagh Murphy's documentary, *Hey, Boo: Harper Lee and To Kill a Mockingbird*, which aired on PBS as part of the *American Masters* series on July 10, 2015.

24. "That Calpurnia led a modest double life [had] never [previously] dawned on me," Scout muses (*TKAM*, 167); W. E. B. Du Bois, *The Souls of Black Folk* (Mineola, N.Y.: Dover, 1994), 2.

25. *TKAM*, 167, 162.

26. Dean Shackelford, "The Female Voice in *To Kill a Mockingbird*: Narrative Strategies in Film and Novel," *Mississippi Quarterly* 50, no. 1 (Winter 1996/97): 105.

27. Bradley Shaw, "Baptizing Boo: Religion in the Cinematic Southern Gothic," *Mississippi Quarterly* 63, no. 3 (Summer 2010), 458.

28. Ryu Spaeth, "Is *To Kill a Mockingbird* racist?" *The Week*, July 17, 2015, http://the-week.com/articles/566893/kill-mockingbird-racist. See also Isaac Chotiner, "A Conversation with Ta-Nehisi Coates," *Slate*, July 13, 2015, http://www.slate.com /articles/arts/culturebox/2015/07/ta_nehisi_coates_the_between_the_world_and _me_author_on_charleston_obama.single.html.

29. James Farmer, *Lay Bare the Heart: An Autobiography of the Civil Rights Movement* (Fort Worth: Texas Christian University Press, 1985), 14.

30. Eric J. Sundquist, "Blues for Atticus Finch: Scottsboro, *Brown*, and Harper Lee," in *The South as an American Problem*, ed. Larry J. Griffin and Don H. Doyle (Athens: University of Georgia Press, 1995), 183.

31. Andrew Young quoted in Michiko Kakutani, "Kind Hero of Mockingbird Is Cast as Racist in New Book," *New York Times*, July 11, 2015, A3.

32. Robert Mulligan, "Production Notes," Special Features, *To Kill a Mockingbird* (dir. Robert Mulligan), DVD: Universal Studios, 2008.

33. May, "In Defense of *TKAM*," 64; Sundquist, "Blues for Atticus Finch," 197, 199.

34. *TKAM*, 294.

35. *TKAM*, 117.

36. *TKAM*, 323.

37. Joseph Crespino, *Atticus Finch: The Biography* (New York: Basic Books, 2018), 17–18.

38. Isaac Saney, "The Case against *To Kill a Mockingbird*," *Race and Class* 45, no. 1 (July 2003): 103.

39. *TKAM*, 273–74, 313.

40. Chura also points out that the Works Progress Administration (WPA) is men-

tioned in the novel's fourth chapter, set in 1933, despite the fact that the WPA was not established until 1935. See Patrick Chura, "The Historical Conditions of the Novel," in *Harper Lee's To Kill a Mockingbird*, ed. Harold Bloom (New York: Infobase Publishing, 2010), 48.

41. Sundquist, "Blues for Atticus Finch," 185–86.

42. Mamie Till-Mobley, with Christopher Benson, *Death of Innocence: The Story of the Hate Crime that Changed America* (New York: Penguin Random House, 2003), 188–89.

43. William Bradford Huie, "The Shocking Story of Approved Killing in Mississippi," *Look*, January 24, 1956.

44. Heather Pool, "Mourning Emmett Till," *Law, Culture, and the Humanities* 11, no. 3 (October 2015): 425.

45. Most white Americans did not see the images of Till's body until the seminal civil rights documentary *Eyes on the Prize* (PBS, 1987). See Pool, "Mourning Emmett Till," 432.

46. Pool, "Mourning Emmett Till," 420, 426.

47. *Brown v. Board of Education*, 347 U.S. 483, 494 (1954).

48. *TKAM*, 273–74.

49. Lee, *Go Set a Watchman*, 246.

50. Michael J. Klarman, Brown v. Board of Education *and the Civil Rights Movement* (New York: Oxford University Press, 2007), 179.

51. See Alexandra Alter, "Harper Lee, Author of 'To Kill a Mockingbird,' Is to Publish a Second Novel," New York Times, February 3, 2015, http://www.nytimes .com/2015/02/04/books/harper-lee-author-of-to-kill-a-mockingbird-is-to -publish-a-new-novel.html.

52. Lee, *Go Set a Watchman*, 149.

53. Brilliant Books, Michigan, "Go Set a Watchman—An Opinion Piece," accessed May 12, 2019, http://www.brilliant-books.net/go-set-watchman-opinion-piece.

54. Lee, *Go Set a Watchman*, 110.

55. Narration, *Fearful Symmetry: The Making of To Kill a Mockingbird* (dir. Charles Kiselyak), 1998. Special Features, *To Kill a Mockingbird* DVD.

56. For a critique of Atticus in *Mockingbird* and the cultural relativism that others have used to defend him, see Monroe Freedman, "Atticus Finch—Right and Wrong," *Alabama Law Review* 45, no. 2 (Winter 1994): 473–82.

57. Talbot D'Alemberte, president of the American Bar Association in 1991–92, wrote an article for *Legal Times* challenging Freedman's article, arguing that "Finch rose above racism and injustice to defend the principle that all men and women deserve their day in court." See Talbot D'Alemberte, "Remembering Atticus Finch's Pro Bono Legacy," *Legal Times*, April 6, 1992, 26.

58. Joseph Crespino, "The Strange Career of Atticus Finch," *Southern Cultures* 6, no. 2 (Summer 2000): 9–29. See "Letters to the Editors," *Southern Cultures* 6, no. 4 (Winter 2000): 1.

59. Stephen L. Carter, "'Watchman' Is Harper Lee for Grown-Ups," *BloombergView*, July 15, 2015, http://www.bloombergview.com /articles/2015-07-15/-watchman-is-harper-lee-for-grown-ups.

60. Harper Lee to Harold Caulfield, 1961, quoted in Gaby Wood, "Harper Lee: The Inside Story of the Greatest Comeback in Literature," *Telegraph*, February 19, 2016,

http://www.telegraph.co.uk/books/go-set-a-watchman/the-curious-case-of
-harper-lee/.

61. Lee, *Go Set a Watchman*, 238–39.

62. Lee, *Go Set a Watchman,* 242.

63. Allen Mendenhall, "Children Once, Not Forever: Harper Lee's *Go Set a Watchman* and Growing Up," *Indiana Law Journal Supplement* 91, no. 6 (2015): 13.

64. Lee, *Go Set a Watchman*, 97.

65 Lee, *Go Set a Watchman*, 60, 61, 65.

66. Lee, *Go Set a Watchman*, 91–92, 167.

67. Kakutani, "Kind Hero of Mockingbird," A3.

68. Katy Waldman, "Atticus Has Become a Racist Confederate Apologist. It Shouldn't Change Our Opinion of Him," *Slate*, July 15, 2015, https://slate.com /culture/2015/07/go-set-a-watchman-atticus-is-a-racist-confederate-apologist -here-s-why-that-shouldn-t-change-our-opinion-of-him.html.

69. Waldman, "Atticus."

70. Lee, *Go Set a Watchman*, 201.

71. Robert H. Brinkmeyer, "The Dynamics of Segregation in Harper Lee's *To Kill a Mockingbird* and *Go Set a Watchman*," in *New Interpretations of Harper Lee's To Kill a Mockingbird and Go Set a Watchman*, ed. Amy Mohr and Mark Olival-Bartley (Newcastle, UK: Cambridge Scholars, 2019), 14.

72. Sundquist, "Blues for Atticus Finch," 183, 205–6.

73. Phelps, "Margins of Maycomb," 529.

74. W. J. Stuckey, "*To Kill a Mockingbird* Is a Good but Flawed Novel," in *Readings on To Kill a Mockingbird*, ed. Terry O'Neill (New York: Greenhaven Press, 2000), 26.

75. Lesley Marx, "Mockingbirds in the Land of Hadedahs: The South African Response to Harper Lee," in Petry, *On Harper Lee,* 115.

76. *TKAM*, 209, 321. In the novel, Atticus and Calpurnia meet Jem and Dill along the way to Helen Robinson's house, and the boys confirm in their summary of events that Calpurnia was in the back seat.

77. Phelps, "Margins of Maycomb," 529.

78. *TKAM*, 294, 117, 218.

79. *TKAM*, 316.

80. *TKAM,* 316.

81. *TKAM*, 127.

82. *TKAM*, 130, 127, 118, 288–89.

83. Crespino, "Strange Career of Atticus Finch," 18.

84. Tony Badger, "Fatalism, Not Gradualism: The Crisis of Southern Liberalism, 1945–65," in *The Making of Martin Luther King and the Civil Rights Movement*, ed. Brian Ward and Tony Badger (New York: New York University Press, 1996), 89.

85. *TKAM*, 310.

86. Crespino, "Strange Career of Atticus Finch," 18.

87. *TKAM*, 124.

88. "Only about 15% of the novel is devoted to Tom Robinson's rape trial, whereas in the film, the running time is more than 30% of a two-hour film." See Shackelford, "The Female Voice in *To Kill a Mockingbird*," 102–3.

89. See Nicole Hahn Rafter, *Shots in the Mirror: Crime Films and Society* (New York: Oxford University Press, 2000), 102–3. Although Rafter's book provides a welcome and lively introduction to the history of American crime drama, she makes

some mistakes in her presentation of the 1950s and 1960s. She states that *To Kill a Mockingbird* is set in Georgia (98), rather than Alabama, and in her discussion of *Inherit the Wind* argues that many of the tensions evident in the film had "already been addressed in *To Kill a Mockingbird*" despite the fact that *Mockingbird* was released over two years after *Inherit the Wind* (104).

90. *TKAM*, 305, 307.

91. *TKAM*, 308–9.

92. *TKAM*, 310–12.

93. Mark Newman, *Getting Right with God: Southern Baptists and Desegregation, 1945–1995* (Tuscaloosa: University of Alabama Press, 2001), 129.

94. A. C. Miller, "Forty-Sixth Annual Report of the Christian Life Commission," published in the *Annual of the Southern Baptist Convention 1954: Proceedings June 2–5 1954, St. Louis, Missouri*, http://media2.sbhla.org.s3.amazonaws.com/annuals/SBC_Annual_1954.pdf, 404.

95. J. Marse Grant, "Stern Challenges Prod Convention Leadership," *Biblical Recorder*, June 3, 1961, 3.

96. Carolyn Dupont, *Mississippi Praying: Southern White Evangelicals and the Civil Rights Movement, 1945–1975* (New York: New York University Press, 2013), 54–57.

97. Markey, "Natural Law," 225.

98. Alan Pakula, Director's Commentary, DVD Special Features.

99. *TKAM*, 132, 135.

100. Mark Twain argued that Sir Walter Scott had done "measureless harm" to the American South, infecting the region with "the jejune romanticism of an absurd past that is dead." See Mark Twain, *Life on the Mississippi* (Kindle Edition, 2012), 82–83. Walter Scott may not have "man[ned] the batteries that fired on Fort Sumter," Scott Horton contended more recently in *Harper's*, but he did encourage "a whole generation of southerners [to think] about the idyllic life and plantation agriculture, with its natural order of aristocracy and slavery." See Scott Horton, "How Walter Scott Started the American Civil War," *Harper's Magazine*, July 29, 2007, https://harpers.org/2007/07/how-walter-scott-started-the-american-civil-war/.

101. *TKAM*, 149.

102. *TKAM*, 146–48.

103. Thomas Shaffer, "Growing Up Good in Maycomb," *Alabama Law Review* 45 (1993–94), 541.

104. Sundquist, "Blues for Atticus Finch," 193.

105. *TKAM*, 296.

106. Another character omitted from the film, Braxton Bragg Underwood was named for a Confederate general and, according to Atticus, "despises Negroes, won't have one near him." Yet he lurked in the shadows with his shotgun, determined to protect Atticus (and therefore Tom) from the lynch mob, emerging as a complex, if relatively minor, character. *TKAM*, 323, 209.

107. Andrew Sarris, "A Negro Is Not a Mockingbird," *Village Voice*, March 7, 1963, 15.

108. See Zoe A. Colley, *Ain't Scared of Your Jail: Arrest, Imprisonment, and the Civil Rights Movement* (Gainesville: University Press of Florida, 2012).

109. Sarris, "A Negro Is Not a Mockingbird," 15; *TKAM*, 315.

110. Martin Luther King Jr., "Letter from Birmingham Jail." The letter appeared in the *Birmingham News* and *Birmingham Post-Herald* on April 13, 1963. The follow-

ing day, it appeared in the *New York Times*. See S. Jonathan Bass, *Blessed Are the Peacemakers: Martin Luther King Jr., Eight White Religious Leaders, and the "Letter from Birmingham Jail"* (Baton Rouge: Louisiana State University Press, 2001), appendix 2.

111. Pakula, Director's Commentary.
112. *TKAM*, 22.
113. Diann L. Baecker, "The Africanist Presence in *To Kill a Mockingbird*," in Mancini, *Social Issues in Literature*, 109, 106; Laura Fine, "Structuring the Narrator's Rebellion in *To Kill a Mockingbird*," in Petry, On Harper Lee, 72.
114. Theodore R. Hovet and Grace-Anne Hovet, "Contending Voices in *To Kill a Mockingbird*," in Mancini, *Social Issues in Literature*, 118. *Forrest Gump* presents a similar narrative in which the motherless Jenny and her sister are abused by their white trash father. Jenny prays to God for deliverance: "Dear God, make me a bird so I can fly away."
115. *TKAM*, 296. Atticus also encourages Jem, but never Scout, to pursue a legal career.
116. *TKAM*, 227; Allison Graham, *Framing the South: Hollywood, Television, and Race during the Civil Rights Struggle* (Baltimore: Johns Hopkins University Press, 2001), 161.
117. Butler, "The Religious Vision," 125–26.
118. Shaw, "Baptizing Boo," 458. Readers' understanding of Boo's theological and family background comes from Scout's discussions with Miss Maudie, which do not appear in the film.
119. *TKAM*, 373.
120. Shaw, "Baptizing Boo," 456.
121. Sundquist, "Blues for Atticus Finch," 187.
122. *TKAM*, 376.
123. Sundquist, "Blues for Atticus Finch," 206.
124. Pakula, Director's Commentary.
125. *TKAM*, 210.
126. Freedman, "Atticus Finch," 476.
127. *TKAM*, 298.
128. Cleophus Thomas Jr., interviewed in *Fearful Symmetry: The Making of To Kill a Mockingbird* (dir. Charles Kiselyak), 1998.
129. Claudia Durst Johnson quoted in *Fearful Symmetry*.
130. Pakula, Production Notes.
131. Peck's previous production company, Melville Productions, produced *Cape Fear* (1962), after Peck purchased the rights to John D. MacDonald's novel *The Executioners*. He asked J. Lee Thompson to direct after working with him on *The Guns of Navarone* (1961) and came up with the title *Cape Fear* himself. *The Making of Cape Fear*, DVD Featurette.
132. Gregory Peck, letter to George Chasin and Mel Tucker, June 18, 1962, quoted in Gary Fishgall, *Gregory Peck: A Biography* (New York: Scribner, 2002), 236.
133. Peck, letter to Mel Tucker, July 6, 1962, quoted in Fishgall, *Gregory Peck,* 236.
134. Gregory Peck quoted in James Bacon, "Although Women's Hearts May Flutter, Gregory Peck Claims They Scare Him," *Reading Eagle* (Pa.), March 27, 1963, 53.
135. See Michael Freedland, "I'm the Only Journalist Alive to Have Interviewed Harper Lee—and It's All Thanks to Gregory Peck," *The Guardian*, July 13, 2015,

https://www.theguardian.com/commentisfree/2015/jul/13
/interviewed-harper-lee-to-kill-a-mockingbird-sequel-go-set-a-watchman.

136. Bob Thomas, "One Dixie Film That Isn't Sick," *Birmingham News*, March 26, 1962, 4.

137. Lee quoted in Charles Leerhsen, "Harper Lee's Novel Achievement," *Smithsonian Magazine*, June 2010, http://www.smithsonianmag.com/arts-culture /harper-lees-novel-achievement-141052/?no-ist.

138. Lee quoted in "Literary Laurels for a Novice," *Life*, May 26, 1961, 78A.

139. Robert Mulligan, "Production Notes," Special Features, *To Kill a Mockingbird* DVD.

140. Peck quoted in "Peck Applauded after Racial Quiz," *The Spokesman-Review*, May 20, 1963, 9.141. Thomas, "One Dixie Film That Isn't Sick," 4.

142. Allen Rivkin quoted in "Peck Applauded after Racial Quiz."

143. See Richard Roud, "The International Gravy Train," The Guardian, December 11, 1971, reprinted in *Decades Never Start on Time: A Richard Roud Anthology*, ed. Michael Temple and Karen Smolens (London: British Film Institute/Palgrave Macmillan, 2014), 123.

144. Here, Atticus's speech is almost verbatim from the novel. See *TKAM*, 273.

Chapter 2. "How Come the Only Cheek Gets Turned in This Country Is the Negro Cheek?"

1. President Barack Obama, Eulogy for Senator Reverend Clementa Pinckney, TD Arena, College of Charleston, South Carolina, June 26, 2015. Transcript accessed July 23, 2019, https://www.whitehouse.gov/the-press-office/2015/06/26 /remarks-president-eulogy-honorable-reverend-clementa-pinckney.

2. Ed Pilkington, "Obama Gives Searing Speech on Race in Eulogy for Charleston Pastor," *The Guardian*, June 26, 2015, http://www.theguardian.com/us-news/2015 /jun/26/obama-charleston-eulogy-pinckney-amazing-grace.

3. Margaret Talev and Mike Dorning, "The Audacity of Obama," *Bloomberg Politics*, June 28, 2015, http://www.bloomberg.com/politics/articles/2015-06-28/ the-audacity-of-obama.

4. R. Drew Smith, ed., *From Every Mountainside: Black Churches and the Broad Terrain of Civil Rights* (Albany: State University of New York Press, 2013), 1.

5. John Dittmer, *Local People: The Struggle for Civil Rights in Mississippi* (Urbana: University of Illinois Press, 1994); Adam Fairclough, *Race and Democracy: The Civil Rights Struggle in Louisiana, 1915–1972,* 2nd ed. (Athens: University of Georgia Press, 2008).

6. Taylor Branch, *Pillar of Fire: America in the King Years 1963–65* (New York: Simon and Schuster, 1998), 25.

7. Wallace Best, "'The Right Achieved and the Wrong Way Conquered': J. H. Jackson, Martin Luther King Jr., and the Conflict over Civil Rights," *Religion and American Culture* 16, no. 2 (Summer 2006): 197.

8. E. Wilbur Bock, "The Decline of the Negro Clergy: Changes in Formal Religious Leadership in the United States in the Twentieth Century," *Phylon* 29, no. 1 (1968): 57.

9. Barbara Dianne Savage, *Your Spirits Walk beside Us: The Politics of Black Religion* (Cambridge, Mass.: Harvard University Press, 2008), 270.

10. Eddie Glaude, "Publics, Prosperity, and Politics: The Changing Face of African American Christianity and Black Political Life," in *Crediting God: Sovereignty and*

Religion in the Age of Global Capitalism, ed. Miguel E. Vatter (Bronx: Fordham University Press, 2011), 287–88.

11. Monteith notes that TV movies *The Road to Freedom: The Vernon Johns Story* (Kenneth Fink, 1994), *Freedom Song* (Phil Alden Robinson, 2000), *Boycott* (Clark Johnson, 2001), and *The Rosa Parks Story* (Julie Dash, 2002) "fall outside of the broad (predominantly white) mainstream cinematic tradition." See Sharon Monteith, "The Movie-Made Movement: Civil Rites of Passage," in *Memory and Popular Film,* ed. Paul Grainge (Manchester, UK: Manchester University Press, 2003), 121.

12. Although SNCC's original formation and ethos owed much to the religious outlooks of leading figures such as James Bevel and John Lewis, this emphasis had begun to evaporate as early as 1963. See Claybourne Carson, *In Struggle: SNCC and the Black Awakening of the 1960s* (Cambridge, Mass.: Harvard University Press, 1981), 95.

13. Scott Romine, *The Real South: Southern Narrative in the Age of Cultural Reproduction* (Baton Rouge: Louisiana State University Press, 2008), 132.

14. Loren Miller, "Uncle Tom in Hollywood," *The Crisis,* 1934. Republished in *The Crisis: 60th Anniversary Issue,* November 1970, 347.

15. Mellonee V. Burnim, "Gospel," in *African American Music: An Introduction,* 2nd ed., ed. Mellonee V. Burnim and Portia K. Maultsby (New York: Routledge, 2015), 189–90.

16. Teresa L. Reed, *The Holy Profane: Religion in Black Popular Music* (Lexington: University Press of Kentucky, 2003), 69.

17. Wallace Best, *Passionately Human, No Less Divine: Religion and Culture in Black Chicago, 1915–1952* (Princeton: Princeton University Press, 2005), 38.

18. See Milton C. Sernett, "When Chicago Was Canaan," in *Bound for the Promised Land: African American Religion and the Great Migration* (Durham: Duke University Press, 1997), 154–79.

19. Daniel R. Bare, *Black Fundamentalists: Conservative Christianity and Racial Identity in the Segregation Era* (New York: New York University Press, 2021), 49.

20. Bare, *Black Fundamentalists,* 49–55.

21. Ira Reid, "Let Us Prey," *Opportunity: Journal of Negro Life* (September 1926), quoted in Sernett, *Bound for the Promised Land,* 191–92.

22. Robert Jackson, "The Secret Life of Oscar Micheaux: Race Films, Contested Histories, and Modern American Culture," in *Beyond Blackface: African Americans and the Creation of American Popular Culture, 1890–1930,* ed. W. Fitzhugh Brundage (Chapel Hill: University of North Carolina Press, 2011), 224; Donald Bogle, *Toms, Coons, Mulattoes, Mammies, and Bucks: An Interpretive History of Blacks in American Films* (New York: Continuum, 2001), 115.

23. Reed, *The Holy Profane,* 64–65.

24. Lerone A. Martin, *Preaching on Wax: The Phonograph and the Shaping of Modern African American Religion* (New York: New York University Press, 2014), 5.

25. William John Mahar, *Behind the Burnt Cork Mask: Early Blackface Minstrelsy and Antebellum American Popular Culture* (Champaign: University of Illinois Press, 1999), 84–85.

26. Reed, *The Holy Profane,* 71.

27. Judith Weisenfeld, *Hollywood Be Thy Name: African American Religion in*

American Film, 1929–1949 (Berkeley: University of California Press, 2007), 235, 20–21.

28. Bogle, *Toms, Coons, Mulattoes*, 30.

29. Weisenfeld, *Hollywood Be Thy Name*, 30, 42–44, 236, 49.

30. Anna Siomopoulos, *Hollywood Melodrama and the New Deal: Public Daydreams* (New York: Routledge, 2012), 83.

31. Curtis J. Evans, "The Religious and Racial Meanings of *The Green Pastures*," *Religion and American Culture: A Journal of Interpretation* 18, no. 1 (Winter 2008): 84–85.

32. "No Time for Green Pastures," *Ebony*, July 1951, 100.

33. "'Pastures' Boycott Is Asked by Bishop," *New York Times*, March 26, 1951, 24.

34. *Purlie Victorious*'s stage run was directed by Howard Da Silva. Blacklisted as a Communist during the 1950s, Da Silva would go on to direct the stage adaptation of *My Sweet Charlie* in 1966. See Thomas S. Hischak, *Enter the Playmakers: Directors and Choreographers on the New York Stage* (Lanham, Md.: Scarecrow, 2006), 28.

35. One planned venture included a biopic of George Washington Carver. See "'Neglecting' 20,000,000 People," *Variety*, March 20, 1963, 3.

36. Walter Kerr, "Review of *Purlie Victorious*—New York, Cort Theater," New York Herald-Tribune, September 29, 1961.

37. Christopher Sieving, *Soul Searching: Black-Themed Cinema from the March on Washington to the Rise of Blaxploitation* (Middletown, Conn.: Wesleyan University Press, 2011), 26.

38. Susan M. Black, "Review of *Purlie Victorious*," Theatre Arts 45, no. 12 (December 1961); Jesse H. Walker, "'Gone Are the Days' Is a Howl a Minute," *New York Amsterdam News*, September 28, 1963, 16.

39. Carol Bunch Davis, "Troubling the Boundaries: 'Blacknesses,' Performance and the African American Freedom Struggle of the 1960s" (PhD diss., University of Southern California, 2007), 55.

40. Sieving, *Soul Searching*, 25. Davis served as master of ceremonies at the March on Washington. He would later eulogize both Malcolm X and Martin Luther King Jr.

41. Ossie Davis quoted in Sieving, *Soul Searching*, 25. The film's original distributors offered the film for charity screenings to raise money for the victims of the Birmingham bombing. See Howard Thompson, "Davis Film Draws Slim Attendance: 'Gone Are the Days' May Have to Be Withdrawn," *New York Times*, September 27, 1963, 16.

42. Douglas Gomery, *Shared Pleasures: A History of Movie Presentation in the United States* (Madison: University of Wisconsin Press, 1992), 166–67.

43. Sieving, *Soul Searching*, 24.

44. Ossie Davis quoted in "What Negro Needs Is Screen Success; Film Showmen Strictly Imitative," *Variety*, March 20, 1963, 3. *Black like Me* was rushed into production because of its perceived "topicality." See Sieving, *Soul Searching*, 22. Sieving's overarching argument is that emphasis on "realism" and "authenticity" in Black-centered cinema of the 1960s limited industry and public understanding of what Black cinema could or should be.

45. See Howard Thompson, "'Gone Are Days [sic]' Closes Monday: Racial Folk Fantasy Fails to Draw Support," *New York Times*, October 24, 1963, 37.

46. Sieving, *Soul Searching*, 27. See p. 29 for detailed discussion of the film as featured in the Black press.

47. "Purlie and His Friends Return in a Film, 'Gone Are the Days!'" *New York Times,* September 24, 1963.

48. Sieving, *Soul Searching,* 29–35.

49. Edward Mapp, *Blacks in American Films: Today and Yesterday* (Metuchen: Scarecrow, 1972), 77.

50. Sieving, *Soul Searching,* 36.

51. See Sharon Monteith, "Civil Rights Movement Film," in *The Cambridge Companion to American Civil Rights Literature,* ed. Julie Armstrong (New York: Cambridge University Press, 2015), 130.

52. Otto Preminger quoted in Larry Still, "Negroes Could Dominate Industry!: Preminger Lists Religion, Race Bias, Sex as Top Movie Themes," *Jet,* January 16, 1964, 58–59.

53. Quoted in A. H. Weiler, "Dr. King to Play Georgia Senator in Movie of 'Advise and Consent,'" *New York Times,* October 20, 1961, 1.

54. See "To Tom Roland," *The Papers of Martin Luther King, Jr.,* vol. 7: *To Save the Soul of America, January 1961–August 1962,* ed. Clayborne Carson and Tenisha Armstrong (Berkeley: University of California Press, 2014), 314; Sharon Monteith, *American Culture in the 1960s* (Edinburgh: Edinburgh University Press, 2008), 11.

55. "*The Cardinal,*" *Ebony,* December 1963, 127. Preminger quoted in Still, "Negroes Could Dominate Industry!" 58.

56. Although many Christians wear plain crosses, the wearing of crucifixes (complete with corpus) is almost exclusively a symbol of Catholicism.

57. Preminger quoted in "*The Cardinal,*" *Ebony,* 127.

58. Harper Lee, *To Kill a Mockingbird* (New York: Grand Central/Hachette, 2010), 196.

59. Ossie Davis quoted in Foster Hirsch, *Otto Preminger: The Man Who Would Be King* (New York: Knopf Doubleday, 2011), unpaginated ebook; Bosley Cowther, "Screen: Episodes of a Man of the Cloth: 'The Cardinal' Opens at the DeMille The Cast," *New York Times,* December 13, 1963, https://www.nytimes.com/1963/12/13/archives/screen-episodes-of-a-man-of-the-cloththe-cardinal-opens-at-the.html.

60. Aired February 20, 1960.

61. Michael Roemer, "Filmmakers' Statements," in *The Politics and Poetics of Black Film: Nothing but a Man,* ed. David C. Wall and Michael T. Martin (Bloomington: Indiana University Press, 2015), 25–26, 36.

62. Bogle, *Toms, Coons, Mulattoes,* 204.

63. Moira Walsh, "Films," *America* 112, no. 2 (1965): 62–63. Roemer's experiences as a Jewish refugee from Nazi Germany influenced his decision to write about racialized outsiders. See Roemer, "Filmmakers' Statements," 25–39. Duff's was "not really a Negro story," Roemer argued—'it's the story of the search for identity and that is everyone's story." Quoted in "'Nothing but a Man': Triumph on a Budget," *Ebony,* April 1965, 200.

64. Thomas J. Goldthwaite, "'Nothing but a Man' Rated Good Theater," *Spokesman -Review,* February 11, 1966, 3. This fear of alienating white audiences, especially in the South, was also reflected in television. When David W. Rintels proposed an episode of *The FBI* (aired 'ABC', 1965–74) on the contemporaneous investigation into the Sixteenth Street Church bombing in Birmingham, Alabama, he was told that the sponsor (Ford Motor Company), the network, and the FBI "would be delighted to have me write about a church bombing subject only to these stipula-

tions: The church must be in the North, there could be no Negroes involved, and the bombing could have nothing at all to do with civil rights." Quoted in Todd Gitlin, *Inside Prime Time* (Berkeley: University of California Press, 2000), 160.

65. Hoyt W. Fuller, "*Nothing but a Man* Reconsidered," *Negro Digest*, May 1965, 49.

66. Albert Johnson, "The Negro in American Film: Some Recent Works," *Film Quarterly* 18, no. 4 (Summer 1965): 25.

67. Brian O'Doherty, "Classic of a Negro Who Stopped Running," *Life*, February 19, 1965, 15.

68. Fuller, "*Nothing but a Man* Reconsidered."

69. Roemer, "Filmmakers' Statements," 35.

70. Michael T. Martin and David Wall, "Historicity and Possibility in *Nothing but a Man*: A Conversation with Khalil Muhammad," in Martin and Wall, *The Politics and Poetics of Black Film*, 150, 165.

71. Martin and Wall, "Historicity and Possibility," 151–52, 168.

72. Johnson, "The Negro in American Film," 15, 23. See Sharon Monteith, "Exploitation Movies and the Freedom Struggle of the 1960s," in *American Cinema and the Southern Imaginary*, ed. Deborah E. Barker and Kathryn McKee (Athens: University of Georgia Press, 2011).

73. See Monteith, "Movie-Made Movement," 127.

74. Martin Luther King Jr., "Address to the First Montgomery Improvement Association (MIA) Mass Meeting," December 5, 1955, Holt Street Baptist Church, Montgomery, Alabama. Transcript accessed May 16, 2019, http://www.digitalhistory.uh.edu/disp_textbook.cfm?smtid=3&psid=3625.

75. Kirt H. Wilson, "Interpreting the Discursive Field of the Montgomery Bus Boycott: Martin Luther King, Jr.'s Holt Street Address," *Rhetoric and Public Affairs* 8, no. 2 (Summer 2005): 301, 305, 312–14, 320.

76. Janet Maslin, "A Personalized View of the Civil Rights Struggle," *New York Times*, December 21, 1990.

77. See Megan Hunt, "Segregation as Southern Anomaly: The Help and Hollywood's Deflection of American Racism," in *Like One of the Family: Domestic Workers, Race and In/visibility in "The Help,"* ed. Fiona Mills (Newcastle upon Tyne, UK: Cambridge Scholars, 2016), 95–105.

78. Jo Ann Robinson quoted in Lynne Olson, *Freedom's Daughters: The Unsung Heroines of the Civil Rights Movement from 1830 to 1970* (New York: Simon and Schuster, 2001), 118. See also Jo Ann Gibson Robinson, *The Montgomery Bus Boycott and the Women Who Started It*, ed. David J. Garrow (Knoxville: University of Tennessee Press, 1987).

79. Herbert Buffum, "I'm Going Through," 1914.

80. For example, Parks's lawyer, Fred Gray, remembered that Parks instilled in him "the feeling that I was the Moses that God had sent to the Pharaoh and commanded him to 'Let my people go'" (quoted in Olson, *Freedom's Daughters*, 111). Activist Mildred Forman Page recalls, "As I look back over the many times we have put our lives on the line and came out unharmed, I say only God could have saved us." See "Two Variations on Nonviolence," in *Hands on the Freedom Plow: Personal Accounts by Women in SNCC*, ed. Faith S. Holsaert, Martha Prescod Norman Noonan, Judy Richardson, Betty Garman Robinson, Jean Smith Young, and Dorothy M. Zellner (Champaign: University of Illinois Press, 2012), 55.

81. Rosa Parks, quoted by Elaine Dutka, "Driving Miss Odessa: Rosa Parks Calls

the Film Important because the United States Has Neglected the Subject for Too Long," *Los Angeles Times*, December 20, 1990, http://articles.latimes .com/1990-12-20/entertainment/ca-9576_1_rosa-parks.

82. George F. Will, "'*Mississippi Burning*': A Flawed Account," *Washington Post*, January 12, 1989, A19.

83. Paul Harvey, *Freedom's Coming: Religious Culture and the Shaping of the South from the Civil War through the Civil Rights Era* (Chapel Hill: University of North Carolina Press, 2005), 4.

84. See Internet Movie Database, *Mississippi Burning*, Full Cast and Crew, accessed June 23, 2019, http://www.imdb.com/title/tt0095647 /fullcredits?ref_=tt_cl_sm#cast.

85. Roger A. Fischer, "Hollywood and the Mythic Land Apart, 1988–1991," in *A Mythic Land Apart: Interpreting Southerners and Their History*, ed. John David Smith and Thomas H. Appleton Jr. (Westport, Conn.: Greenwood, 1997), 180.

86. Philip Tagg, "Open Letter about 'Black Music,' 'Afro-American Music' and 'European Music,'" accessed May 23, 2019, http://tagg.org/articles/opelet.html. This letter was reedited and published in the journal *Popular Music* 8, no. 3 (1989): 285–98. Ruth Doughty, "African American Film Sound: Scoring Blackness," in *Sound and Music in Film and Visual Media: A Critical Overview*, ed. Graeme Harper, Ruth Doughty, and Jochen Eisentraut (New York: Bloomsbury, 2014), 325.

87. Doughty, "African American Film Sound," 325.

88. Indeed, many gospel songs owe much of their form to secular styles, which proved problematic for many Baptist and Methodist traditionalists. For some established congregations, gospel was often too closely identified with Pentecostalism, projecting what C. Eric Lincoln and Lawrence H. Mamiya call "problematic theology," as performers interpret and compose songs based on their own "personal theology" rather than from accepted dogma. See C. Eric Lincoln and Lawrence H. Mamiya, *The Black Church in the African American Experience* (Durham, N.C.: Duke University Press, 2003), 377.

89. Brian Ward, *Just My Soul Responding: Rhythm and Blues, Black Consciousness and Race Relations* (London: Routledge, 1998), 197.

90. Charles Hobson, "The Gospel Truth," *Down Beat*, May 30, 1968, 19.

91. W. E. B. DuBois, *The Souls of Black Folk* (Mineola, N.Y.: Dover, 1994), 155.

92. Ron Eyerman and Andrew Jamison, *Music and Social Movements: Mobilizing Traditions in the Twentieth-Century* (Cambridge: Cambridge University Press, 1998), 75.

93. Doughty, "African American Film Sound," 326.

94. See David R. Jansson, "'A Geography of Racism': Internal Orientalism and the Construction of American National Identity in the Film *Mississippi Burning*," *National Identities* 7, no. 3 (September 2005): 265–85.

95. George Lipsitz, "The Possessive Investment in Whiteness: Racialized Social Democracy and the 'White' Problem in American Studies," *American Quarterly* 47, no. 3 (September 1995): 380–81.

96. George Lipsitz, *The Possessive Investment in Whiteness: How White People Benefit from Identity Politics* (Philadelphia: Temple University Press, 1998), 19.

97. Kelly J. Madison, "Legitimation Crisis and Containment: The 'Anti-racist-White-Hero' Film," *Critical Studies in Mass Communication* 16, no. 4 (1999): 406.

98. Jennifer Fuller, "Debating the Present through the Past: Representations of the

Civil Rights Movement in the 1990s," in *The Civil Rights Movement in American Memory*, ed. Leigh Raiford and Renee C. Romano (Athens: University of Georgia Press, 2006), 169.

99. Evans, "The Religious and Racial Meanings of *The Green Pastures*," 60, 63.

100. Jansson, "A Geography of Racism," 270.

101. Bogle, *Toms, Coons, Mulattoes*, 303.

102. Dave Dennis, Eulogy for James Chaney, First Union Church, Meridian, Mississippi, August 7, 1964, recorded by Pacifica Radio. Transcript in William H. Lawson, "A Righteous Anger in Mississippi: Genre Constraints and Breaking Precedence" (master's thesis, Florida State University, 2004), 56–58, http://diginole.lib.fsu.edu /islandora/object/fsu:181562/datastream/PDF/view.

103. Suzanne E. Smith, *To Serve the Living: Funeral Directors and the African American Way of Death* (Cambridge, Mass.: Harvard University Press, 2010).

104. Lawson, "A Righteous Anger," 30.

105. James D. Williams, "*Mississippi Burning* Offers Distorted View of History" (NAACP Focus), *The Crisis* 96, no. 4 (April 1989): 27.

106. Alan Parker, "A Conviction in Mississippi," *The Times*, June 2005, http://alanparker .com/essay/a-conviction-in-mississippi/.

107. Allison Graham, *Framing the South: Hollywood, Television, and Race during the Civil Rights Struggle* (Baltimore: Johns Hopkins University Press, 2001), 152.

108. For the typical reading of *Mississippi Burning*, see Henry Bourgeois, "Hollywood and the Civil Rights Movement: The Case of *Mississippi Burning*," *Howard Journal of Communications* 4, no. 1–2 (1992): 157–63; and Robert Brent Toplin, "*Mississippi Burning*: 'A Standard to Which We Couldn't Live Up,'" in *History by Hollywood: The Use and Abuse of the American Past* (Champaign: University of Illinois Press, 1996), 25–44.

109. Ralph Ellison, "The Shadow and the Act," *The Reporter*, December 6, 1949, reprinted in Ralph Ellison, *Shadow and Act* (New York: Vintage, 1973), 277.

Chapter 3. "When Things Made Sense, When We Were the Good Guys"

1. Michael A. Fletcher, "U.S. Investigates Suspicious Fires at Southern Black Churches," *Washington Post*, February 8, 1996, A3.

2. Deval L. Patrick and Randolph Scott-McLaughlin quoted in Kevin Sack, "Links Sought in an 'Epidemic of Terror,'" *New York Times*, May 21, 1996, http://www .nytimes.com/1996/05/21/us/links-sought-in-an-epidemic-of-terror.html.

3. Timothy J. Minchin, "One America? Church Burnings and Perceptions of Race Relations in the Clinton Years," *Australasian Journal of American Studies* 27, no. 2 (December 2008): 4.

4. Both quoted in Michael A. Fletcher, "Christian Coalition Plans to Cooperate with Black Churches to Squelch Fires," *Washington Post*, June 19, 1996, A6.

5. Arrest rate of 35.6 percent compared to 16 percent for other arsons, reported in National Church Arson Task Force, "Third Year Report for the President," January 2000, https://www.hsdl.org/?view&did=1410, 2.

6. Christopher B. Strain, *Burning Faith: Church Arson in the American South* (Gainesville: University Press of Florida, 2008), 19.

7. Fred Bayles, "Burning Churches," *Free-Lance Star* (Fredericksburg, Va.), July 5, 1996, A4. For a retrospective analysis of the rise of hate groups in the 1990s, see

Carol M. Swain, *The New White Nationalism in America: Its Challenge to Integration* (Cambridge: Cambridge University Press, 2002), 75–76.

8. Michael Fumento, "A Church Arson Epidemic? It's Smoke and Mirrors," *Wall Street Journal*, July 8, 1996, https://www.wsj.com/articles/SB836760439744561500; Michael Kelly, "Playing with Fire," *New Yorker*, July 15, 1996, 28.

9. William Jefferson Clinton, "The President's Radio Address on June 8, 1996," *Clinton Digital Library*, accessed September 7, 2021, https://clinton.presidentiallibraries.us/items/show/13030.

10. Jim Campbell, "America's Long History of Black Churches Burning," *Los Angeles Times,* June 16, 1996, M1.

11. Minchin, "One America?" 8.

12. Clinton's battles in Congress were especially significant after the 1994 midterms, where Republicans gained control of both houses for the first time since 1954. However, George C. Edwards III writes that this opposition "eased [Clinton's] burden," as "new Republican majorities overplayed their hands and refused to budge on their proposals." Congressional Republicans were thus publicly culpable for subsequent government shutdowns, while Clinton characterized himself as the "reasonable" alternative to Republican "radicalism," using executive orders and vetoes to promote his own policy and "to defend moderation." George C. Edwards III, "Bill Clinton and His Crisis of Governance," *Presidential Studies Quarterly* 28, no. 4 (1998): 757.

13. Jennifer L. Pierce, *Racing for Innocence: Whiteness, Gender, and the Backlash against Affirmative Action* (Stanford: Stanford University Press, 2012), 137.

14. Stokely Carmichael and Charles V. Hamilton, *Black Power: The Politics of Liberation in America* (New York: Vintage, 1967), 28; Joseph Crespino, "The Strange Career of Atticus Finch," Southern Cultures 6, no. 2 (Summer 2000): 22.

15. Allison Graham, *Framing the South: Hollywood, Television, and Race during the Civil Rights Struggle* (Baltimore: Johns Hopkins University Press, 2001), 190.

16. Roopali Mukherjee, *The Racial Order of Things: Cultural Imaginaries of the Post-Soul Era* (Minneapolis: University of Minnesota Press, 2006), 151.

17. Bernard Beck quoted in Teresa Wiltz, "Whose History?" *Chicago Tribune,* January 13, 1997, http://articles.chicagotribune.com/1997-01-13/features/9701130093_1_medgar-evers-beckwith-myrlie-evers.

18. Sharon Monteith, "The Movie-Made Movement: Civil Rites of Passage," in *Memory and Popular Film*, ed. Paul Grainge (Manchester, UK: Manchester University Press, 2003), 125; Mark Wheeler, *Hollywood: Politics and Society* (London: British Film Institute, 2006), 145.

19. Stephen Powers, David Rothman, and Stanley Rothman, *Hollywood's America: Social and Political Themes in American Motion Pictures* (Boulder: Westview, 1996), 3, 5.

20. Jennifer Fuller, "Debating the Present through the Past: Representations of the Civil Rights Movement in the 1990s," in *The Civil Rights Movement in American Memory,* ed. Leigh Raiford and Renee C. Romano (Athens: University of Georgia Press, 2006), 167.

21. Hungry for land and profits, televangelist Jimmy Lee Farmsworth (R. Lee Ermey) exploits elderly church members in *Fletch Lives* so that he can expand Bibleland Amusement Park, the centerpiece of which is the "Jump for Jesus" trampoline area. Ermey also played Mayor Tilman in *Mississippi Burning.*

22. "Conspiracy Theory Fades, but Racism Smolders," *USA Today*, July 2, 1996, 10A.

23. Kevin Sack, "Links Sought in an 'Epidemic of Terror,'" *New York Times*, May 21, 1996, A12.

24. Minchin, "One America?" 9.

25. Mark Whitaker, "A Crisis of Shattered Dreams," *Newsweek*, May 6, 1991, http://www.newsweek.com/crisis-shattered-dreams-203930.

26. Josephine Metcalf and Carina Spaulding, "Introduction: 'Out of the Frying Pan and into the Fire,'" in *African American Culture and Society after Rodney King: Provocations and Protests, Progression and Post-racialism*, ed. Josephine Metcalf and Carina Spaulding (Farnham, UK: Ashgate, 2015), 1–2.

27. Linda Deutsch and Michael Fleeman, *Verdict: The Chronicle of the O. J. Simpson Trial* (Kansas City, Mo.: Andrews and Meel, 1995), 2–4.

28. Oran P. Smith, *The Rise of Baptist Republicanism* (New York: New York University Press, 1997), 2.

29. Andrew Manis, *Southern Civil Religions: Civil Rights and the Culture Wars* (Macon, Ga.: Mercer University Press, 2002) 171–72.

30. Gary Scott Smith, Religion in the Oval Office: The Religious Lives of American Presidents (New York: Oxford University Press, 2015), 340; Richard Vara, "SouthernBaptists Set Sights on Clinton," Sun Sentinel, June 12, 1998,http://articles.sun-sentinel.com/1998-06-12/news/9806110511_1_southern-baptists-clinton-s-home-church-combat.

31. Richard Land quoted in Tom Strode, "*Newsweek* Article: Baptist Moderates Laid Groundwork for Clinton Morality," *Baptist Press*, October 30, 1998, http://www.bpnews.net/2780/newsweek-article-baptist-moderates-laid-groundwork-for-clinton-morality; Emma Green, "Southern Baptists and the Sin of Racism," *The Atlantic*, April 7, 2015, http://www.theatlantic.com/politics/archive/2015/04/southern-baptists-wrestle-with-the-sin-of-racism/389808/; Lillian Kwon, "So. Baptist Leader Richard Land Reprimanded over Trayvon Martin Comments," *Christian Post*, June 1, 2012, http://www.christianpost.com/news/so-baptist-richard-land-reprimanded-over-trayvon-martin-comments-75927/#yrrXYPUloODoqPLT.99.

32. Nancy Tatom Ammerman, *Baptist Battles: Social Change and Religious Conflict in the Southern Baptist Convention* (New Brunswick, N.J.: Rutgers University Press, 1995), 103; Mark Newman, *Getting Right with God: Southern Baptists and Desegregation, 1945–1995* (Tuscaloosa: University of Alabama Press, 2001), 202.

33. Resolution on Racial Reconciliation on the 150th Anniversary of the Southern Baptist Convention, Atlanta, Georgia, 1995, accessed September 23, 2019, http://www.sbc.net/resolutions/899/resolution-on-racial-reconciliation-on-the-150th-anniversary-of-the-southern-baptist-convention; Bill Maxwell, "A Moral Duty to Correct Old Wrongs," *Times Daily* (Florence, Ala.), June 28, 1995, 7B.

34. Jack E. White, "Forgive Us Our Sins," *Time*, July 3, 1995, 29.

35. Thornton quoted in Erik Bauer, "'I'm Pretty Anti-violence. I Don't Want to Do More Movies about Violence'—Billy Bob Thornton," interview for *Creative Screenwriting*, accessed January 3, 2023, http://creativescreenwriting.com/im-pretty-anti-violence-i-dont-want-to-do-more-movies-about-violence-billy-bob-thornton/.

36. Jerry Mitchell, "The Case of the Supposedly-Sealed Files—and What They Revealed," *Nieman Reports: Cold Case Reporting: Revisiting Racial Crimes*,

September 9, 2011, http://niemanreports.org/articles/the-case-of-the-supposedly-sealed-files-and-what-they-revealed/.

37. Fred Zollo quoted in Sean Mitchell, "Waking the Ghosts," *Los Angeles Times*, December 15, 1996, http://articles.latimes.com/1996-12-15/entertainment/ca-9135_1_mississippi-burning.

38. Quoted in Renee C. Romano, *Racial Reckoning: Prosecuting America's Civil Rights Murders* (Cambridge, Mass.: Harvard University Press, 2014), 132.

39. Renee C. Romano, "Narratives of Redemption: The Birmingham Church Bombing Trials and the Construction of Civil Rights Memory," in *The Civil Rights Movement in American Memory*, ed. Leigh Raiford and Renee C. Romano (Athens: University of Georgia Press, 2006), 98.

40. Gary Younge, "Racism Rebooted," *The Nation*, July 11, 2005, https://www.thenation.com/article/archive/racism-rebooted/.

41. Romano, "Narratives of Redemption," 99–100.

42. Andrew Hartman, *A War for the Soul of America: A History of the Culture Wars* (Chicago: University of Chicago Press, 2015), 121.

43. Janet Maslin, "Review: In John Grisham's 'The Whistler,' a Serious Woman and Serious Crime," *New York Times*, October 26, 2016, https://www.nytimes.com/2016/10/27/books/review-john-grishams-the-whistler.html.

44. John Grisham, "Most N.C. Death Row Inmates Did Not Receive a Fair Trial," *Raleigh News and Observer*, October 12, 2018.

45. Quoted in Holly Baxter, "John Grisham: 'There Are Tens of Thousands of Innocent People in Prison and You Don't Believe It because You're White,'" *The Independent*, May 22, 2022, accessed October 14, 2022, https://www.independent.co.uk/news/world/americas/john-grisham-innocence-project-prison-b2084503.html.

46. Graham, *Framing the South*, 189.

47. Bernard Beck quoted in Wiltz, "Whose History?" Several critics have argued that Hollywood's increasing fascination with the civil rights movement and Vietnam reflected baby boomer nostalgia, as both contemporary racial tensions and the Gulf War encouraged comparisons with the events of the 1960s. Yet, as Sharon Monteith has argued, if filmmakers were so concerned with attracting baby boomer audiences in the late twentieth century, why did they prove so reluctant to engage with student involvement in the civil rights movement, especially the voter registration drives that brought Goodman and Schwerner to Mississippi in the first place? See Sharon Monteith, "Exploitation Movies and the Freedom Struggle of the 1960s," in *American Cinema and the Southern Imaginary*, ed. Deborah E. Barker and Kathryn McKee (Athens: University of Georgia Press, 2011), 195.

48. Godfrey Cheshire, "Review: *Ghosts of Mississippi*," *Variety*, December 21, 1996, https://variety.com/1996/film/reviews/ghosts-of-mississippi-1117436727/.

49. Harper Lee, *Go Set a Watchman* (London: William Heinemann, 2015), 149.

50. Tom Wicker, "Toward the Ideal," *New York Times*, December 26, 1991, A25.

51. Justin Gomer, *White Balance: How Hollywood Shaped Colorblind Ideology and Undermined Civil Rights* (Chapel Hill: University of North Carolina Press, 2020), 172.

52. Michael A. Fletcher, "Affirmative Action Tops NAACP List," *Washington Post*, July 14, 1998, A3.

53. Gomer, *White Balance*, 174.

54. Terry Anderson, *The Pursuit of Fairness: A History of Affirmative Action* (New York: Oxford University Press, 2005).

55. Mukherjee, *The Racial Order of Things*, 183–84.

56. Gomer, *White Balance*, 190.

57. Roger Ebert, "Review: *A Time to Kill*," July 26, 1996, https://www.rogerebert.com /reviews/a-time-to-kill-1996.

58. Mukherjee, *The Racial Order of Things*, 179–80.

59. Monteith, "The Movie-Made Movement," 121, 138.

60. DeLaughter here engenders his potential usurper as male, though it has previously been established that Pat Bennett is a woman.

61. Graham, *Framing the South*, 187.

62. Amy Dawes, "Emotional 'Ghosts,'" *Daily News* (Los Angeles), December 24, 1996, 3–6.

63. A senior member of the Jackson Citizens' Council, Judge Moore had conspired to have Evers arrested along with NAACP executive secretary Roy Wilkins in 1959, when the two activists planned to mark the fifth anniversary of the *Brown* decision with a desegregation suit in Jackson. Moore was a spectator at Beckwith's original trials in the 1960s and kept the murder weapon as a souvenir. DeLaughter was able to retrieve the rifle from his mother-in-law prior to the 1994 retrial. See Maryanne Vollers, *Ghosts of Mississippi: The Murder of Medgar Evers, the Trials of Byron de la Beckwith, and the Haunting of the New South* (Boston: Little, Brown, 1995), 75–77, 279.

64. Jake Brigance suffers from similar marital strain in both the novel and film *A Time to Kill* when his wife, Carla, leaves town with their daughter as the result of Klan intimidation. Although this is primarily for their safety, it is suggested that the marriage is under strain as a result of the case. This marital uncertainty is exacerbated by Brigance's developing friendship with liberal, northern law student Ellen Roark (Sandra Bullock).

65. "I would always tuck my kids in at night," the real DeLaughter explained, "but no, I didn't sing 'Dixie.'" See Mitchell, "Waking the Ghosts."

66. See Willie Morris, *Ghosts of Medgar Evers: A Tale of Race, Murder, Mississippi, and Hollywood* (New York: Random House, 1998), 131.

67. Amy Dawes, "Emotional 'Ghosts,'" *Daily News* (Los Angeles), December 24, 1996, 3.

68. Tina Daunt, "Reiner Casts His Lot with Clinton," *Los Angeles Times,* September 27, 2007, https://www.latimes.com/archives/la-xpm-2007-sep-27-na-reiner27 -story.html.

69. Reiner quoted in Dawes, "Emotional 'Ghosts,'" 3, 6; Martin Grove, 'Evers Case Let Reiner Travel to Mississippi,' *Hollywood Reporter,* November 15, 1996, 6.

70. Reiner quoted in Dawes, "Emotional 'Ghosts,'" 3, 6.

71. Bobby DeLaughter quoted in Morris, *The Ghosts of Medgar Evers*, 68; Peter T. Chattaway, "Setting the Record Straight," *The Ubyssey* (University of British Columbia), January 10, 1997, 4, http://www.library.ubc.ca/archives/pdfs/ubyssey /UBYSSEY_1997_01_10.pdf.

72. Random House, "Teacher's Guide: A Time to Kill," question 2, chaps. 11–15: "Compare the Brigance church with the Hailey family's Mt. Zion CME." Accessed

December 14, 2019, https://www.randomhouse.com/catalog/teachers
_guides/9780440245919.pdf.

73. John Grisham, *A Time to Kill*, Kindle ed. (London: Cornerstone Digital
Publishing, 2010), 117–18. In reality, First Presbyterian of Canton, Mississippi,
the real town in which Joel Schumacher directed his adaptation, proved the
only local white congregation to welcome northern activists and clergy during
Freedom Summer of 1964, "guided by their cerebral and theologically liberal—by
Mississippi standards—pastor, Richard T. Harbison." However, few of Harbison's
parishioners shared his enthusiasm for such "newcomers," which, combined with
Citizens' Council intimidation, prevented further integration of the northern students and prompted Harbison's resignation. "First Presbyterian Church [subse-
quently] joined the rest of Canton in its policy of 'no hospitality.'" See Carolyn
Dupont, *Mississippi Praying: Southern White Evangelicals and the Civil Rights
Movement, 1945–1975* (New York: New York University Press, 2013), 183–85.

74. Monteith, "The Movie-Made Movement," 135. Most coverage of the 1987 rally
focuses on the pre-empted anti-Klan demonstrations. See "600 March in North
Carolina to Protest Klan's Rally Today," *Los Angeles Times*, June 7, 1987, http://
articles.latimes.com/1987-06-07/news/mn-1091_1_klan-s-rally-today; William E.
Schmidt, "Klan's Carolina March Kindling Fear and Unity," *New York Times*,
June 5, 1987, http://www.nytimes.com/1987/06/05/us/klan-s-carolina-march
-kindling-fear-and-unity.html.

75. Leonard Zeskind, *Blood and Politics: The History of the White Nationalist
Movement from the Margins to the Mainstream* (New York: Farrar, Straus and
Giroux, 2009), 35.

76. Tyler Bridges, *The Rise of David Duke* (Jackson: University of Mississippi Press,
1994), 45.

77. Nancy Bishop Dessommes, "Hollywood in Hoods: The Portrayal of the Ku Klux
Klan in Popular Film," *Journal of Popular Culture* 32, no. 4 (Spring 1999): 18.

78. Romano, *Racial Reckoning*, 239n56.

79. The original interview lasted ninety minutes and aired on WLBT in Jackson.

80. Morris describes the intricacies of Woods's transformation, writing that "everything was rubber except his nose, eyeballs, and eyelids. . . . A crew member was
assigned to hold an umbrella over him so he would not melt" in the Mississippi
sun. See Morris, *Ghosts of Medgar Evers*, 87, 155.

81. Janet Maslin, "For a True Story, Dipping into the Classics," *New York Times*,
December 20, 1996, https://www.nytimes.com/1996/12/20/movies/for-a-true
-story-dipping-into-the-classics.html?rref=collection%2Fcollection%2Fmovie
-guide.

82. Margaret A. McGurk, "Mississippi Smouldering," *Cincinnati Enquirer*, accessed
July 12, 2014, http://enquirer.com/columns/mcgurk/010397b_mm.html; Matthew
Gilbert, "The Perfect Villain," *Spokesman-Review* (Spokane, Wash.), January 5,
1997, E3.

83. Butler quoted in Michael Newton, *The Ku Klux Klan in Mississippi: A History*
(Jefferson, N.C.: McFarland, 2010), 186.

84. See Amy Dawes, "Making Film an Emotional Trip for Rob Reiner," *Sun Sentinel*,
January 3, 1997, https://www.sun-sentinel.com/fl-xpm-1997-01-03-9612310140
-story.html. A transcript of the original interview shows that Beckwith was committed to "Dixie" as "a white Christian republic." He denied his role in Evers's

murder but admitted that as an Episcopalian, "I was trained from my youth to make war for the enemies of this white Christian republic." Interview with Byron De La Beckwith, April 30, 1990, Bobby De Laughter Papers, Mississippi Department of Archives and History, Jackson, Box 4, Folder 27, pp. 40, 18. Although Beckwith's disdain for Judaism is evident in the transcript of his actual interview with Ed Bryson (who plays himself in the film), Beckwith's refusal to speak to Jews in the film was based on producer Fred Zollo's conversations with the real Beckwith at Hinds County Jail before the film was made. When asked if he was a Jew, Zollo, who also produced *Mississippi Burning,* responded that he was Catholic, to which Beckwith demanded that he recite the "Hail Mary" before he would speak to him. See Morris, *Ghosts of Medgar Evers,* 144.

85. Morris, *Ghosts of Medgar Evers,* 144.
86. Matthew Gilbert, "James Woods Is So Good at Being Bad," *Los Angeles Times,* January 1, 1997, http://articles.latimes.com/1997-01-01/entertainment /ca-14352_1_james-woods.
87. See George Lipsitz, The Possessive Investment in *Whiteness: How White People Benefit from Identity Politics* (Philadelphia: Temple University Press, 1998), 222–23. In more recent years, Woods has used his Twitter account to attack prominent Democrats and forward inflammatory themes and conspiracy theories. Publication of a Twitter dataset in 2022 demonstrated that Woods was the most persistent purveyor of misinformation about the 2020 election. See Justin Hendrix, "Researchers Release Comprehensive Twitter Dataset of False Claims about the 2020 Election," *Just Security,* June 15, 2022, https://www.just security.org/81913/researchers-release-comprehensive-twitter-dataset-of-false -claims-about-the-2020-election/; Jim Treacher, "James Woods: 'I'll Probably Never Work in That Town Again,'" *Daily Caller,* September 10, 2013, http://daily caller.com/2013/10/09/james-woods-ill-probably-never-work-in-that-town -again/; Katie Scott, "James Woods Returns to Twitter, Goes after Hillary Clinton, Elizabeth Warren," *Global News,* February 7, 2020, https://globalnews.ca/ news/6520818/james-woods-twitter/.
88. Lipsitz, *The Possessive Investment in Whiteness,* 220–22.
89. Lipsitz, *The Possessive Investment in Whiteness,* 220–22, 114–15.
90. Lewis R. Gordon, "A Lynching Well Lost," *Black Scholar* 25, no. 4 (Fall 1995): 37–38.
91. Mukherjee, *The Racial Order of Things,* 177.

Chapter 4. "Jimmy Swaggart Meets Huey Long in Hell"

1. Wesley Strick interviewed in "The Making of the 1991 *Cape Fear,*" DVD Special Features, *Cape Fear* Boxset, J. Lee Thompson, Martin Scorsese (dir.), Universal Pictures UK, 2001. I refer to Max Cady simply as "Cady" and other characters by their first names. This reflects how they are commonly referred to in the film and magnifies the sense of "otherness" constructed around Cady.
2. "Burlesque" here reflects the derisive and overblown nature of De Niro's character-ization of Cady. As Linda Hutcheon has noted, burlesque, unlike parody, "necessi-tates the inclusion or concept of ridicule." See Hutcheon, *A Theory of Parody: The Teachings of Twentieth-Century Art Forms* (Urbana: University of Illinois Press, 2000), 32.
3. Strick quoted in Mary Pat Kelly, *Martin Scorsese: A Journey* (London: Secker and Warburg, 1992), 286.

4. Melanie Friesen, letter to Martin Scorsese cc. De Niro, August 20 1990, box 29, file 5: "Melanie Friesen: Memoranda and Associated Research Material," Robert De Niro (RDN) Papers, Harry Ransom Center, University of Texas at Austin, 1.

5. Melanie Friesen, letter to Martin Scorsese cc. De Niro, August 20 1990, 2.

6. Robert Casillo, "School for Skandalon: Scorsese and Girard at *Cape Fear,*" *Italian Americana* 12, no. 2 (Summer 1994): 202.

7. Jem Cohen, "Research Materials: Pentecostal," box 30, folder 8, RDN Papers.

8. Randall J. Stephens, *The Fire Spreads: Holiness and Pentecostalism in the American South* (Cambridge, Mass.: Harvard University Press, 2008), 3–5.

9. Elaine J. Lawless, "Brothers and Sisters: Pentecostals as a Religious Folk Group," *Western Folklore* 42, no. 2 (April 1983): 85–86.

10. Richard J. Callahan Jr., "The Work of Class in Southern Religion," *Journal of Southern Religion* 13 (2011), http://jsreligion.org/issues/vol13/callahan.html.

11. Stephens, *The Fire Spreads*, 230–32.

12. Kate Bowler, *Blessed: A History of the American Prosperity Gospel* (New York: Oxford University Press, 2013), 11, 226.

13. Casillo, "School for Skandalon," 214.

14. Ilona Herman, notes and designs sent to Robert De Niro, "Tattoo Design and Correspondence," box 28, file 1, RDN Papers.

15. Considered "self-imposed scars," tattoos have proven crucial to projections of masculinity, indicative of what Helen Stoddart calls "a kind of machismo-driven heroism" that signals a character's unique ability to endure pain. This is particularly apparent in *Cape Fear,* Stoddart continues, because of the way in which De Niro's commitment to "Method" acting and almost "masochistic" bodily transformation was "fetishised in press coverage." See Helen Stoddart, "'I Don't Know Whether to Look at Him or Read Him': *Cape Fear* and Male Scarification," in *Me Jane: Masculinity, Movies and Women,* ed. Pat Kirkham and Janet Thumin (London: Lawrence and Wishart, 1995), 194–96.

16. Strick quoted in Kelly, *Martin Scorsese,* 290.

17. Thomas Nesbit, *Henry Miller and Religion* (New York: Routledge, 2007), 24.

18. Michael J. Giuliano, *Thrice Born: The Rhetorical Comeback of Jimmy Swaggart* (Macon, Ga.: Mercer University Press, 1999), 28–29.

19. Although Bakker was originally from Michigan, PTL was established in Charlotte, North Carolina. With his wife, Tammy Faye, Bakker also opened a religious theme park and television production facility in Fort Mill, South Carolina.

20. Giuliano, *Thrice Born,* 30.

21. Giuliano, *Thrice Born,* 38.

22. Quentin Schultze, *Televangelism and American Culture: The Business of Popular Religion* (Eugene, Oreg.: Wipf and Stock, 2003), 39.

23. Giuliano, *Thrice Born,* 31, 29.

24. Joshua Gamson, "Normal Sins: Sex Scandal Narratives as Institutional Morality Tales," *Social Problems* 48, no. 2 (May 2001): 189.

25. Art Harris and Jason Berry, "Jimmy Swaggart's Secret Sex Life," *Penthouse,* July 1988, 104–7.

26. Melanie Friesen, letter to Robert De Niro, November 10, 1990, box 29, folder 5, RDN Papers.

27. "Scandals: No Apologies This Time," *Time,* October 28, 1991, http://content.time .com/time/magazine/article/0,9171,974120,00.html.

28. In 1980, 19 percent of respondents were "more likely" to vote for an evangeli-

cal candidate, compared with 9 percent who claimed to be "less likely." By 1987, 15 percent were "more likely" to vote for an evangelical candidate, but 29 percent were "less likely." Thirteen percent of those interviewed in 1987 did not want fundamentalists as neighbors, a figure 10 percent higher than those who did not want to live beside Jews, a more traditional target of religious prejudice. Princeton Religion Research Center, *Emerging Trends*, April 1987, 5.

29. Wayne King, "Pat Robertson: A Candidate of Contradictions," *New York Times*, February 27 1988, http://www.nytimes.com/1988/02/27/us/pat-robertson-a -candidate-of-contradictions.html.

30. Pat Robertson, on NBC News, report by Lisa Myers, "Miracle Man," December 21 1987, https://www.youtube.com/watch?v=zJsgAEQAvis; Wayne King, "The Record of Pat Robertson on Religion and Government," *New York Times,* December 27 1987, http://www.nytimes.com/1987/12/27/us/the-record-of-pat-robertson-on -religion-and-government.html?pagewanted=all&src=pm.

31. "Beware of false prophets, which come to you in sheep's clothing, but inwardly they are ravening wolves" (Matthew 7:15). Quoted at the beginning of the *Penthouse* article on Swaggart and also the opening sequences of the films *The Night of the Hunter* (Charles Laughton, 1955) and *The Miracle Woman* (Frank Capra, 1931).

32. J. W. Williamson, *Hillbillyland: What the Movies Did to the Mountains and What the Mountains Did to the Movies* (Chapel Hill: University of North Carolina Press, 1995), 156.

33. Indeed, middle- and upper-class white southerners had been busting "undesirables" for "vagrancy" since the end of the Civil War, sweeping many newly emancipated, formerly enslaved people into chain gangs. See Daniel A. Novak, *The Wheel of Servitude: Black Forced Labor after Slavery* (Lexington: University Press of Kentucky, 1983).

34. Grant Wacker, *Heaven Below: Early Pentecostals and American Culture* (Cambridge, Mass.: Harvard University Press, 2009), 267.

35. Lawless, "Brothers and Sisters," 86.

36. Kirsten Thompson, *Apocalyptic Dread: American Film at the Turn of the Millennium* (Albany: State University of New York Press, 2007), 162n20. Cady makes several allusions to being raped in prison, and there is considerable literature regarding prison rape among De Niro's research materials, including Susan Brownmiller, *Against Our Will: Men, Women and Rape* (New York: Simon and Schuster, 1975); Richard T. Rada, "Psychological Factors in Rapist Behavior," from *Clinical Aspects of the Rapist* (New York: Grune and Stratton, 1978); Timothy Beneke, "Rape Language," from *Men on Rape: What They Have to Say about Sexual Violence* (New York: St. Martin's, 1983). Most of this literature implies that rape was a prevalent and almost inevitable experience for many incarcerated men, especially younger and less physically threatening inmates.

37. Original screenplay by Wesley Strick, November 2, 1989, box folder 22.4, RDN Papers, 1.

38. These practices reflect a literal reading of a passage in the Gospel of Mark, which many Signs Following churches identify as the words of the resurrected Jesus: "In my name shall they cast out devils; they shall speak with new tongues; They shall take up serpents; and if they drink any deadly thing, it shall not hurt them, they shall lay hands on the sick and they shall recover" (Mark 16:17–18 [King James Version]).

39. Michael J. McVicar, "Take Away the Serpents from Us: The Sign of Serpent Handling and the Development of Southern Pentecostalism," *Journal of Southern Religion* 15 (2013), http://jsreligion.org/issues/vol15/mcvicar.html. See Joel Christie, "Reality TV Snake Pastor Died of Snake Bite after Refusing Treatment because 'It Was God's Plan,'" *Daily Mail*, February 16, 2014, http://www.dailymail.co.uk/news/article-2560727/Kentucky-Pastor-famous-practicing-rare-Christian-snake-handling-tradition-KILLED-bitten-rattlesnake-refusing-treatment-Gods-plan.html; Anugrah Kumar, "Snake Salvation Church to Continue Snake Handling after Pastor Coots' Death from Bite; Son Takes Over," *Christian Post*, February 23, 2014, http://www.christianpost.com/news/snake-salvation-church-to-continue-snake-handling-after-pastor-coots-death-from-bite-son-takes-over-115068/.

40. Cohen, note dated November 1 1990, "Research Materials: Pentecostal," box 30, folder 8, RDN Papers.

41. Stephens, *The Fire Spreads*, 254; Ralph H. Wood Jr. and W. Paul Williamson, *Them that Believe: The Power and Meaning of the Christian Serpent-Handling Tradition* (Berkeley: University of California Press, 2008), 8–9.

42. Strick, Screenplay: *Cape Fear*, October 24, 1990, box 23, folder 8, RDN Papers.

43. Jem Cohen, note dated November 1 1990, "Research Materials: Pentecostal," box 30, folder 8, RDN Papers.

44. See Kenneth Archer, *A Pentecostal Hermeneutic for the Twenty First Century: Spirit, Scripture and Community* (London: T & T Clark, 2004), 23; Robert M. Anderson, *Visions of the Disinherited: The Making of American Pentecostalism* (Peabody, Mass.: Hendrickson, 1992).

45. "I got the judge to postpone the alimony hearing for another twenty-one days," Sam tells Tom Broadbent (Fred Dalton Thompson), who replies, "I've still got 'til Monday to find out which S&L, in which municipality my son-in-law stashed all that money. . . . But I thank you, and my daughter thanks you."

46. American Bar Association, *Model Code of Professional Responsibility* (1964), Ethical Consideration, 7–1, accessed December 4 2018, http://www.law.cornell.edu/ethics/aba/mcpr/MCPR.HTM.

47. Philip E. Wegner, *Life between Two Deaths, 1989–2001: U.S. Culture in the Long Nineties* (Durham, N.C.: Duke University Press, 2009), 114–15.

48. Elizabeth Hinton, *From the War on Poverty to the War on Crime: The Making of Mass Incarceration in America* (Cambridge, Mass.: Harvard University Press, 2016).

49. See Michelle Alexander, *The New Jim Crow: Mass Incarceration in the Age of Colorblindness,* rev. ed. (New York: New Press, 2012), 59, 96; Nicole D. Porter, "Unfinished Project of Civil Rights in the Era of Mass Incarceration and the Movement for Black Lives," *Wake Forest Journal of Law and Policy* 6, no. 1 (2016): 1–34.

50. Williamson, *Hillbillyland*, 156.

51. Baker would go on to play Jim Folsom, two-time liberal populist Alabama governor, in John Frankenheimer's docudrama *George Wallace* (1998) in a performance Dan Carter described as "histrionic." See Dan Carter, "Fact, Fiction, and Film: Frankenheimer's George Wallace," *Perspectives on History: The Newsmagazine of the American Historical Association,* January 1998, https://www.historians.org/publications-and-directories/perspectives-on-history/january-1998/fact-fiction-and-film-frankenheimers-george-wallace.

52. Wegner, *Life between Two Deaths*, 86.
53. Kirsten Thompson, *"Cape Fear* and Trembling: Familial Dread," in *Literature and Film: A Guide to the Theory and Practice of Film Adaptation*, ed. Robert Stam and Alessandra Raengo (New York: Blackwell, 2004), 144.
54. George Eells, "The Life Story of Robert Mitchum," *Good Housekeeping* 198, no. 5 (May 1984): 197. Mitchum was also arrested and convicted for marijuana possession in 1948 in a high-profile case.
55. Quoted in Allison Graham, *Framing the South: Hollywood, Television, and Race during the Civil Rights Struggle* (Baltimore: Johns Hopkins University Press, 2001), 162. Director J. Lee Thompson admitted that Mitchum had something of a "chip on his shoulder" when filming in Savannah, demonstrating "a bitterness against the whole place, against the community. . . . He was explosive, always ready to explode, which was great for the picture. I mean, I didn't try to stop that (laughs)." Interview, *The Making of the 1962 Cape Fear*, DVD Special Features.
56. Norman Mailer, "The White Negro: Superficial Reflections on the Hipster," *Dissent* (Fall 1957), 278.
57. Wegner, *Life between Two Deaths*, 88.
58. Kirsten Thompson, *"Cape Fear* and Trembling," 127.
59. Deborah E. Barker, *Reconstructing Violence: The Southern Rape Complex in Film and Literature* (Baton Rouge: Louisiana State University Press, 2015), 155.
60. Allison Graham and Sharon Monteith, eds., "Southern Media Cultures," *The New Encyclopedia of Southern Culture, vol. 18: Media* (Chapel Hill: University of North Carolina Press, 2011), 14.
61. Wegner, *Life between Two Deaths*, 100.
62. Neil R. McMillen, "Black Enfranchisement in Mississippi: Federal Enforcement and Black Protest in the 1960s," *Journal of Southern History* 43, no. 3 (August 1977): 356.
63. For example, see "Question and Answer Period Following Remarks of Senator John F. Kennedy," Bean Feed, Minneapolis, October 1, 1960, via *The American Presidency Project,* ed. Gerhard Peters and John T. Woolley, accessed December 14, 2018, https://www.presidency.ucsb.edu/documents/remarks-senator -john-f-kennedy-bean-feed-minneapolis-mn.
64. *Moses v. Kennedy,* 219 F. Supp. 762 (D.D.C. 1963).
65. Wegner, *Life between Two Deaths*, 101.
66. Kirsten Thompson, *"Cape Fear* and Trembling," 131.
67. Rape shield laws limit the cross-examination of rape victims, specifically regarding their previous sexual history, and were adopted by all U.S. jurisdictions across the 1970s and 1980s. In Georgia, where Cady was tried and convicted, a rape shield law was adopted in 1976.
68. Sticky note removed from De Niro's copy of the 1962 continuity script. Reel 4A, p. 4 and Reel 6A, p. 7, box 22, folder 1 RDN Papers.
69. Annette Wernblad, *The Passion of Martin Scorsese: A Critical Study of the Films* (Jefferson, N.C.: McFarland, 2010), 14. See Ben Child, *"The Wolf of Wall Street* Criticized for 'Glorifying Psychopathic Behavior,'" *The Guardian*, December 30, 2013, http://www.theguardian.com/film/2013/dec/30/wolf-of-wall-street -christina-mcdowell-letter-martin-scorsese; Adam White and Jason Stolworthy, "Martin Scorsese Says He 'Doesn't Have Time' to Write Female Characters," *The Independent*, October 22, 2019, https://www.independent.co.uk/arts

-entertainment/films/news/martin-scorsese-female-characters-irishman
-casino-sharon-stone-marvel-a9165991.html.

70. Stoddart, "I Don't Know Whether to Look at Him or Read Him," 198–99. See also Eve Sedgwick, *Between Men: English Literature and Male Homosocial Desire* (New York: Columbia University Press, 1985).

71. See Jeffrey Couchman, *The Night of the Hunter: A Biography of a Film* (Evanston, Ill.: Northwestern University Press, 2009), 72.

72. Strick, Production Notes, *Cape Fear* Press Kit, November 1991, box 29, folder 1, RDN Papers.

73. Flannery O'Connor, "A Good Man Is Hard to Find," in *The Complete Stories* (New York: Farrar, Straus and Giroux, 1971), 133.

74. Strick, Original Screenplay, November 2, 1989, box 22, folder 4, p. 64.

75. Strick, Original Screenplay, November 2, 1989, box 22, folder 4, p. 4; Strick quoted in Kelly, *Martin Scorsese,* 287.

76. Flannery O'Connor, "Some Aspects of the Grotesque in Southern Fiction," in *Mystery and Manners: Occasional Prose,* ed. Robert and Sally Fitzgerald (New York: Farrar, Straus and Giroux, 1970), 44.

77. Flannery O'Connor, "The Catholic Novelist in the Protestant South," in *Mystery and Manners,* 204; Strick, Production Notes, *Cape Fear* Press Kit.

78. Wegner, *Life between Two Deaths,* 87.

79. George M. Marsden, *Fundamentalism in American Culture* (New York: Oxford University Press, 2006), 235–39; Mark Shibley, "The Southernization of American Religion: Testing a Hypothesis," *Sociological Analysis* 52, no. 2 (Summer 1991): 159–74.

80. Strick, Interview, "The Making of the 1991 *Cape Fear.*"

81. Thomas G. Long, "Preaching about Evangelism—Faith Finding Its Voice," in *Preaching in and out of Season,* ed. Thomas G. Long and Neely Dixon McCarter (Louisville: Westminster John Knox Press, 1990), 77–78.

82. Strick, Original Screenplay, November 2, 1989, p. 109, box 22, folder 4, RDN Papers.

83. Arthur M. Schlesinger Jr., "The Messiah of the Rednecks," in *Huey Long,* ed. Hugh Davis Graham (Englewood Cliffs: Prentice-Hall, 1970), 146; J. Michael Hogan and Glen Williams, "The Rusticity and Religiosity of Huey P. Long," *Rhetoric and Public Affairs* 7, no. 2 (2004): 151.

84. Elton Abernathy, "Huey Long: Oratorical 'Wealth Sharing,'" *Southern Speech Journal* 21 (1955): 102; Schlesinger, "Messiah of the Rednecks," 48. For a more nuanced account of Long's career, see Anthony J. Badger, "Huey Long and the New Deal," in *Nothing Else to Fear: New Perspectives on America in the Thirties,* ed. Stephen W. Baskerville and Ralph Willett (Manchester, UK: Manchester University Press, 1985), 65–103.

85. See Garry Boulard, *Huey Long: His Life in Photos, Drawings, and Cartoons* (Gretna, La.: Pelican, 2003), 42; John T. Edge, "The State of the Broth," *Oxford American,* no. 84 (Spring 2014), http://www.oxfordamerican.org/magazine /item/143-the-state-of-the-broth.

86. Strick, Original Screenplay, November 2, 1989, box folder 22.4, RDN Papers, 8.

87. Strick, Original Screenplay, 5–9.

88. Benjamin Tillman quoted in Waldo W. Braden, *The Oral Tradition in the South* (Baton Rouge: Louisiana State University Press, 1983), 90.

89. Kirsten Thompson, *"Cape Fear* and Trembling," 139.
90. "Debauchery, it's a three-syllable word," Lori patronizes Cady in the bar. "You making fun of me? OK, no problem," he responds. "I'm drinking a Sea Breeze. I hope you can afford them," she says later. Diane Taylor had also demeaned Cady in the 1962 film, calling him "an animal—coarse, rough, barbaric. . . . You're rock bottom. . . . It's a great comfort to a girl to know she can't possibly sink any lower."
91. Wegner, *Life between Two Deaths,* 107.
92. Thompson, *Apocalyptic Dread,* 49.
93. See M. V. Hood III, Quentin Kidd, and Irwin L. Morris, *The Rational Southerner: Black Mobilization, Republican Growth, and the Partisan Transformation of the American South* (New York: Oxford University Press, 2012), 182, table 9.1, based on decennial U.S. census data.
94. Thomas Frank, *The Conquest of Cool: Business Culture, Counterculture, and the Rise of Hip Consumerism* (Chicago: University of Chicago Press, 1997), 1.
95. Thomas Carsey and Geoffrey Layman, "How Our Partisan Loyalties Are Driving Polarization," *Washington Post,* January 27, 2014, http://www.washingtonpost .com/blogs/monkey-cage/wp/2014/01/27/how-our-partisan-loyalties-are -driving-polarization/. See also Bill Scher, "How the Republicans Lost the Culture War," *Politico,* October 12 2014, http://www.politico.com/magazine/story/2014/10 /how-republicans-lost-the-culture-war-111822_Page2.html#.VIbSnKSsWnM.

Chapter 5. "You Don't See Billy Graham Walking Any Picket Lines"

1. See Kelly J. Madison, "Legitimation Crisis and Containment: The 'Anti-racist-White-Hero' Film," *Critical Studies in Mass Communication* 16, no. 4 (1999).
2. Warren Hinckle and David Welsh, "The Five Battles of Selma," *Ramparts Magazine,* June 1965, 36.
3. Peter Dreier, "*Selma*'s Missing Rabbi," *Huffington Post,* January 17, 2015, http://www .huffingtonpost.com/peter-dreier/selmas-missing-rabbi_b_6491368.html.
4. In *Shelby County v. Holder,* the U.S. Supreme Court ruled that the formula that constituted which electoral jurisdictions were subject to federal preclearance (due to a history of discrimination in voter registration and elections) was outdated and no longer necessary, thus posing a burden to equal sovereignty of states. In her dissenting opinion, joined by Justices Stephen Breyer, Elena Kagan, and Sonia Sotomayor, Justice Ruth Bader Ginsburg wrote that "throwing out preclearance when it has worked and is continuing to work to stop discriminatory changes is like throwing away your umbrella in a rainstorm because you are not getting wet." *Shelby County v. Holder,* 570, U.S. 529 (2013).
5. Sharon Waxman, "Why 'Selma' Director Ava DuVernay Joined #BlackFridayBlackout over Ferguson," *The Wrap,* November 26, 2014, https://www .thewrap.com/why-selma-director-ava-duvernay-joined-blackfridayblackout -over-ferguson/.
6. Mark Newman, *Getting Right with God: Southern Baptists and Desegregation, 1945–1995* (Tuscaloosa: University of Alabama Press, 2001); Carolyn Dupont, *Mississippi Praying: Southern White Evangelicals and the Civil Rights Movement, 1945–1975* (New York: New York University Press, 2013); Randall J. Stephens, "'It Has to Come from the Hearts of the People': Evangelicals, Fundamentalists, Race, and the 1964 Civil Rights Act," *Journal of American Studies* 50, no. 3 (August 2016): 559–85.

7. Jon Speed, "You Will Hate Selma but Should Watch It Anyway," *Gospel Spam*, January 14, 2015, http://gospelspam.com/selma-movie-review/.

8. J. Russell Hawkins quoted in Justin Taylor, "Jim Crow, Civil Rights, and Southern White Evangelicals: A Historian's Forum," *Gospel Coalition*, February 9, 2015, http://www.thegospelcoalition.org/blogs/justintaylor/2015/02/09/jim-crow-civil-rights-and-southern-white-evangelicals-a-historians-forum-rusty-hawkins/#_ftn2.

9. Carolyn Dupont quoted in Justin Taylor, "Jim Crow, Civil Rights, and Southern White Evangelicals: A Historian's Forum," *Gospel Coalition*, February 10, 2015, http://www.thegospelcoalition.org/blogs/justintaylor/2015/02/10/jim-crow-civil-rights-and-southern-white-evangelicals-a-historians-forum-carolyn-dupont/.

10. Jay Reeves, "Billy Graham Had Pride and Regret on Civil Rights," *AP News*, February 25, 2018, https://apnews.com/20d646efe23c469fbbc83cd04ec2fc17.

11. Michael G. Long, *Billy Graham and the Beloved Community: America's Evangelist and the Dream of Martin Luther King, Jr.* (New York: Palgrave Macmillan, 2006), 127, 113–14; Steven P. Miller, *Billy Graham and the Rise of the Sunbelt South* (Philadelphia: University of Pennsylvania Press, 2009), 105.

12. Long, *Billy Graham*, 114.

13. Long, *Billy Graham*, 115, 110–11.

14. Martin Luther King Jr., Letter to Billy Graham, July 23, 1958, accessed January 3, 2023, https://kinginstitute.stanford.edu/king-papers/documents/billy-graham-0.

15. Anthea D. Butler, *White Evangelical Racism: The Politics of Morality in America* (Chapel Hill: University of North Carolina Press, 2021), 37–44.

16. "Billy Graham Urges Restraint in Sit-Ins," *New York Times,* April 18, 1963, 21. See also S. Jonathan Bass, *Blessed Are the Peacemakers: Martin Luther King Jr., Eight White Religious Leaders, and the "Letter from Birmingham Jail"* (Baton Rouge: Louisiana State University Press, 2001).

17. President John F. Kennedy, "Radio and Television Report to the American People on Civil Rights," June 11, 1963, https://www.jfklibrary.org/archives/other-resources/john-f-kennedy-speeches/civil-rights-radio-and-television-report-19630611.

18. Martin Luther King Jr., Address at the Freedom Rally in Cobo Hall, Detroit, Michigan, June 23, 1963, https://kinginstitute.stanford.edu/king-papers/documents/address-freedom-rally-cobo-hall.

19. Chuck Stone, "Silly Billy Graham Magnificent Phony," *Chicago Defender*, April 18, 1964, 2.

20. Speed, "You Will Hate Selma."

21. Stone, "Silly Billy Graham," 1.

22. Matthew Avery Sutton, "Billy Graham Was on the Wrong Side of History," *The Guardian,* February 21, 2018, https://www.theguardian.com/commentisfree/2018/feb/21/billy-graham-wrong-side-history.

23. Jemar Tisby, "Moving beyond Graham's Legacy: Raising the Bar on Evangelical Participation in Civil Rights," *The Witness*, June 27, 2018, https://thewitnessbcc.com/moving-beyond-grahams-legacy-raising-the-bar-on-evangelical-participation-in-civil-rights/.

24. Long, *Billy Graham*, 117.

25. Martin Luther King Jr., "Nonviolence and Social Change," in *The Trumpet of Conscience* (New York: Harper and Row, 1968), 59. Aaron Griffith points out that Graham also preached that "Congress should immediately drop all other legislation and devise new laws to deal with riots and violence such as we have wit-

nessed in Los Angeles." This was a marked change for the "evangelist who had previously proclaimed personal conversion as the ideal response to crime." See Aaron Griffith, *God's Law and Order: The Politics of Punishment in Evangelical America* (Cambridge, Mass.: Harvard University Press, 2020), 120.

26. Martin Luther King Jr., "Draft of Chapter XV, 'The Answer to a Perplexing Question,'" in *The Papers of Martin Luther King, Jr.*, volume 6: *Advocate of the Social Gospel, September 1948–March 1963*, ed. Clayborne Carson, Susan Carson, Susan Englander, Troy Jackson, and Gerald L. Smith (Berkeley: University of California Press, 2007), 550.

27. Eddie Glaude, "The Black Church Is Dead," *Huffington Post Religion Blog*, April 26, 2010, http://www.huffingtonpost.com/eddie-glaude-jr-phd/the-black-church-is-dead_b_473815.html.

28. Suzanne E. Smith, *To Serve the Living: Funeral Directors and the African American Way of Death* (Cambridge, Mass.: Harvard University Press, 2010), 179, 169.

29. See Alexander Remington, "King Adviser James Bevel, 72; Incest Sentence Clouded Legacy," *Washington Post*, December 20, 2008, http://www.washington-post.com/wp-dyn/content/article/2008/12/19/AR2008121903432_2.html. In a deleted scene, Bevel implores King to "be aggressive," lamenting that his colleague is "too soft." Bevel's idea that "we lay Jimmie Lee's body down on George Wallace's door in Montgomery" is met by King's repeated assurance: "We need to remain calm." See Bryan Alexander, "Common Snaps in This Deleted 'Selma' Scene," *USA Today*, April 21, 2015, http://www.usatoday.com/story/life/movies/2015/04/21/selma-deleted-scene-common-martin-luther-king/26112273/.

30. James Bevel at Brown Chapel AME, Selma, Alabama, February 26, 1965. See Taylor Branch, *Pillar of Fire: America in the King Years 1963–65* (New York: Simon and Schuster, 1998), 599; Smith, To Serve the Living, 177.

31. Mark Blankenship, "Can Public Enemy Make 'Selma' Feel Modern?" *Tribeca*, November 7, 2014, https://tribecafilm.com/stories/public-enemy-selma-trailer-song.

32. Morgan Rhodes, interviewed by Alex Cohen and Jacob Margolis, "The Music of 'Selma': Scoring the Civil Rights Movement," *Take Two*, Southern California Public Radio, January 9, 2015, http://www.scpr.org/programs/take-two/2015/01/09/41040/the-music-of-selma-scoring-the-civil-rights-moveme/.

33. Aniko Bodroghkozy, *Equal Time: Television and the Civil Rights Movement* (Champaign: University of Illinois Press, 2013), 128.

34. Aniko Bodroghkozy, "Oscars 2015: What 'Selma' Got Right and Got Wrong," NBC Storyline, February 22, 2015, http://www.nbcnews.com/storyline/oscars/oscars-2015-what-selma-got-right-got-wrong-n310361.

35. Kenn Rabin quoted in Sheila Curran Bernard, "A Conversation with Selma Archive Producer Kenn Rabin," *American Historian* (February 2015), http://tah.oah.org/february-2015/conversation-with-kenn-rabin/.

36. Bodroghkozy, "Oscars 2015."

37. Bodroghkozy notes that DuVernay's camera angles differed from those in the original news footage, which situated viewers as onlookers rather than participants. See Bodroghkozy, "Oscars 2015."

38. Rhodes, "The Music of 'Selma.'"

39. Rhodes clarified her understanding of "tedious" in a Twitter post, January 3, 2015, 3:11 p.m.: https://twitter.com/morganrhodes/status/683787883711299584.

40. Rhodes, "The Music of 'Selma.'"
41. Sister Gertrude Morgan, "I Got the New World in My View," *Selma—Music from the Motion Picture*, Paramount Pictures/Pathé Productions, Digital Download, 2015.
42. Rhodes, "The Music of 'Selma.'"
43. Twenty-six-year-old Jimmie Lee Jackson was shot by a white Alabama state trooper during a peaceful protest in Marion, Alabama, on February 18, 1965. His murder is depicted in *Selma* and proves central to the decision to march to Montgomery.
44. Rhodes, "The Music of 'Selma.'"
45. Robert Darden, "The Missing Songs of 'Selma,'" *On Faith*, January 16, 2015, http://www.faithstreet.com/onfaith/2015/01/16/the-missing-songs-of-selma/35899.
46. Ann Powers, "How One of Gospel's Essential Songs Gave 'Selma' Its Soul," The Record: Music News from NPR, January 15, 2015, http://www.npr.org/sections/therecord/2015/01/15/377427650/how-one-of-gospels-essential-songs-gave-selma-its-soul.
47. Rhodes, "The Music of 'Selma.'"
48. "Ben Branch, 59, Leader in Civil Rights, Business," *Chicago Tribune*, August 28, 1987, http://articles.chicagotribune.com/1987-08-28/news/8703050549_1_mr-branch-ben-branch-southern-christian-leadership-conference.
49. Powers, "How One of Gospel's Essential Songs."
50. Shannon M. Houston, "Violence and Glory in Ava DuVernay's *Selma*," *Paste*, January 5, 2015, http://www.pastemagazine.com/articles/2015/01/violence-and-glory-in-ava-duvernays-selma.html. It is undoubtedly because of its connection with King that "Take My Hand, Precious Lord" has featured so prominently in civil rights filmmaking. Mahalia Jackson's version opens *Mississippi Burning*, while a searching rendition by the Jones Sisters soundtracks the most dramatic moments of *A Time to Kill,* as Carl Lee (Samuel L. Jackson) assassinates the white men who raped his daughter on the steps of the courthouse as they make their way to their trial. Whereas Black gospel music often soundtracks white violence inflicted on innocent, peaceful African Americans, the use of "Take My Hand" in *A Time to Kill* accompanies scenes of Black vigilantism and murder, potentially reflecting the limitations of nonviolent, Christian patience. "America is a war," Carl Lee concludes. By its conclusion, however, *A Time to Kill* elicits hope in a more positive future, as white and Black families come together suggesting that the promise of the civil rights movement has been reborn in Canton, Mississippi. As the credits begin, a large choral rendition of "Take My Hand, Precious Lord" begins to play at a faster tempo than the song's previous appearance in the film.
51. The Impressions, "Keep on Pushing," *Selma—Music from the Motion Picture.*
52. Peter Burns, *Curtis Mayfield: People Never Give Up* (London: Sanctuary, 2003), 29.
53. Tammy L. Kernodle, "'I Wish I Knew How It Would Feel to Be Free': Nina Simone and the Redefining of the Freedom Song of the 1960s," *Journal of the Society for American Music* 2, no. 3 (2008): 296.
54. Fink, "Yesterday Was Hard on All of Us," *Selma: Music from the Motion Picture.*
55. Martin Luther King Jr., *Where Do We Go from Here: Chaos or Community?* (Boston: Beacon, 2010).
56. Ann Powers interviewed by Renee Montagne, *Morning Edition,* NPR, February 20,

2015, http://www.npr.org/sections/therecord/2015/01/15/377427650/how-one-of
-gospels-essential-songs-gave-selma-its-soul.

57. "The movement is a rhythm to us / Freedom is like religion to us / . . . That's why Rosa sat on the bus / That's why we walk through Ferguson with our hands up," Common and John Legend, "Glory," *Selma: Music from the Motion Picture*.

58. Anthony Puccinelli, "Designer Rage: *A Time to Kill,* Directed by Joel Schumacher, with Matthew McConaughey, Samuel L. Jackson, Sandra Bullock, Kiefer Sutherland, and Ashley Judd," *Chicago Reader*, August 15,1996, http://www .chicagoreader.com/chicago/a-time-to-kill-directed-by-joel-schumacher-with -matthew-mcconaughey-samuel-l-jackson-sandra-bullock-kiefer-sutherland -and-ashley-judd/Content?oid=891305.

59. Michael Eric Dyson, "Whose President Was He?" *Politico Magazine*, January/ February 2016, https://www.politico.com/magazine/story/2016/01 /barack-obama-race-relations-213493/.

60. Ed Pilkington, "Obama Gives Searing Speech on Race in Eulogy for Charleston Pastor," *The Guardian*, June 26, 2015, http://www.theguardian.com/us-news/2015 /jun/26/obama-charleston-eulogy-pinckney-amazing-grace.

61. Douglas Thomas Woodhouse, "Cinematic Blackness in the Age of Obama and #BlackLivesMatter" (master's thesis, Harvard University, 2018), 3–4, https://dash .harvard.edu/handle/1/42004063.

62. Reginald Hudlin, "'Django Unchained' Producer on 'Selma' Oscar Snubs: Did Voters Have 'Racial Fatigue'?" *Hollywood Reporter,* January 15, 2015, https://www .hollywoodreporter.com/news/general-news/django unchained-producer-selma -oscar-764888/; Michael Shulman, "Shakeup at the Oscars," *New Yorker,* February 19, 2017, https://www.newyorker.com/magazine/2017/02/27/shakeup -at-the-oscars.

63. Shulman, "Shakeup at the Oscars."

64. David Sims, "The Oscars Haven't Been This White in 17 Years," *The Atlantic,* January 15, 2015, https://www.theatlantic.com/entertainment/archive/2015/01 /the-oscars-havent-been-this-white-in-17-years/384550/.

65. Lamont H. Yeakey, "Introduction: The Film and History of Selma, Alabama, 1965," *Black Camera* 10, no. 2 (Spring 2019): 161. *Selma* made $66.8 million at the box office and was produced on a budget of $20 million. *Detroit* took just $23.3 million worldwide, a loss on its budget of $34 million. Figures from Box Office Mojo, www.boxofficemojo.com.

66. Sims, "The Oscars Haven't Been This White in 17 Years."

67. Ben Dalton, "David Oyelowo Calls for BAFTA Changes: 'It Cannot Be a Road Trip for Hollywood,'" *ScreenDaily*, June 4, 2020, https://www.screendaily.com /news/david-oyelowo-calls-for-bafta-changes-it-cannot-be-a-road-trip-for -hollywood/5150368.article.

68. Joseph A. Califano Jr., "The Movie 'Selma' Has a Glaring Flaw," *Washington Post*, December 26, 2014.

69. Califano, "The Movie 'Selma.'"

70. Vincent Dowd, "Oscars: *Selma* Writer Tells His Side of Row with Director," *BBC News*, February 20, 2015, https://www.bbc.co.uk/news/entertainment-arts-31539526.

71. Martin Luther King Jr., *The Autobiography of Martin Luther King, Jr.*, chap. 26:

Selma, edited by Clayborne Carson, accessed August 4, 2022, https://kinginstitute
.stanford.edu/chapter-26-selma.

72. Yeakey, "Introduction: The Film and History of Selma," 173–74.

73. Peniel Joseph, "'Selma' Backlash Misses the Point," Code Switch, NPR, January 10,
2015, https://www.npr.org/sections/codeswitch/2015/01/10/376081786/selma
-backlash-misses-the-point?t=1659445214187.

74. Jonathan Scott Holloway, "Selma: History as Entertainment or Entertainment as
History?" *AHA Today*, March 18, 2015, https://www.historians.org
/publications-and-directories/perspectives-on-history/march-2015/selma
-history-as-entertainment-or-entertainment-as-history; Yeakey, "Introduction:
The Film and History of Selma," 174–75.

75. Barbara Reynolds, "The Biggest Problem with 'Selma' Has Nothing to Do with LBJ
or the Oscars," *Washington Post,* January 19, 2015, https://www.washingtonpost
.com/posteverything/wp/2015/01/19/the-biggest-problem-with-selma-has
-nothing-to-do-with-lbj-or-the-oscars/.

76. Andrew O'Hehir, "'Lee Daniels' The Butler': An Oscar-Worthy Historical Fable,"
Salon, August 14, 2013, https://www.salon.com/2013/08/14/lee_daniels_the_butler
_an_oscar_worthy_historical_fable/.

77. *Selma* made $66.8 million at the box office and was produced on a budget of $20
million. *The Butler* made $176.6 million, with a production budget of $30 million.
Figures from Box Office Mojo, www.boxofficemojo.com.

78. Allison Graham draws particular attention to the film's initial setup in which
Forrest tells his life story to an African American woman at a bus stop. "Although
the scene is set in present-day Savannah, the Rosa Parks connotations are unmis-
takable," Graham writes, especially when the woman complains of her tired feet.
See Allison Graham, *Framing the South: Hollywood, Television, and Race during
the Civil Rights Struggle* (Baltimore: Johns Hopkins University Press, 2001), 192.

79. Robert Zemeckis, *Through the Eyes of Forrest Gump,* documentary directed by
Peyton Reed, 1994. Available on *Forrest Gump,* 2 disc Special Collector's Edition
(2001).

80. Will Haygood, "A Butler Served Well by This Election," *Washington Post*,
November 7, 2008, https://www.washingtonpost.com/wp-dyn/content
/article/2008/11/06/AR2008110603948_pf.html.

81. Andrew Friedman, "Decolonization's Diplomats: Antiracism and the Year of
Africa in Washington, D.C.," *Journal of American History* 106, no. 3 (2019): 616.

82. Jeanne Theoharis, "Hidden in Plain Sight: The Civil Rights Movement outside
the South," in *The Myth of Southern Exceptionalism*, ed. Matthew D. Lassiter and
Joseph Crespino (New York: Oxford University Press, 2009), 50.

83. Peniel E. Joseph, "The Black Power Movement: A State of the Field," *Journal of
American History* 96, no. 3 (December 2009): 752.

84. Woodhouse points out that by 1965, the year of his assassination, Malcolm X had
converted to Sunni Islam and repudiated the Nation of Islam and their message.
Woodhouse argues, therefore, that "Louis' characterization of the speech is incongruous with what [Malcolm X] was likely to have been speaking about at this
time in his life." See Woodhouse, "Cinematic Blackness in the Age of Obama and
#BlackLivesMatter," 32n2.

85. David G. Holmes, "Seen and Heard: Negotiating the Black Female Ethos in *Selma*," *Black Camera* 10, no. 2 (Spring 2019): 186.

86. Loren King, "Ava DuVernay's March to Direct 'Selma,'" *Boston Globe,* February 20, 2015, https://www.bostonglobe.com/arts/movies/2015/01/03/ava-duvernay-march-direct-selma/aYNxrN3gPjhbalF4QEnO7M/story.html.

87. David J. Garrow, *Bearing the Cross: Martin Luther King Jr. and the Southern Christian Leadership Conference* (New York: Open Road Media, 2015), E-book, 693–96.

88. Dupont, *Mississippi Praying,* 6.

Conclusion. "Why There's This Desire to Write about All These Horrible Things That Happened over Civil Rights, I Don't Know"

1. Peter Baker, *The Breach: Inside the Impeachment and Trial of William Jefferson Clinton* (New York: Scribner, 2000), 103; Janet Maslin, "Critic's Notebook; The Year's Best Films: Risks Furnish Rewards," *New York Times,* December 26, 1997, https://www.nytimes.com/1997/12/26/movies/critic-s-notebook-the-year-s-best-films-risks-furnish-rewards.html.

2. Robert Marquand, "'The Apostle' Rewrites How Religion Is Depicted on Big Screen," *Christian Science Monitor,* February 5, 1998, https://www.csmonitor.com/1998/0205/020598.us.us.1.html.

3. Patton Dodd, "How *The Apostle* Gets Religion," *CrossCurrents* 65, no. 2 (June 2015): 191, 197; "'The Apostle': An Interview with Robert Duvall by Bill Blizek and Ronald Burke," *Journal of Religion and Film* 2, no. 1 (1998): 3.

4. Robert Duvall interviewed by Mark Morning, "The 'Low-Down' on Robert Duvall," *Christianity Today,* July 27, 2010.

5. Robert Duvall quoted in Pete Hammond, "Duvall on 'The Judge': It Felt like Making a Studio Film from the '70s," *Deadline,* December 4, 2014, http://deadline.com/2014/12/the-judges-robert-duvall-tops-an-already-stellar-career-with-one-of-his-best-roles-to-date-1201269748/.

6. Thornton quoted in Erik Bauer, "'I'm Pretty Anti-violence. I Don't Want to Do More Movies about Violence'—Billy Bob Thornton," interview for *Creative Screenwriting,* accessed January 3, 2023, http://creativescreenwriting.com/im-pretty-anti-violence-i-dont-want-to-do-more-movies-about-violence-billy-bob-thornton/.

7. Rita Kempley, "Who Is That Guy?" *Washington Post,* March 23, 1996, http://www.washingtonpost.com/wp-srv/style/longterm/movies/review97/fbillythornton.htm.

8. Kempley, "Who Is That Guy?"; Allison Graham, *Framing the South: Hollywood, Television, and Race during the Civil Rights Struggle* (Baltimore: Johns Hopkins University Press, 2001), 185.

9. See Matthew McEver, "The Messianic Figure in Film: Christology beyond the Biblical Epic," *Journal of Religion and Film* 2, no. 2 (October 1998), https://www.unomaha.edu/jrf/McEverMessiah.htm; Mark Roncace, "*Sling Blade,*" in *Bible and Cinema: Fifty Key Films,* ed. Adele Reinhartz (London: Routledge, 2013), 238–42.

10. Thornton quoted in Kempley, "Who Is That Guy?"

11. Like *Cool Hand Luke* and *The Green Mile, Sling Blade* contributes to a body of work testament to Hollywood's obsession with crime and punishment in the South. *Cool Hand Luke* focuses on a southern chain gang in the 1940s, while *The Green Mile* depicts an innocent man (and Christ figure) facing the death penalty in Depression-era Louisiana. Another more humorous examination is *O Brother, Where Art Thou?* (Joel and Ethan Coen, 2000) in which three men es-

cape a Mississippi chain gang. "While the most sadistic aspects of the South's penal system have never ceased to enthrall, they also have never seemed to surprise," historian Heather Ann Thompson writes. See Heather Ann Thompson, "Blinded by a 'Barbaric' South: Prison Horrors, Inmate Abuse, and the Ironic History of American Penal Reform," in *The Myth of Southern Exceptionalism*, ed. Matthew D. Lassiter and Joseph Crespino (New York: Oxford University Press, 2009), 74, 84.

12. Kempley, "Who Is That Guy?"

13. Bradley Shaw, "Baptizing Boo: Religion in the Cinematic Southern Gothic," *Mississippi Quarterly* 63, no. 3 (Summer 2010): 464.

14. After surviving a homemade abortion, the younger Childers son was handed over to Karl (who "wasn't but six or eight" years old), who was instructed to "throw it away." With no way to care for the baby, Karl admits that he buried him alive in a shoebox, figuring it was better to "return him to the good Lord right off the bat."

15. Kempley, "Who Is That Guy?"

16. Harper Lee, *To Kill a Mockingbird* (New York: Grand Central/Hachette, 2010), 60.

17. Quoted in Kempley, "Who Is That Guy?"

18. Thornton quoted in Bauer, "'I'm Pretty Anti-violence.'"

19. Thornton quoted in Bauer, "'I'm Pretty Anti-violence.'"

20. Jonathan Rosenbaum, "Soul Brothers (A FAMILY THING)," *Chicago Reader*, April 12, 1996.

21. Kenneth Turan, "'Family Thing': A Sensitive Journey of Self-Discovery," *Los Angeles Times,* March 29, 1996, https://www.latimes.com/archives/la-xpm-1996-03-29-ca-52443-story.html.

22. Tom Epperson, "True Hollywood Stories: A Family Thing," accessed February 24, 2020, http://www.tomepperson.com/a-family-thing—-true-hollywood-stories.html.

23. Godfrey Cheshire, "A Family Thing," *Variety,* March 21, 1996, https://variety.com/1996/film/reviews/a-family-thing-1200445263/.

24. Steven G. Kellman, "Review of *A Family Thing*," *Southern Quarterly* 35, no. 1 (Fall 1996): 143.

25. "Movie Review: *Down in the Delta*," *Movieguide*, 1998, https://www.movieguide.org/reviews/down-in-the-delta.html.

INDEX

Brigance, Jake (*continued*)
and, 101–2; southern lawyer trope and, 19–20, 82, 98, 107
Brilliant Books, 30–31
Brinkmeyer, Robert H., 35
"brittle secularist" critiques (Mencken), 6–7
Brooks, Cleanth, 22
Brown, Michael, 140
Brown v. Board of Education, 28–31, 33, 37
Brundage, W. Fitzhugh, 6–7
Burden of Southern History (Woodward), 7–8
Burr, Ty, 19
Burton, Tom, 119
Bush, George W., 10
Butler, Anthea D., 143
Butler, Robert, 24, 45
Butler, The: awards and, 159–60; Black Power and, 164–65; box office numbers, 213n77; depiction of presidents in, 159–61, 163–64; evolution of civil rights genre and, 17; issues of race in, 161; MLK and, 166; Obama and, 160, 161–62; southern exceptionalism and, 162–64

Cady, Max (character): characterization of, 108, 117–18, 202nn1–2, 203n15, 208n90; civil rights and, 125–26; conflation of religion and sexual violence, 113–14, 128; cultural bias against, 133–34, 136–37; incarceration of, 122; introductory scenes of, 112; Mitchum version of, 123–24; "othering" of, 120; Pentecostalism and, 110–12, 118–21, 129–31, 132; rape of, 204n36; reconceptualization of, 1, 16, 109–10; as southern demagogue, 133–35; southern gothic and, 116–17; tattoos, 112–13; treatment of women, 127–28; white anxieties and, 122–23, 131. See also *Cape Fear;* De Niro, Robert
Califano, Joseph A., Jr., 155
Callahan, Richard, Jr., 111
Calpurnia (character), 23, 24, 25, 36, 38. See also *To Kill a Mockingbird*
Campbell, Jim, 81
Cape Fear (1962), 109–10, 123–25, 127, 189n131
Cape Fear (1991): Cady incarceration in, 122; Cady reconceptualization in, 1, 16; court scenes in, 125–26; divided whiteness and, 117, 120–22; gender and sexuality in, 113, 126–28; 1960s and, 135–36; Pentecostalism in, 119–20; racial intolerance and, 134, 135; religion and rape in, 128; religiosity in, 116–17, 129–30; southern backwardness and, 2, 4,

202n11; South in, 109–10, 129–30; televangelist scandals and, 115–17; white anxieties in, 122–23, 131–32. See also Cady, Max
Cardinal, The, 62–63
Carmichael, Stokely, 83
Carsey, Thomas, 136
Carter, Stephen L., 33
Cash, W. J., 7
Casillo, Robert, 110
Cayhall, Sam (character), 88–92
Chamber, The, 88–92
Chaney, James, 76–77
Chappell, David, 11
Childers, Karl (character). See *Sling Blade*
Chura, Patrick, 28, 185–86n40
church burnings, 80–82, 84, 103
cinema in the Age of Obama: awards and, 154–55; Obama and, 152–53; representation of LBJ and, 155–59. See also *Butler, The; Selma*
civil rights cinema: agenda of civil rights movement and, 93–96; awards and, 154–55; baby boomer nostalgia and, 199n47; Black directors and evolution of, 17; Black lives and civil rights activity in, 69–70; divided whiteness in, 78–79; focus of, 166–67; Hollywood narratives and, 4, 138–39; key tropes of, 16; music and, 211n50; Reiner and, 100; religiosity versus political mobilization in, 5; scholarship on, 5–6; white liberalism and, 84; white moderates and, 142; whiteness and, 3. See also civil rights melodramas; white redemption narratives; *and individual films*
civil rights melodramas: Black agency and, 16; color blindness and, 108; death penalty and, 89–91; Hollywood tropes and religion in, 177–78; music and, 73–75; racism in, 106–7; role of whites and national culture in, 75; southern religiosity and exceptionalism in, 170–71, 175–76; Thornton on, 173–74, 176; white "authenticity" in, 17; white redemption narratives and, 91–92; white resentment in, 107. See also civil rights cinema; stereotypes and tropes; white redemption narratives; *and individual films*
civil rights movement: Black religiosity and, 51–53, 194n80; *The Butler* and, 164–65; *The Cardinal* and, 63–64; church burnings and, 84; cinematic reshaping of, 15; cold cases, 87–88; film and agenda of, 93–95; *Gone Are the Days!* and, 58–62; Billy Graham and, 143–45;

Hollywood and dangers of, 67; Hollywood tropes and, 53; *The Long Walk Home* and, 68–69; made-for-TV movies and, 13–14; *Mississippi Burning* and, 67–68; Montgomery bus boycott and, 68–70; national integration and, 75; *Nothing but a Man* and, 64–67; Protestant individualism and, 10; *Selma* and white involvement in, 12–13; southern religiosity and, 11–12, 139, 168, 178; *To Kill a Mockingbird* and, 26, 37, 48; white savior narrative and, 20–21

class. *See* divided whiteness; poverty as trope; southern exceptionalism; white trash villains

Clinton, Bill, 80–84, 86, 89, 93, 197n12

Coates, Ta-Nehisi, 26

Cochran, Johnnie, 106

Cohen, Jem, 110–11, 118–19

Colick, Lewis, 99

color blindness, 4, 82, 92–96, 107–8

Common, 151

Confederate battle flag, 11, 34–35

conservative-liberal divide, 136–37; Republican revolution, 16, 85–87. *See also* divided whiteness

Cotter, Odessa (character), 69–70

Crespino, Joseph, 27–28, 32, 37, 38

Crisis at Central High, 14

crossover films, interracial, 56, 62, 65–66

culture wars, 15–17, 84–88, 137, 178

Dailey, Jane, 11

D'Alemberte, Talbot, 186n57

Daniels, Lee. *See Butler, The*

Darden, Robert, 149–50

Davis, Carol Bunch, 59

Davis, Ossie, 58–62, 64, 192n40

death penalty, 89–91

DeLaughter, Bobby, 100–101, 139

DeLaughter, Bobby (character), 19–20, 82–83, 89–90, 92, 96–100, 139. *See also Ghosts of Mississippi*

De Niro, Robert, 1, 109–10, 112–13, 116–19, 127. *See also* Cady, Max; *Cape Fear* (1991)

Dennis, Dave, 76–77

desegregation, 11, 14, 28–29, 60–64, 162–63. *See also Brown v. Board of Education*; civil rights movement

Dessommes, Nancy Bishop, 103

Detroit, 154–55, 212n65

Dewey, Sonny (character), 169

Dionne, E. J., 6

"diseased whiteness," 5, 8

District of Columbia, 162

Dittmer, John, 52

divided whiteness: *Cape Fear* and, 117, 120–22; civil rights cinema and, 3; color blindness and, 78–79, 82; "diseased whiteness," 5, 8; hillbillies and, 8; individual responsibility and, 88; religion and, 11; religiosity and, 177–78; *To Kill a Mockingbird* and, 43–47; white anxieties, 122–25, 131; white liberalism and, 107–8. *See also* Pentecostalism; white liberalism; white redemption narratives

"Dixie," 19, 63–64, 99

Dodd, Patton, 170

Doughty, Ruth, 74, 75

Down in the Delta, 176

Duke, David, 103

Dupont, Carolyn, 40, 142, 168

Duvall, Robert, 169, 172, 175

DuVernay, Ava, 17, 140–41, 166–67. *See also Selma*

Dyson, Michael Eric, 153

Elder, Lonne, 14

Emberton, Carole, 11

eulogies, 76–77, 146, 153

Evangelicalism, 8–10, 54, 116, 128–29, 139, 179n2

Evangelism, 132–33

Evans, Curtis J., 76

Evers, Medgar, 87, 100. *See also Ghosts of Mississippi*

Evers-Williams, Myrlie, 87, 98, 99

Evers-Williams, Myrlie (film portrayal), 97–98. *See also Ghosts of Mississippi*

Ewell, Bob (character), 15, 32, 43–45. *See also To Kill a Mockingbird*

Eyerman, Ron, 74

Fade In, Crossroads (R. Jackson), 5

Fairclough, Adam, 52

Family Thing, A, 17, 174–77

Farmer, James, 26

Farrakhan, Louis, 85

Faulkner, William, 20, 22, 116, 171–72, 183n64

Fearful Symmetry, 32, 47

Federal Bureau of Investigation (FBI). *See Mississippi Burning*

Fermoyle, Stephen (character), 63–64

Finch, Alexandra (character). *See To Kill a Mockingbird*

Finch, Atticus (character): character of, 19–

Selma (*continued*)

147–49, 155; box office numbers, 213n77, 212n65; camera angles and, 210n37; critiques of, 155, 159; deleted scenes, 210n29; evolution of civil rights genre and, 17; Hollywood interpretation of civil rights and, 4; LBJ in, 155–56; MLK and, 167–68; music in, 147–52; Obama-era films and, 153; release context of, 140; religiosity in, 53, 139–40, 141–42, 145–46; significance of, 167–68, 178; George Wallace and, 158; white involvement and, 12–13

Shackelford, Dean, 25

Shaffer, Thomas, 41

Shaw, Bradley, 25, 46, 173

Shelby County v. Holder, 208n4

Sieving, Christopher, 60–61, 62, 192n44

Signs Following, 117, 118, 119, 204n38. *See also* Pentecostalism

Simpson, O. J., 85, 105–7

Sims, David, 154, 155

Sixteenth Street Baptist Church, 58–59, 142, 193–94n64

sixties (era), 135–36

Sling Blade, 2, 17, 171–73, 214–15n11, 215n14

Smith, Gary Scott, 86

Smith, Oran P., 85

Smith, R. Drew, 51

Smith, Suzanne E., 77, 146

"social problem pictures," 4, 13–15, 48, 62, 79, 154. *See also* Hollywood's South; southern exceptionalism

Sounder, 14

soundtracks: *Cape Fear*, 115–16, 131; civil rights melodramas and, 73–74; gospel/spiritual, 33–34, 56–57, 71–75, 195n88; *Mississippi Burning*, 16, 54, 71–75; *Selma* and, 139–40, 147–52; *A Time to Kill*, 96, 152, 211n50

South, Hollywood portrayal of. *See* Hollywood's South

Southern Baptist Convention (SBC), 85–87. *See also* Baptists

southern exceptionalism: Beckwith and, 104–5; Black music and, 75; *The Butler* and, 162–64; *Cape Fear* research and, 110; civil rights cold cases and, 88; class and racism in, 41–42; construction of, 3; divided whiteness and, 107–8; David Duke and, 103; gender and, 126–28; Hollywood whiteness and, 82; neutrality of whiteness and, 176; political realignment, 6; political shifts of, 6; post–civil rights era and, 6; religiosity and, 2–3, 7,

8, 12, 132–33; secular, consensus liberalism versus, 78; segregation and, 11; Thornton and, 174; *To Kill a Mockingbird* and, 48–49; Twain and Scott on, 188n100; white liberalism and, 84; white preoccupations and, 6. *See also* Appalachia; Hollywood's South; Ku Klux Klan; southern religiosity; stereotypes and tropes; *and individual films*

"southernization" in United States, 4, 16

southern religiosity: *The Apostle* and, 169–70; boundaries of South and, 10; *Cape Fear* and, 1, 128–32, 137; *The Cardinal* and, 62–63; characterization of South and, 15; church attendance in *To Kill a Mockingbird* and, 23–24; civil rights melodramas and, 170–71; civil rights movement and, 139; DeLaughter and, 100–101; *A Family Thing* and, 177; film and, 2–3; Florida and, 10; fundamentalism in, 1, 6–7; *Ghosts of Mississippi* and, 104–5; *Go Set a Watchman* and, 33–34; historians and, 7–8; "holiness movement," 110–11, 119; Hollywood narratives and, 138–39; hypocrisy in, 40; as integral trope of South, 3–4; Louisiana and, 10; Mississippi and, 9; *The Night of the Hunter* and, 128–29; outsider status and, 12; politics and, 6, 132–33, 203–4n28; portrayal of African Americans and, 5; poverty and, 111; prevalence of, 8–10; as problematic, 7; Protestantism and, 3; race and, 24; references to specific movements and, 179n2; religious feeling and, 9; Republican revolution and, 85–87; segregation and, 11–12; *Selma* and, 139–40, 141, 167–68; semiotics of, 8; as signifier of South, 2–3; *Sling Blade* and, 172–73; southern "authenticity" and, 17; southern studies and, 8; stereotypes and tropes, 5, 16–17; symbolic secularity of United States and, 4; televangelist scandals and, 114–16; in *To Kill a Mockingbird*, 22–23; understaing of civil rights movement and, 178; white Christian nationalism and, 11; white redemption narratives and, 14–15, 16, 101–2, 178; white trash villains and, 5. *See also* Black religiosity; Evangelicalism; Hollywood's South; Pentecostalism; southern exceptionalism

Spaeth, Ryu, 25

Speed, Jon, 141, 144

Stephens, Randall, 111

stereotypes and tropes: cinematic use of, 3, 15–17; civil rights cold cases and, 88; Ossie Davis and, 59; race and, 53–54, 56–57; southern demagogue, 133–35; southern lawyer, 19–22; southern rape myth, 27, 39; white bravery narrative, 68; white civil rights hero, 38; white savior narratives, 20, 138, 167. *See also* Hollywood's South; poverty as trope; white redemption narratives; white trash villains

Stevens, John (character), 20, 184n15
Stoddart, Helen, 128, 203n15
Stone, Chuck, 144
Strick, Wesley, 1, 110, 113–14, 129–30, 132–34, 137
Student Nonviolent Coordinating Committee (SNCC), 191n12
Sundquist, Eric J., 26, 46
Sutton, Matthew Avery, 144
Swaggart, Jimmy, 115–16

Tagg, Philip, 74
"Take My Hand, Precious Lord" (Dorsey), 150, 211n50
televangelist scandals, 114–16
Theoharis, Jeanne, 163
Thomas, Cleophus, Jr., 47
Thompson, Heather Ann, 214–15n11
Thompson, J. Lee, 124, 206n55
Thompson, Kirsten, 118, 123, 124, 126, 134–35
Thornton, Billy Bob, 17, 171–74, 176
Till, Emmett, 28–29, 163
Till-Bradley, Mamie, 28–29
Tillman, Ben, 134
Time to Kill, A (film): Black church and, 53; civil rights heroes and, 15; as civil rights melodrama, 171; color blindness and, 94–96; death penalty and, 89–90; divided whiteness and, 82; KKK and, 102–3; marital strife in, 200n64; music in, 211n50; NAACP and, 92, 94–95, 96; southern backwardness and, 2, 4; southern religiosity in, 16, 101–2; *To Kill a Mockingbird* and, 19–20; white resentment and, 107
Tisby, Jemar, 144
To Kill a Mockingbird (film): awards and, 154; civil rights melodrama and, 15–16, 49; civil rights movement and, 26, 48; courtroom speech in, 30–31; criticism of and, 25; distortions and omissions in, 21, 25, 39, 40–42, 188n106, 189n118; films borrowing from, 19; freedom struggle and, 4; *Inherit the Wind* and, 187–88n89; Peck influence on, 47–48; Prix Gary Cooper for, 49; race in, 24–25, 31–32; Tom Robinson's death in, 42–43; southern

religiosity in, 22–23; symbolic Atticus in, 38; trial in, 187n88; white savior narratives and, 20–21. *See also* Finch, Atticus; Finch, Scout; Maycomb, Ala.; *To Kill a Mockingbird* (Lee)

To Kill a Mockingbird (Lee): Bible and, 23–24; courtroom speech in, 30–31; criticism of, 21–22, 25, 30, 184n11; divided whiteness and, 43–47, 49–50; Mrs. Dubose in, 41–42; gender in, 25, 39–40, 45; *Go Set a Watchman* and, 184n10; missionary circle in, 39–41; neighborhood in, 45–46; rabid dog scene in, 36–38; race in, 24–25, 29–32, 35–38; reception of, 26; Tom Robinson in, 42–43; Roosevelt and, 28; Scottsboro and, 26–28; trial in, 187n88; in white imagination, 32; WPA in, 185–86n40. *See also* Finch, Atticus; Finch, Scout; *Go Set a Watchman*; Maycomb, Ala.; *To Kill a Mockingbird* (film)

True Blood, 2, 10–11
Trump, Donald, 152
Tryon, Tom, 63, 64
Twain, Mark, 188n100
12 Years a Slave, 154

Victorious, Purlie (character), 58–59, 61–62
Vision of the Disinherited (Anderson), 119
voting: baby boomers and, 199n47; civil rights movement and, 37; *The Long Walk Home* and, 70; Million Man March and, 85; *Mississippi Burning* and, 77; religion and, 116; Republican Party and, 93; *Selma* and, 53, 139–40, 146, 151, 156–58, 162, 168; white juries and, 27

Wacker, Grant, 117
Waldman, Katy, 35
"Walk with Me" (Bass), 147, 149
Ward, Brian, 74
War on Drugs, 122
Webb, Paul, 155
Wegner, Philip, 121–22, 123, 125, 131, 135
Weisenfeld, Judith, 56–58
Welsh, David, 139
Wernblad, Annette, 127
Where Do We Go from Here? (King), 151
White, Jack E., 87
white anxieties, 122–25, 131. *See also* divided whiteness
white liberalism, 21, 82–84, 107–8, 121–22, 136–37. *See also* divided whiteness; stereotypes and tropes

Printed in the United States
by Baker & Taylor Publisher Services